Amazing Grace for Families

Amazing Grace
for Families

101 Stories of Faith, Hope, Inspiration, & Humor

Edited by
Jeff Cavins, Matthew Pinto, and
Patti Maguire Armstrong

West Chester, Pennsylvania

Ascension Press
Post Office Box 1990
West Chester, PA 19380
Orders: 1-800-376-0520
www.AscensionPress.com

Cover design: Kinsey Caruth

Printed in the United States of America
08 09 10 11 7 6 5 4 3 2

ISBN 978-1-934217-35-1

This book is dedicated to our children:

Carly, Jacqueline, and Antonia
–Jeff Cavins

Michael, Andrew, James, Thomas, and David
–Matthew Pinto

Aaron, Luke, Calvin, Tyler, Joash, Jacob, Mary,
Teresa, John, and Isaac
–Patti Maguire Armstrong

Contents

Chapter 2 – **A Family's Wisdom**

Chapter 3 – A Family's Hope

Chapter 4 – A Family's Humor

Chapter 5 – A Family's Faithfulness

Chapter 6 – A Family's Character

Chapter 7 – A Family's Strength

∽

Introduction

In my family, each and every day presents a multitude of opportunities to experience the love of God. I experience the love and care of God through my wife as she loves me with her whole heart. In turn, I experience the joy of loving my wife as Christ loves the Church. Most days provide me with opportunities to nurture my children and receive from them a beautiful, simple love. Both my wife and I have ample opportunities to exercise patience, mercy, and sacrifice as we interact with each member of our family. In short, our family is a small world where we learn, love, and grow. We also do this in the outside world, but we first experience life at home.

The family—or as Pope John Paul II calls it, the "domestic church"—lives, interacts within, and is strengthened by the universal Church. It is within the framework of God's larger family that the domestic church receives grace and instruction on how to be faithful. For example, a family that is centered on the Eucharist will find its source of apostolic zeal, and the family that is centered upon the cross will have before it a daily example of love. Through the Catholic Church, the domestic church receives patterns for living that can change the world. As Pope John Paul II said, "As the family goes, so goes the world."

In today's popular culture, there is an assault on the domestic church, with movies, television, and pop music undermining the integrity of the family. Since the family is an example of the love and fidelity of the Trinity to the world, this assault is blurring or masking the true intent of the family as a school of love and clouding God's communication to a needy world. This is one of the reasons we decided to publish *Amazing Grace for Families*.

We think that it is important that people read about families who have struggled but overcame obstacles and found concrete ways of participating in the life of the Trinity.

By reading *Amazing Grace for Families,* you will have a greater understanding of your importance within the larger Church, and you will be prompted to make the choices that influence your family for good. After reading these stories, Emily and I have taken ideas from some of these beautiful families and incorporated them into our own family life. You will find stories about heart-wrenching decisions that had to be made, miraculous outcomes, and simple daily life that will inspire you and encourage you. It is our hope that through these stories you will find inspiration for your family and perhaps come away with ideas on how to overcome various family issues.

Within these pages are situations that you may face one day. Perhaps there are stories with which you find common ground. Questions you may want to keep in mind as you read these stories are: *What is the focus of my family? What are the priorities we have set for ourselves? What is our eternal goal?*

I've traveled the country and heard from many people past their child-raising years that their children have left the faith. I like to encourage them that though they feel a sense of regret, there is something they can do to influence their families. God's grace is still available through prayer and continued interaction with loved ones, even though your physical proximity has changed. There are still stories to be written of the grace of God working in families even when each member has gone his or her own way.

Though families today may find themselves in many situations that are less than ideal, knowing and doing the will of God will move them toward conformity with Christ. It has been said that we choose our friends, but God chooses our family members. May we all come to a deeper appreciation for the masterpiece that God has assembled in our homes. My prayer is that *Amazing Grace for Families* will give you ideas, hope, and courage to be the family God created you to be, resulting in a renewed sense of purpose and joy. For some of you, the lessons learned in this book may be a confirmation of the virtues you are instilling in your family. For others, this book may be a lifesaver. Enjoy!

—Jeff Cavins

Chapter 1
A Family's Love

Focused on the Family

It was two a.m. when I stood at the edge of the window of the Frontier Hotel, a filthy, brick high-rise where pimps, prostitutes, and addicts walked the halls. The burden that had been placed on my young shoulders for eight years suddenly overcame me. I had been a fighter, determined to take care of my six brothers and sisters in the absence of any responsible adults. But on this night, taking my life seemed a better alternative than living to see my sixteenth birthday, which was only a few weeks away.

For as long as I could remember, my mother had blamed me for ruining her life. Pregnant at fifteen, she had been given an ultimatum by her father: get rid of the baby or get out and don't look back. My mom dropped out of school to support me, but she repeatedly told me: "Without you, my life would have been different." She made it no secret that she regretted the decision to keep me.

My father, Fonso, was in prison for drug dealing when I was born. I was four when he came to live with us upon his release. He was a six-foot-five, three-hundred-pound Vietnam veteran with mental problems. His discipline was strict and often irrational. In spite of his frequent brutality, he gave me some strong values that pulled me through my darkest times. Early on, my father instilled in me that I was to be the man in the family and that family was important. He was fanatical about school attendance to the point that I was not allowed to miss even when I was sick. And even though their lives did not

5

always reflect it, my parents believed in God, and they taught me to pray. When I was young, if my mother was gone from home for any length of time, I used to pray. Praying always made me feel better. Sometimes my mother attended church on Sundays, but whether she made it or not, my brothers and sisters and I always went to Sunday school. It was a way to relax, have fun, and learn about God. We loved it.

Shortly after I turned eight, my father was murdered in a disagreement with drug dealers. By that time, my brother was four, my sister was one, and my mom was pregnant again. She worked at a series of respectable jobs, including being a transit worker and secretary for the Los Angeles Police Department. It seemed as if we were doing all right. But then, she hooked up with a cocaine addict named Marcel.

I knew he was bad news from the start. "Mom, we're doing fine without him," I pleaded. "Why do we need him?"

But as a young widow with four children to take care of, my mom found something attractive in him. He moved in and regularly inflicted abuse on us. Once, when I asked him what he had done with our mother's paycheck, he punched me hard enough to break my jaw. It was not long before my mother was also hooked on cocaine. The two of them would leave us locked in a closet while they left on drug binges. Soon, they just left us alone at home while they disappeared for weeks.

I had taken my father's words "to be a man" to heart. Instinctively, I fed, bathed, and cared for my siblings and made sure they got to school. I did not dare tell anyone the truth because my mother had warned me that we would all be separated into different foster homes if anyone were to find out. I always made excuses and covered for my mother's absences. Whatever it took, I was determined to keep our family together.

Marcel and my mother's drug habit was consuming them. They sold anything of value. My grandmother sometimes brought diapers, clothes, and toys for the kids, but they would end up being sold for drug money. My grandfather had not reconciled with my mother, but my grandmother kept in touch with us. She worked long hours, and it was a multiple-bus commute to see us, so her visits were rare. However, my grandmother did often call on the phone. Her unconditional love gave me emotional support, but I did not dare let her in on the truth. I feared the shock would be too much for her or that she would confront Marcel and get hurt in the process.

By the time I was nine, I dropped out of school. We moved around so much that no one ever noticed. I had started finding odd jobs to do early in the morning or in the evening, so the older kids could take care of the babies when I was not there. I was creative and often aggressive in finding work. I convinced a store owner to let me empty his garbage cans and stock his shelves for fourteen dollars a week. I used to buy T-shirts with a Jesus picture or religious sayings on them. I could get four for ten dollars and then re-sell them outside of church on Sunday for ten dollars each.

With one scheme, I risked my life. I bought macadamia nuts and dried them out with baking soda so that they looked like crack-cocaine rocks. I sold them on the streets for thirty dollars each. Eventually, I was tracked down, beaten up, stabbed, and robbed of the little stuff I had.

When my mother and Marcel had gone through all the money, sometimes we slept under freeway overpasses, outside movie theaters, in abandoned cars, or at the Salvation Army. When Marcel ran out of drugs, my mother often hooked up with other addicts. At such times, it was not unusual for Marcel to force his way into our room and demand money or information about my mother's whereabouts. One time, he put a plastic bag over my two-year-old sister's head. Pleading and hitting, I couldn't get Marcel to loosen his death grip. Finally, I had to bite him. Marcel threw me through a window and broke my arm, but at least he let my sister go.

During the day, if our living situation permitted it, I made sure the older kids went to school. I kept them clean and well groomed and even washed their clothes for them, often in sinks. I tried to teach them to have good values, to believe in God, to get good grades, and to never, never use drugs. "You do not want to end up like Marcel and Mom," I warned them. "You don't have to end up on the streets. Stay in school and study hard." I tried to shield them from as much as I could. Before their eyes, I acted as if everything was under control and there was nothing to worry about. I wanted them to grow up strong and good and to believe in themselves. "Even if you think you have nothing, you have something to be grateful for because you are alive," I would say. I told them to have goals and expect to achieve them. I wanted to give them the strength and the faith to escape the streets.

My mother was often jailed for drugs and other crimes. She also had three more babies until there were seven children, including me. I could not afford formula, so I just bought milk for them. I kept working and taking care of the kids, but it was getting harder. I bought a Styrofoam cooler and a hot plate so that I could buy lunchmeat or cook simple meals like macaroni and cheese.

We ended up settling in the Frontier Hotel for thirteen dollars a night or forty-five for the week. Although it was not much, sometimes that money was out of my reach. Instead of getting thrown out on the streets, I figured out that I could find a vacant apartment and kick the door in. Then, I would replace the broken hardware on that door from hardware of the door of the apartment we had left. The building was large enough that no one would realize we were squatting in another apartment. One time, a Hollywood movie starring Nick Nolte was being filmed and the roof of the hotel was being used in one of the scenes. I helped a set director with props and carried things around for him. He didn't have to, but he paid me two hundred dollars for my help. It was a fortune to me.

Although the hotel provided a roof over our heads, it was a scary, rat-infested place where drug deals took place in the halls. We had even witnessed a murder in the lobby. I always took my brothers and sisters down the hall to the bathroom to keep an eye on them and wipe off the filthy toilet seat for them. We could never feel safe so I kept a screwdriver and knife on hand to protect us. One time, a crazed drug dealer came to the door looking for my mother, who was not there. I had the chain lock on the door, but he could fit his arm through the thin opening. He threatened to break the door down. I took a knife and held it against his arm and told him to leave or I'd cut his arm. Still, he would not leave. Not until the blade cut his skin did he finally leave us alone.

As hard as it may seem to believe, for many years, I just thought of surviving and never considered that my life was harder than any other kid's. But the stress and so many sleepless nights at the hotel finally took their toll on me One night, I looked over at my brothers and sisters huddled on the floor under one blanket. My youngest sister was crying, but I had no food for her. "I can't do this anymore," I thought. "I have nothing more to give."

It was then, looking at the concrete, fifteen stories below, that I envisioned leaving this world behind. I closed my eyes and hoped that my family would forgive me for leaving them. I was tottering on the edge, ready to jump, when a woman across the street let out a scream after she looked up and realized what I was going to do.

Instinctively, I stepped back. The reality that I could be dead at that very moment hit me. I collapsed onto the floor, sobbing. With tears still streaming down my face, I went to my little sister, rocked her in my arms, and remembered God. "Dear God, I don't know what to do. Please help us." I prayed and rocked her through the night. I felt better in the morning.

A few days later, my prayers were answered. A church group had set up a kitchen on the streets on the eve of Thanksgiving. I took advantage of the free food and brought all the kids with me. Sitting with some of the church volunteers, I was comforted by their kindness and warm conversation. They were interested in me and complimentary of how well behaved my brothers and sisters were. For the first time, I opened up about my life. Before, I had worked so hard to hide the reality, but I was so very tired by then. I knew I needed help.

Right away, these volunteers went to work, trying to find a secure home for us. But there was no foster family willing to take in all seven of us. I had not come this far to let my family be split up in the end. I knew my only hope was to call my grandmother and let her know the truth of the past eight years. She was horrified. I had covered so well that no one had ever suspected the depravity of our lives.

She and my grandfather agreed to take us all in, but the Los Angeles County welfare system was concerned that my grandmother was retired and my grandfather was in poor health with diabetes. I threatened to hide the children if the courts did not agree to let them take us all. Finally, my grandparents were granted legal custody of everyone.

My grandfather had never reconciled with my mother or accepted me, so I decided it was best to accept an offer from one of the church members to stay with him. I had petitioned the courts when I was sixteen and was granted emancipation. I missed not living with my family, but I was determined to show my grandfather that I was a hard worker. My friend owned a fire protection company and gave me a job installing sprinkler heads. I also joined him for a while in a Christian rap group. We actually traveled with secular bands and performed before large audiences in cities throughout the United States and in England.

Renowned writer Paula McDonald had learned of my story. She wrote a *Reader's Digest* article about my life, and the media picked up on it. There was an outpouring of offers to help in many ways, including counseling and tutoring. Since I had dropped out of school at such a young age, I could barely read or write. Eventually, I earned my GED and went on to receive an associate degree in business administration.

The CEO of Costco read about my story in *Reader's Digest* and offered me a job collecting the carts in the parking lot. I studied at night and worked during the day at Costco, but I had no intention of staying outside. I paid attention to what the cashiers were doing, because that was my next goal. Another employee who knew my background laughed when he heard of my desire. "That's never going to happen," he said. But before long, I became a cashier. Then I paid attention to what the supervisors did. Soon, I was promoted to supervisor. By the time I was twenty, I became the youngest manager ever at Costco and was assigned with opening new stores. Ironically, the guy who had once laughed at my desire to be a cashier ended up working under me.

When I was twenty-seven, I left the company and started my own trucking business, RDM Transportation, named for my brother Raf, my uncle David, and myself. I have gone from being homeless and having no education to owning a Fortune 500 company.

I have also returned to music and just started my own record label, Openfire Entertainment. My goal is to give opportunities to talented young musicians with positive messages.

Several years before my grandfather died, I had moved back with my family. My grandfather told me he was proud of me. For so long, he had feared that I would fail and turn out like my mother. But after watching how hard I worked and seeing my successes, he came to realize how wrong he had been.

In 2002, as my grandfather lay dying in a hospice, I drove with my brother Raf to a skid-row area in Los Angeles. "Dear God, please help me find my mother if she is out here," I prayed, not really sure where I might find her. I spotted her on one of the streets and called out her name. She looked up at me, more confused than surprised. We took her to see our grandfather. She sat at his bedside, and my grandfather finally made peace with his daughter after all those years. He died the next day.

My mother kept in touch with us for a time afterwards. She tried to straighten out her life again, but she unfortunately drifted back to the streets. We keep her in our prayers. Looking back on my life, I do not feel that it was harder than a lot of what many other people have had to survive. I have been on church mission trips to Mexico and seen great suffering there. But through it all, my faith in God has been strengthened. It was through His grace that I was able to take care of my family and have lived to see so many of my prayers answered. Life is not always easy, but God can pull us through.

— Mike Powell

Mike and his family live in Murrieta, California, with their grandmother. She is now sixty-three and works for Los Angeles County. She commutes by train every morning, nearly one hundred miles round-trip. Mike owns and operates RDM Transportation and Openfire Entertainment, a record label. His brother Raphael, twenty-five, works with him. Amber, twenty-two, Chloe, twenty, Shanice, eighteen, Ebony, sixteen, Michelle, fourteen, Eunique, thirteen, are college or high school students.

Editors' Note: *After her story appeared in* Reader's Digest, *author Paula McDonald and Mike appeared on national media interview shows. Everywhere they went, she received the same astonished question: How could this kid have survived? Paula says he is the most amazing person she has ever met. According to her, "Mike has a guardian angel of some kind looking out for him so that he can keep looking out for that family. He's on this earth to do something important and nothing, seemingly, is going to take him out until that work is done. I've never seen anything like it." Paula has seen the scars from his eight bullet wounds, verified the ER stories, and heard how he would get treated and then sneak out of the hospital so that the kids would not be left alone. Paula is working on a book about Mike's life and has a movie option.*

Putting My Life on the Line

"Come on, Mom. Let's go," my kids begged. It was a typical plea from kids painfully waiting for the adults to finish up so that they could get on with their own activity. It had been a beautiful weekend in the Colorado mountains, where we were visiting my parents. It was hard to leave on this crisp, clear morning, so my husband, Christophe, and I promised our children, Chloe, seven; Annie, five; and Elliot, two, one last swim in the hot springs before we headed home to McAllen, Texas. But first, my parents were excited to show us the mountain cabin they were thinking of buying.

My husband had gone ahead with Dad so that they could make a close inspection of the cabin. When I pulled into the driveway with my mom and the kids, we all rushed out. Mom and I absentmindedly left both front doors to my car open, thinking we would be just a few minutes. The empty cabin held little interest for my children. Putting their swimsuits to use was all they could think of. "Can we go yet?" they pleaded.

"OK, let's go," I announced. The adults kept talking and slowly walking to our Chevy Suburban while the children piled in. Then, without warning, the gear slipped and the car began moving forward. It was headed straight toward the deep canyon below.

"God, no!" I screamed. My dad and I had seen it first and instantly began sprinting toward the car. It was headed toward a tree. "God, let it hit the tree, let it hit the tree," I prayed. Instead, it actually seemed to veer away from the tree. With nothing else in its path, the car was headed unimpeded towards the cliff.

Although everything was happening so fast, I felt as if it were all in slow motion. The doors closed, and I saw my three children looking at me, frozen in fear. Chloe looked at the canyon and then tried to get her brother and sister to buckle up in the back. I realized she knew she was going over. Adrenaline and horror surged through me. A burst of speed led me to the front of the car. It seemed there was no time to open the door and jump in, so my instincts took over. I could not just watch my children plunge to their death, so I threw my body in front of the vehicle. I was the only thing in its path now, fifteen yards from the edge. Leaning into it was my only hope of stopping the car's progression.

My small frame was no match for a truck with three tons of steel that kept gaining ground. I felt myself being pulled under, so I grabbed onto the hood—but still I fell back. The bumper ran over me, taking my legs and pushing me over as if I were doing a sommersault. The tires slowly trod on me. The moment the tires hit my lower back, my legs instantly felt as if they were floating above me. The car moved on. My ribs were crushed, and my clavicle was broken. The tire missed my head because it was tilted to the side; otherwise, my skull would have been crushed. But the intense pressure broke the blood vessels in my eyes, and I went blind. Although it felt like I was in a dream, I thought of my kids. "God, don't let me hear the crash," I prayed. "I can't bear it."

My dad had not seen me go under the car. All he saw was that the car kept moving toward the canyon. Perhaps because the car bumped over my body, the passenger side door swung open. It must not have latched. My dad dove into the car, landing on the floorboard and fearing that he would be going down with the children. Instead, he was able to reach over and put the car into park. The car stopped six or seven yards from the edge.

Dad got the children out, and I could hear him shouting, "Thank you, God! Thank you, God."

Then I heard my mother scream my name. Until then, no one had realized what had happened to me. My dad reached me first. "Joy, I'm going to move your leg," he said, his voice panting and shaking. Although I could feel nothing, my left calf was twisted above my thigh.

"Don't touch me," I cried. I had no idea what would become of me, but I had heard many times never to move someone after an accident, but to wait for help. "I'm paralyzed and I'm blind," I cried. "I don't want to live. I can't handle both."

"Don't say that, honey," my Dad pleaded. "We're getting you help."

I thought of the children. "Get the kids," I gasped. "I need to say good-bye. I need to tell them I love them." I did not expect another chance. In spite of the shock and the severity of my injuries, peace came over me. I was ready to go. At that moment, I heard a powerful but calm voice that came from somewhere outside of me. I knew it was God. "It's your choice if you live or die, but if you choose to stay, you'll have to fight."

Then, I heard Chloe screaming for me. "My mommy's dying. I want to see her." I loved my children so much. That love pulled me back. I chose to stay and then lost consciousness.

I was taken by stretcher on a helicopter. My husband and parents feared they would never see me alive again. A policeman offered to take my children to his home while they drove down the mountain to the hospital. I faded in and out of consciousness. I heard the emergency technician tell the pilot that my veins were blown so he could not get an IV in me. "There's nothing I can do," he said frantically.

Thinking I was really going to die, I actually felt happy. I'm so close to my kids that this thought would normally have caused me to panic, but instead, an unbelievable peace washed over me again. The voice returned. "No, it's not your time." Then, immediately I experienced the horrible pain of my injuries for the first time. Again I lost consciousness.

In the emergency room, I came to. I learned that I would never walk again. Yet, in spite of my critical condition, there were little miracles. The radiologist had never seen ribs crushed to the extent that mine were, and yet my heart was untouched. If the car had stopped on me or if my head had not been tilted, I would be dead. My vision returned that same day, but my life was in danger for the first week. Friends, relatives, and entire church congregations reached out to others to create a prayer chain for me that linked across the country. I felt their prayers lift me up and get me through moment to moment.

There's not much I can remember during the first week. Once I was stabilized, I was taken to surgery. Afterward, I ran a high fever and was extremely uncomfortable, but I was no longer in danger of dying. Still, I became agitated and feared death. My mom, who had been at my side, left the room for a short while. While she was gone, a man dressed in a white jacket like a nurse or doctor came into the room. He looked to be in his fifties and had long silvery-blond hair and beautiful blue eyes. He smiled at me and reached for my medical chart, which was hanging on the back of the bed.

The man looked at my chart and then looked at me. "Joy," he said in a strong but gentle voice, "you are going to be OK." His words calmed me. It was as if he was telling me not only about my medical condition but about my life. He was telling me that even with my handicaps, I was going to be OK. When my mom returned, I excitedly told her about the man and that I was going to be okay. My mom ran out in the hallway, but no one was there. She went to the nurse's station and asked who had come in to see me. The nurse on duty said no one had gone past her. I feel certain that it was my angel who had come to lift my spirits and give me hope.

I was in the hospital for another five months and in rehabilitation for two months. It's been seven years now since the accident, and I continue to do physical therapy. I have not given up hope of one day walking again.

There have been many struggles, but my family pulled me through. My kids still needed a mom. I wanted to take care of them and not just sit in my room and cry. I had to learn to maneuver my wheel chair and drive and be the mom I was before.

Some times were tougher than others. One day, I told Christophe it was not fair for him to have a wife in a wheelchair. "I'm holding you back," I said. "This isn't what you bargained for."

"Joy, if you had no arms or legs, I'd carry you," he said with tears in his eyes. "You're still the woman I love."

Another time, when I was frustrated with struggling to do even basic things such as dress myself, I asked my dad if throwing myself in front of the car even made a difference in the end.

"The police said that you slowed the car just enough," he said. "In another second, it would have crashed down onto the rocks. Honey, you saved your children's lives."

At that moment, I knew I would do it all over again if given the choice.

Amazingly, many good things have come out of this. I believe that my children are more understanding and compassionate with others because of what they've been through with me. It's brought out a lot of love and mercy in them. My daughter Annie and I even keep a list of all the good things that have come out of this. We've been on *Oprah,* and we've met so many people. Our "good list" has grown long.

I have learned that there is good in everything, no matter what you go through. I did not want it to happen, and there are days I want to throw my wheelchair across the room, but through the grace of God, I can take the good and use it.

—Joy Veron

Joy Veron lives in Mission, Texas, with her husband and three children. She teaches "children's church" at Sts. Peter and Paul Parish. Joy and her family are involved in the outreach committee at their parish, helping several orphanages in Reynosa, Mexico. Their mission is to make sure the children are warm, well fed, and, most of all, loved.

Free at Last

Humming softly, I looked down at my young daughter and let out a deep sigh. Thankfully, Angelina had drifted off to sleep. I tucked her in bed and tiptoed out of her bedroom and into the horror from which I was trying to protect my little girl. The police had paid our family yet another visit. With a search warrant in hand, they had free reign of our house, searching for drugs and illegal weapons. Edmund, age eight, stood with my husband, Willie Lee. I did not want him to be a witness to the scene, but being two years older than his sister, Edmund was not so willing to let me whisk him away under my protective wing.

It wasn't supposed to be this way, I thought angrily. I had gone from living the American dream to waking up in my worst nightmare. There was nothing my husband and I would not do for our four children, yet our two oldest sons, Andre and Avery, were teenage delinquents. They had become entangled with drugs and gangs.

I had wanted to do everything right for my children. I took a leave from my work as a model and interior designer in order to stay home to raise them. My husband provided for the family as a dentist. His love and willingness to care for us knew no bounds. We lived in a comfortable four-bedroom home in a suburb of Orlando, Florida. Playgrounds and story time filled my days while the boys were little. When they reached school age, we sent them to private Christian schools. I drove to every field trip and rarely missed a Home and School meeting. I never thought I'd have to fight with the streets, but the lure of the wild side enticed my boys. Venturing out of the sanctuary of our loving family, they were smitten with fast-talking, hard-driving hoods. Andre was first arrested in 1992 for breaking into a car. Then, months later, Avery was arrested for breaking and entering. In time, the police were banging at our door on a weekly basis.

Sometimes the boys ran into our house shaking with fear that some gang member was going to shoot them.

It was our oldest son who blazed the trail by joining a cousin in criminal activity. Avery, ever the gentle soul, had been a "square" and called a sissy until it broke him down and he turned to the dark side. As the boys' lives unraveled, a wedge was driven between my husband and me. The love that had been our glue was strained when he responded to them with love and indulgence. I felt he was sabotaging my efforts at discipline when he bailed them out of trouble. The clashes between us were many.

How did we get to this point? I kept asking myself. I prayed relentlessly. The boys were in and out of jail. Finally, I decided I could not let pride get in my way. Instead of trying to hide my pain, I began asking everyone I knew to pray for them.

It did not happen overnight, but gradually, they surrendered to God. While they were in their twenties, both began to turn to prayer and the Bible. For a time, Andre straddled a line between God and the streets. He was married with a two-year-old son and two weeks away from receiving a dental technician degree when he was arrested one last time. In the halls of the court room, his son ran up to "Daddy," but a guard stopped the two from having any contact. Seeing the pain and confusion on his little boy's face broke Andre's heart. While serving his six-month jail sentence, his wife gave birth to their little girl. He knew his own pain was nothing compared to the pain he had caused others. Andre knew he had to choose to serve God and God alone. He turned his back on the streets nine years ago and has never looked back.

Andre, age thirty-two, is now a loving husband and father of three. God has turned his life around so completely that he is a church and youth leader and works with senior citizens. Andre has also been a keynote speaker for correction programs. As a motivational speaker, he has spoken before judges and police officers that once knew him as a criminal.

Avery currently suffers from a mental disability, and is in a state hospital. Thus far, medication has not been able to help him. But my heart is at peace. One of the nurses told me that when he is in reality, he reads his Bible and is often on his knees praying. During their days in trouble, I often prayed: "If my sons should die in the street and I am not there, let them call Your name before they close their eyes." Avery knows God and loves Him, so my prayer has been answered. I know that Avery's suffering is not wasted. I am as proud of him as my other children.

But my story is not just one of conversion for my sons. Their experience has converted me in a way that never would have happened without the pain. When we turn to God, He does not just end the bad; He can use it for good.

During my years of anguish, I learned of so many other mothers whose hearts were being ripped apart by sons involved in crime. Typically, they were embarrassed and felt like failures. I came to believe that God was asking me to give these women the support of each other and of God. With my husband's emotional and financial support, I started Mothers of Incarcerated Sons on Mother's Day in 2001. On a shoestring budget and with volunteers, we are now in 120 prisons in thirty-two states. MIS does everything from starting support groups for mothers (and fathers are welcomed, too) to helping find jobs for paroled prisoners. Sons who have been released from prison are encouraged to come to the support groups and pray with the other mothers who still have sons incarcerated. Prayer and a mother's love are powerful gateways to a new life.

I often visit prisons and tell the inmates, "You mean so much to God that He set you aside from the distractions of the world. You are in a university of learning now, where you can listen to God and prepare yourself for His service." They can make their failure temporary and move from pain to providence to power, by the grace of God.

This grassroots effort just keeps growing. We have not received any major grants, but we appeal to churches to make a monthly financial commitment to help us do God's work in the prisons. God is our CEO. It is He who can change hearts and set us free.

In 2002, *Essence* magazine listed me among the "Fifty Most Inspiring African Americans" and then in 2004 selected me as one of the "Thirty Most Beautiful Women in the World." Like so much of my life, it is something I never dreamed of. I accept the title most humbly because it helps publicize our program and focuses on my own source of inspiration—God and love of family. With such inspiration, anything is possible.

— Sherry Grace

Sherry Grace is the founder and executive director of Mothers of Incarcerated Sons, Inc. (www.misons.org). She has dedicated her life to turning the misfortune that plagued her household into a launching pad of success for countless families and men in prisons across the country. Sherry is the wife of Dr. Willie L Grace, Jr., and they have four children, Andre, thirty-two, Avery, thirty, Edmund, twenty-five, and Angel, twenty-three. She is the grandmother of Ashley, Dante, and Allurah Grace.

Our Daughter, Betsy

Betsy squealed as she tried to slip past my husband, Ben. "I've got you now," he laughed, grabbing her leg as she collapsed into a heap of giggles. But then the wrestling stopped.

"Diane," he called to me from our family room to the adjoining kitchen. "What is this lump on Betsy's calf?" The bike ride from the previous day crossed my mind. At five years old, Betsy had been so proud that she made it around a two-mile trail on her bike.

"Did you fall off your bike and hurt your leg yesterday?" Ben questioned her.

"No," she answered.

"Call her pediatrician and see if you can get her in today," he said.

"Yeah, right," I laughed, assuming Ben was still clowning around. As an emergency room physician, not even a serious gash in one of the kids could ruffle his feathers. As long as they were conscious and breathing, Ben did not worry.

"I'm serious, Diane," he said with an edge that made me nervous. "Kids don't have lumps."

I made an appointment for that afternoon. Betsy had been given a clean bill of health for her annual physical earlier that summer. I told myself that it was probably nothing, but either way, we would soon find out. Since Ben had worked the night shift at the emergency room, he could stay home with one-year-old John and seven-year-old Luke.

The doctor examined Betsy. "I'm going to have an ultrasound done so we can have a better look," he explained. By then, it was getting harder to convince myself that it was nothing. I called Ben. He took the boys to a neighbor's and joined me at the doctor's office.

The ultrasound revealed only that it was a mass of some kind. Cancer was suspected, so the next step was to biopsy it.

Betsy needed to have a chest x-ray first as part of the standard pre-op procedure.

I tried to calm myself. Well, in a worse-case scenario, if it was cancer, it was below her knee joint. Even if she had it amputated, she could still run and play sports with a prosthesis.

With Betsy in another room, the doctor flipped the x-rays up on the wall. A big shadow of white behind Betsy's heart and along her lymphatic system in her neck was visible. I looked at the doctor for an interpretation. He looked stricken. I looked over at Ben. His face had gone white.

"Oh, this changes everything," the doctor said in a whispered tone.

"What does this mean?" I demanded, frantic to understand what I was looking at.

Ben choked back tears. "Betsy has tumors in her chest and neck." Ben paused as his voice caught. "That means she probably has a tumor in her leg too."

Ben and I sat down. My legs were too weak to hold me up. We cried and held each other. Only hours earlier, our house had been filled with Betsy's laughter. She had always been a healthy, happy little girl. It seemed impossible that she could have cancer.

"Will we still do a biopsy?" I asked.

"No, we need a new plan now," the doctor explained. The cancer had spread throughout Betsy's small body. Removing a lump was no longer a possible treatment plan.

Ben and I had to go back into the room where Betsy sat waiting for us. "The doctors are not sure what's wrong with your leg yet," I explained. "We need to see another doctor first." Before we told her everything, we wanted to know exactly what we were dealing with. An appointment was made to see an oncologist the next day.

"Dear God," I prayed, "Please get us through this. Don't let Betsy suffer. Please, God," I begged, "let her survive."

The oncologist diagnosed Betsy with a muscle-cell tumor, rhabdomyosarcoma. We gently explained to Betsy that cells divide, but with cancer, they divide too much. She was going to have medicine to kill those cells.

Betsy began chemotherapy right away. The drugs were given during the night, and on the first night, she vomited seventeen times as her fragile little body shook and heaved. Ben and I stayed at her side. My mom and sisters helped with our boys. By the third day the doctor explained that Betsy needed to feel like she was safe. If we were afraid to leave the room, that was giving her the wrong message.

Ben and I left and sat together in church for an hour. We cried and prayed, sometimes separately and sometimes together. It was the longest hour of my life until I could return to Betsy's side.

In between chemo treatments, Betsy began kindergarten. She attended on days she felt well enough. When her hair began falling out, she was not surprised, since the doctor had told her to expect it. "Hey Luke," she called to her big brother. "As long as it's coming out, we might as well have fun with it." She had her brother help her brush and pull it out in clumps and put it into a plastic bag. Betsy accepted it, but that night, I lay in bed and sobbed, the plastic bag on my dresser.

Betsy had picked out a wig to wear for when she went bald. She wore it to school the next day after being absent for a couple weeks.

"Hey," one of the kids shouted. "Teacher said you were going to lose your hair, but you didn't."

Betsy smiled impishly. "You think this is my hair, but it isn't. See?" she said and pulled off the wig. "This is the way my head really looks. If you want to come up and touch it, it's OK; it won't hurt me." The kids all crowded around and felt her head.

"I wore this wig because I thought I would be embarrassed, but I don't really feel embarrassed," Betsy announced. "And it's kind of itchy, so I'm not going to wear it anymore." And she never did.

Betsy went into remission halfway through kindergarten. Then, in October of 1991, as a first grader at Cathedral of the Holy Spirit, her tumors returned. Treatment started up again full force. In January, our pastor, Fr. Thomas Kramer, suggested that Betsy make her First Holy Communion at Mass. She wore a beautiful white dress and white headband with a veil on the back upon her bald head, so she would look beautiful for Jesus. After Mass, it seemed everyone came up to touch and congratulate her. Ben and I were touched by the outpouring of love.

The week before Easter of 1993, our family went to Disney World as a gift from the Make-a-Wish Foundation. Betsy was weak but still able to enjoy it. One evening in the hotel, while I tucked her into her bed, she felt a lump on her back. "That's a tumor, isn't it?" she asked. "I'm going to die, aren't I?" I was not ready to answer yes. I told her we were still fighting it.

We took her to the hospital on Good Friday to see her doctor. "Betsy, we can't stop this cancer anymore. You are going to die from cancer," he gently explained. When Ben and Betsy and I stepped out into the hallway, Betsy saw a favorite nurse. "Carol," she announced matter-of-factly, "it looks like I am going to die. But that's OK because then I'll be in heaven with Jesus and our baby (I'd had a miscarriage years before). Or else I'll get to stay here with my mom and dad and brothers, so either way I'll be OK." Ben and I looked at each other and recognized the shared pain in our eyes. We said nothing, though.

On Monday, we brought Betsy back to the hospital for comfort care. The doctor wanted to try to shrink the tumors so they would not cause so much discomfort. Instead, by Wednesday, Betsy began her final stage of dying. We knew it would be soon, so we had a few close relatives and friends come to say their good-byes. Fr. Kramer came to confirm her and administer the Anointing of the Sick. He said, "Betsy, you're going to see Jesus soon."

Betsy, who had been laying quietly, sat bolt upright and anxiously asked, "When?"

Father Kramer answered, "I don't know exactly, but it will be soon." She seemed satisfied with that answer and lay back down.

Then, wanting to comfort her, I said, "Betsy, are you afraid?" She looked at me in surprise, and quickly replied, "No! Are you?" I felt God's grace come over me as I realized how much Betsy trusted Jesus and what we had taught her about His love and how wonderful being in heaven with Him would be. Thanks to her courage and faith, I could answer truthfully: "No."

Our boys came to be with their sister one last time. "I love you, Betsy," they each said and held her hand. "I love you, too," she responded weakly. After a couple hours, the boys were taken home. Ben and I lay alone with Betsy and stroked her hands and head. It seemed we could not tell her enough times how much we loved her. Betsy remained responsive. Then, her breathing became labored.

We held her in our arms and spoke softly, "Betsy, we love you so much, but we are ready for you to go, if it is your time. If you can see Jesus or a bright light, it's OK to go. We'll be all right." Immediately her body relaxed, her face looked peaceful, and she went on to be with her Jesus.

In the grace of the final moments, I had felt strong and peaceful, but now, I was heart-broken. After her twenty-two-month battle with cancer, Betsy was gone from us. Ben and I held each other and sobbed.

Our grief was intense, but we still had two other children who needed us. It was the reason we could still get out of bed in the morning and get through the day without Betsy. During Betsy's treatment, Ben and I had been a team, but we found that we grieved very differently. I learned that talking to a counselor was very helpful to me during my grieving, whereas Ben preferred to grieve more privately. It was a very painful time, one that could have ended in divorce. Instead, through the grace of God, we slowly began to heal. We feel our marriage became stronger because of what we had survived together.

Three years after Betsy died, we welcomed another baby into our family—our daughter, Mary. Mary looks a lot like her big sister and has her spunky spirit. She is a heavenly blessing and often a sweet reminder of Betsy.

It has been fourteen years now since I've been able to hold Betsy or hear her little voice. Yet I know that if God said to me, "Here, you can have her back," I would not ask that of her. I know that she is with Jesus and that we cannot even imagine the ecstasy that brings. I accept the pain that comes from our temporary separation. Because of my faith in God, I know that Betsy is happier with God than she could ever be on earth. She will never hurt again. And as a parent, my most important job was to get her to heaven. I believe that mission was accomplished.

— Diane Roller

Diane Roller is the mother of four children. She chose to stay home the last twenty-four years to raise her family and has just recently returned to her part-time career as a physical therapist. She is an active volunteer in her church, school, and community and loves to play tennis.

Just Do It!

"The dog's out!"

I blew a gusty sigh from my lips as I watched my eight-year-old son Paul race outside to catch our dog. Cringing inwardly, I pictured our ninety-pound black lab romping through the neighborhood at full speed, scaring little old ladies and innocent children simply by his massive size.

Stirring my three boys' supper on the stove again, I turned the heat up a little, hoping to speed the process along. I glanced at the kitchen clock for the umpteenth time and realized I was running just as late as the last time I'd looked. Feeling more than a little guilty, I grimaced as I pictured my always-punctual husband waiting on me to finish getting ready ... again. We were due to arrive at a dinner banquet in less than an hour, and I was still dressed in my robe with my just-shampooed hair wrapped in a towel. To soothe my conscience, I reminded myself that the phone had been ringing at a near constant rate all afternoon, which added to my tardiness. Having a home-based candle business was a great way of earning extra money, but it certainly created extra commotion during the holiday season, which was now well under way.

If I can just get these noodles simmering, I can put on the lid and go get ready. I turned the heat under the skillet a little higher. Just then, my eldest son, Jerome, signed for the delivery of ten cases of candles that the UPS man was getting ready to unload onto my kitchen floor via the garage door. I released yet another full-cheeked sigh and rolled my eyes as I realized that all ten cases would have to be tagged and marked before they could be put away. *It'll have to get it done tomorrow,* I thought. The customers will just have to wait.

So as not to embarrass myself and shock the UPS man, I escaped from the kitchen and looked out the bedroom window for the dog. As I stood there impatiently scanning the back-yard, a tiny voice crept into my head. Call Laura. I ignored the thought, gave up the window search, and proceeded to lay my clothes out onto the bed.

Call Laura. This time I argued with the thought. "Laura? Who's Laura?"

Ryan's mother. Ryan was the "new kid" in my son Paul's class. The boys had played together once, but I had actually spoken to Laura very little ... mostly just short, friendly conversations while we passed each other in the parking lot at school. As I reached for my pantyhose, I remembered why I had let Paul go home with Laura the first time I met her—it was her smile and friendly face. Sounds naïve, but true. I just knew by way of instinct that she was a good lady. I suddenly recalled chatting with her briefly in the hall at school several days earlier. "We'll have to get together sometime! I'll call you," I remembered saying as we shuffled along with the after-school rush to get outside.

Call Laura. I began yanking on my pantyhose, and inwardly vowed to call Laura soon and set up a lunch date or something fun. Call Laura. "OK, Lord, I'll call Laura later. Right now, I'm late!" I spoke aloud.

Just then, a waft of burning spaghetti sauce filled my nostrils. "Oh, noooo!" I exclaimed, as I envisioned the Hamburger Helper on its way to becoming "hamburger tartar." I rushed toward the kitchen and stumbled through the maze of boxes. After quickly turning the burner to low, I scraped at the gummy noodles that now adhered to the bottom of the pan.

"What next?" I mumbled, as my two-year-old son Roy tugged on my robe and asked me to read him a book. I managed a weak smile and answered, "I can't right now, sweetie. Mommy's very busy right now."

Call Laura.

"Please, Lord ... I'll call her tomorrow ... I promise!" Yet even as the words slipped from my lips, I knew the truth. God was trying to tell me something. This sort of inner calling had happened before, and I knew I should not ignore it.

Having gotten the dinner under control, I hoisted Roy onto my hip and went to look for the cordless phone. When I found it, I just stared at it. What would I say to her? "Uh, Laura, this is Liz ... yeah, Paul's mom. Remember me? Well ... the strangest thing just happened ... God told me to call you." Oh, yeah, sure. That would be perfect. She'll think I'm loony.

I sighed, and then looked up the number while popping a Barney video in the VCR for Roy to watch. As I listened to the ringing, I suddenly became apprehensive as to what I would say. Maybe I should hang up.

"Hello."

I swallowed hard before saying, "Hi, Laura! This is Liz ... Paul's mom. How are you?" I don't recall what she answered, since it took me just a split second to realize she was crying. I asked her what was wrong, and she explained that she had just found out that she had been pregnant for the very first time and had lost the baby. (They had been blessed with their only son, Ryan, through adoption.) To make matters worse, she had just been informed that she had developed an uncommon cancerous condition in her uterus that could be life threatening.

Instantly, my predicament seemed petty. Suddenly, it didn't matter whether we would be late for dinner, or whether someone would call the dogcatcher before we could lasso the dog and bring him home. It really did not matter if all the candles were put away before the customers arrived. I gripped the phone tightly, and closed my eyes in a silent prayer.

When it was my turn to reply to her tearful declaration, I said, "I am so sorry for what you are going through, but I want you to know, you can stop crying because God has taken special care to have me call you tonight. I believe He wants you to know that He is present and in control of your situation. He cares about you very much and will not abandon you."

I then proceeded to tell her about the chaos in which I'd just ventured to call her. We laughed a little, and then talked with all seriousness about the truth ... God had definitely placed her on my heart for a reason. I knew it, but more importantly, she knew it.

Like most people who are dealing with an illness or crisis, Laura went through some difficult times when she felt afraid. Sometimes I felt afraid for her. It was during these times that we would remind each other of the day that God whispered her name into my heart. In the month's that followed, Laura's condition was healed completely. Best of all, we've been good friends and prayer buddies ever since!

As the years go by, I marvel at the way God makes Himself known to us. I have learned to act quickly when He prompts me to do so, even when it's uncomfortable and hard. Even when He has called me to do something difficult, if I obey, I always end up feeling blessed beyond measure. He is Lord of all things, great and small.

—Elizabeth Schmeidler

Elizabeth Schmeidler is happily married and mother to three wonderful sons. Also a singer-songwriter, Elizabeth has composed and recorded three CDs of inspirational music. Her music can be heard on many radio and internet stations and ordered through CDbaby.com. As an author of novels, short stories, children's stories, and poetry, she continues to write and sing in her pursuit to do God's will. She can be contacted at cdmusic@eaglecom.net.

The Simple Life

The Sibling Bond

Last week my oldest son, David, left the house to be measured for his high school graduation cap and gown. I can't believe he's almost eighteen. He looked so strong and handsome and sure of himself as he walked out the door with his sweatshirt slung over his shoulder and his keys jingling in his hands.

What happened to the little boy I brought home from the hospital in the white ducky snow suit that was two sizes too big?

The same week my son was measured for his graduation gown, my youngest daughter, Angela, started sitting up and eating solid food. She's already five months old. She's been in this family for her entire lifetime, but that's only a semester in my older son's world. It really was almost yesterday when we brought her home in her delicate pink gown on a warm evening.

These two kids are a generation apart. Angela is entering this family's daily life, and, in a way, David is exiting. She's just getting to know our faces and voices and personalities. He's ready to leave ours soon for new ones. What kind of relationship, one may ask, can these two have as siblings, so many years and worlds apart?

It's just past seven p.m. Football practice ended a half hour ago, and soon David and his brother Michael will be walking through the door, with hearty appetites and mountains of homework. I hear the door squeak and the thump of equipment hitting the floor. Next I hear David's husky voice cooing, "Come on, baby," to his little sister, whom he has rescued from the swing in the front room.

I peek around the corner to see that she responds by grabbing his face and wiggling toward him. "Shh ... shh ... shh," he says as he cradles her in his arms and bounces her gently back and forth, holding her securely against his chest. Back and forth. Back and forth. They are engaged in a dance, two unlikely companions frozen in a single moment. For a short time they will be under the same roof, in the same world. Then suddenly, their lives will diverge into strikingly separate paths—hers of blocks and abc's and babyhood, his of college term papers, interviews, and adulthood. But for now, they are in the same plane. She is learning, from his strong arms, to trust. He is learning, from her vulnerability, to give. He is a father of tomorrow, in an internship, of sorts, learning gentleness and devotion, all from this little bundle called Sister.

In a minute, David sets Angela down and turns to the refrigerator to look for pizza or apples or leftover dinner and resumes his teenage cares. Will he remember this moment? Probably not. Will she? Even less likely. But the bonds that have been forged run deep, even if the individual moment is forgotten. Link by link the family chain lengthens and strengthens. Angela will be closer in age to David's children than to her own brother. Most likely she will play with her nieces and her nephews as if they were her siblings. And David and Angela are really too far apart in age to experience typical sibling squabbles. By the time Angela wants time to primp in the bathroom, David will be long gone, with his own bathroom in his own apartment or home.

So what do these siblings offer to the other's life? David gives Angela security, protection, and unconditional love. And Angela gives David an opportunity to give and to learn that gentleness is strength. Because of David, Angela has more than just her father to provide a reference in her mind for understanding a gentle, all-loving, and protective God. And David doesn't need a teacher in catechism class to tell him that there is value and beauty in every stage of life. He already knows that, because he lives with Angela.

—Theresa Thomas

Theresa Thomas, wife of David, is a homeschooling mother of ten children, as well as a freelance writer and newspaper columnist for Today's Catholic.

Matthew

Given that we had a new baby in our family every two to three years for twenty years, it seemed like a good idea to have an extra home pregnancy kit tucked in the back of a bathroom shelf. I did not really think I was pregnant, but I was not certain. I remembered the kit and thought, I'll just check to be sure. The pink line that emerged, indicating a positive result, took my breath away. I would be forty-seven when the baby was due. We had recently taken in a boy from Kenya, so now we were a family of eleven.

"Hey, Mark, we're going to have another baby," I announced to my husband, showing him the pink line. We looked at each other, wide-eyed. We shared a strong understanding that each little soul is a gift from God that will last an eternity. Still, I'd be forty-seven and Mark forty-eight. As we gradually adjusted to the news, I discovered that our willingness to accept new life led us closer to God. Instead of thinking of things like money, the opinions of others, and our advanced age, we saw ourselves as co-creators with God. We would trust in Him to provide for both the necessary material needs of this transitory world. New life had begun and would forever be a part of our family.

It had only been the previous week that my daughter Teresa, age eight, had expressed hope that I would have another baby. When I pointed out that older women did not usually have babies, she reminded me that Elizabeth was older when she had John the Baptist. I had just smiled and said: "You never know."

Well, now we knew. The younger kids were ecstatic. I thought the older kids would be taken aback (we had one in college, three in high school, one in junior high, and four younger ones), but they all said that given my track record, they had pretty much expected it.

Friends and family registered surprise. After all, they had been secretly guessing that our nest was full.

The older kids actually had some fun with it. For instance, Luke, who was a senior, was in a class where a picture for the yearbook was being taken. The photographer asked someone to say something funny to get everyone to laugh. "My mom's pregnant again," Luke announced. It got the desired reaction. Although the older kids once had a temporary hesitation to having more children, once baby number seven was in their lives and hearts, they realized how wrong those feelings had been. Everyone had been on board with our last baby, Isaac, and were happily ready again this time.

Then, at three months, I miscarried for the first time. I had some early warnings, so by the time it happened, it was not a surprise. The enormity of my loss did not really hit me until I was alone at morning Mass a couple days later. I had requested that my kids ask God to let us know the sex of the baby. My oldest, Aaron, suggested I give it a unisex name and leave it at that. "I would really like to know who it was," I explained, "so please ask God to somehow let us know."

It was just before Mass, two days after the miscarriage, that I suddenly felt a deep sense of knowing that the baby had been a boy—Matthew. We chose that name to go with our Mark, Luke and John, members of the family. Realizing I had a son suddenly filled me with a deep awareness that my very own child was with God now. I knew there was no greater place to be, but still, a maternal sadness washed over me. My little son Matthew was our only baby I did not get to hold in my arms and have with me. He was the only one that his big brothers and sisters missed out on in this world.

I shed a few tears but was filled with peace because I knew who my baby was now. Then, after Mass, before leaving for home, the thought occurred to me that, although I was convinced

I had a son in heaven, other family members might say, "Mom, you really don't know for sure."

I sent up a quick but heartfelt prayer. "Dear God, I accept that my son is with you now, but it would mean a lot to me if you would somehow let the others know the baby was a boy." I wanted my husband to know his son and the children to have a relationship with a little brother in heaven.

I kept the morning's experience to myself. Then, just a few hours later, Aaron called me from Fargo, where he attended college and was living for the summer. "Mom, I'm in a big hurry, but I just wanted to call to tell you I know the baby was a boy."

Aaron had dreamed two nights in a row of a baby. In the first dream, a baby had died, but he was confused. The next night, he had the same dream, but this time, when he looked at the baby, he knew it was his little brother. In the dream he looked at me, and we nodded at one another because we both knew.

"Oh, Aaron, I just asked God this morning to somehow let everyone else know it was a boy." I explained my own experience to him, marveling at my answered prayer. My oldest had connected with my youngest, from earth to heaven.

There was no time to talk, however, because Aaron was in a hurry to participate in a study that paid very good money to college students. We said good-bye, and I learned the rest of the story later.

Aaron arrived at the study site only minutes after our conversation. By all rights, he should have been disqualified during the screening because his heart started racing when his pulse was taken. Since, the study had been overbooked, they were looking for any reason to start bumping students. Aaron knew from experience that an above-normal heart rate was a typical factor used to bump students. It was Aaron's nervousness that caused his fast heart rate, but he could not get himself to calm down. He began asking his little brother, Matthew, to help him. Aaron really needed the money for expenses. His pulse was taken two more times, each time measuring faster than the previous rate.

It seemed hopeless. The study director looked at him and then at the nurse beside him who was recording the results. "Please, Matthew," Aaron prayed. "Please help me get into this study." But Aaron braced himself, waiting to be told he was dismissed. There's no way, now, he thought.

Looking Aaron in the eyes, the director paused and then stated quietly to the nurse at his side: "Let him in." The nurse registered surprise, but then quickly followed as they went on to the next participant.

Euphoric disbelief and awe filled Aaron's soul. It seemed impossible. He was in! And it was his little brother who had gotten him in. It had to be.

It's been a little over three years now since we lost Matthew—athough, spiritually speaking, we will never lose him. He will always love us, his family, and always hear our prayers. He knows more than we do, and his love is greater than ours. Even though it would have been great to hold him on this earth, it is a grace to have him holding us in his heart now in heaven.

—Patti Maguire Armstrong

Patti Maguire Armstrong is one of the editors of Amazing Grace for Families. *Her biography appears at the end of the book.*

A Modern-Day Holy Family

"Not many priests can say that their personal chapel is located in the same place where, as a boy, they made a consecration to the Sacred Heart of Jesus," said Bishop Paul V. Dudley with a sparkle in his eyes. My wife, Emily, and I stood in the small room of Bishop Dudley's private chapel and looked closely at a picture of the Sacred Heart of Jesus on which his youthful signature was written across the bottom. "On the day of my parents' wedding they consecrated their marriage to the Sacred Heart," Bishop Dudley continued, gently patting the large portrait of Jesus, whose hands were drawn toward his heart encircled with thorns and blazing with love. "I distinctly recall the ceremony that my father would lead each time one of us children became old enough to sign his or her name to the document of consecration to the Sacred Heart. I was about twelve when I signed it."

Emily and I were in awe at the holiness that flooded the simple room of Bishop Dudley's small trailer. It was placed on the original farmstead. There was a view of the old farmhouse out one window and the barn out another. He had invited us to participate in Mass with him, followed by lunch, which he personally served. At seventy-nine years old, he was slowing down, but he was every bit as full of the love of Christ as ever.

On the altar of his chapel he pointed to a small crucifix. "This crucifix is the one my mother held through each one of her ten children's births. All of her children were born at home on our farm, up until the last two. This crucifix was precious to all of us children, and we kissed it often." Emily and I marvelled at the hand-sized crucifix as we each held it. After each of us also kissed it, we returned it to the altar as Bishop Dudley continued, "I am so blessed to have much of my spiritual heritage near me."

He took us to the farmhouse for a tour of each small room. We could just imagine ten children running through while as mother cooked up enough to feed them all and as the father came in from the barn. "This is the room where many important events occurred during my childhood, including our family rosary and our devotion to the Sacred Heart of Jesus," Bishop Dudley told us. The room was hardly larger than an average bedroom, and yet the Dudley family had all fit into it.

Bishop Dudley reminisced about his parents. "I would say their marriage was filled with a spirit of joy. I am so convinced of the holiness of my parents that I ask them to intercede for me. I have always wanted to begin the process of their sainthood. They would be such a saintly model of sanctity and fidelity for the Church. We all attended weekly Mass, Friday holy hour, and biweekly confession.

"With ten children to feed and tend to, plus the rigors of farming, my mother still always managed to have her daily prayer time," he continued. "She had a small black volume secured with a rubber band which none of us ever dared to open. She took it with her for her thirty-minute walk down the main road from the farmhouse or to her room during the long, dark Minnesota winters. I'll never forget her simple but profound prayer she added to the end of our daily family rosary. 'Help my children to do what You created them to do, and to do it well.' My parents didn't pray for us to become priests or sisters. They entrusted us into the care of our Lord and consecrated us to his Blessed Mother. As it turns out, my brother Frank and I became priests in 1946 and 1951, respectively."

By this time I felt so humbled comparing the simple devotion of this holy family to the busy, often scattered life at our own home. With three children it seemed difficult for my family to gather everyone up to get to confession regularly, but this amazing Dudley family had made it a routine part of life for all of them.

As we stood on the front door of the farmhouse, Bishop Dudley said, "I can still vividly see my mother standing on these steps and blessing us with the sign of the cross whenever we drove away. She and my father were continual saintly examples.

"One year after my ordination as a priest, my mother died suddenly at the age of sixty-four. As our grief-stricken father gathered the family together after the burial, he told us something about Mother that we had never known. He said, 'Your mother faithfully, every First Friday of the month, would wake at two a.m. to spend a holy hour.' Years later I chose the two a.m. hour for Eucharistic adoration because it was the only slot open at my parish. When I recalled that this hour was the same one my mother had chosen to spend in prayer before the Blessed Sacrament each month, it made my hour of adoration all the more special."

For my wife and me, our visit to the Dudley farm that day was like receiving a graduate degree in how to raise a family. Now, when I think of Bishop Dudley, the words of the apostle Paul come to mind, "Follow me as I follow Christ." I hope that one day our children will speak as fondly of Emily and me as Bishop Dudley spoke of his faithful parents.

—Jeff Cavins

Jeff Cavins is co-creator of the Amazing Grace *series and an editor of* Amazing Grace for Families. *His biography appears at the end of the book.*

A Mother's Ultimate Sacrifice

Jesus, you've got to breathe for me. I just can't do it anymore.

This was the last thing Jill Hawkins-Scheiter remembered as doctors desperately fought to save her life just five days after she gave birth to her first child, a baby girl. Only three months earlier, a physician had warned that this might happen and strongly recommended that the Scheiters abort their sixteen-week-old infant. Jill refused. She was adamant. She was going to have this baby. But the moment her heart stopped beating, it seemed as if every dire prediction was about to come true.

Jill Hawkins-Scheiter suffers from a muscular disease so rare it is known to exist in a thousand people worldwide. She is the only person with the disease ever known to have conceived and given birth to a child. So rare is this condition that for the first twenty-one years of her life, doctors didn't even know what it was and simply referred to it as, "Jill Hawkins disease."

Pat and Ron Hawkins began to notice something wrong with Jill when she was eighteen months old. "She would fall a lot," said her mother. When they would play Candy Land, Jill would reach forward to move her playing piece and fall forward until her head hit the board. After an examination by a pediatrician, Jill was sent to Children's Hospital in Philadelphia. "That's where it all started," Hawkins said.

Jill spent the next twenty-one years of her life as a walking medical mystery. "At first, they thought she had an unknown form of muscular dystrophy," Pat Hawkins said. In fact, Jill was the poster child for the Jerry Lewis telethon in 1985. But doctors were never sure, and the uncertainty was brutal for Pat. "I just knew that the only thing that was going to release me from this was prayer."

For years she attended the Miraculous Medal Novena at St. Stanislaus Parish in Lansdale, Pennsylvania, and would gaze on the statue of Mary holding Baby Jesus, whose arms are outstretched. One day she prayed, "You're a mother. You'll understand what I'm feeling. All I want is for her to be able to lift her arms like that." Jill was seven years old when she came up to her mother and said, "Look what I can do!" and lifted her arms just like the statue.

Years went by. Jill endured an endless number of tests, biopsies, and surgeries at numerous hospitals and clinics. When she was twelve, two steel rods were inserted into her spine to keep her back straight.

Through it all, Pat Hawkins kept her daughter's life as normal as possible. "I wanted her to know she was different, but not an exception," she said.

She was twenty-one years old when doctors finally arrived at a firm diagnosis—congenital myasthenia gravis syndrome—an unknown disease that causes overall muscle weakness in varying degrees. Thankfully, she was given a drug that greatly improved her muscle strength.

Life was looking up for young Jill, especially when romance began to bloom between herself and long-time friend, John Scheiter.

Susan Middleton, a family friend, remembers, "Pat had been praying for years that Jill would find a good man who would have the patience to take care of Jill." That prayer was answered in John Scheiter, Montgomery County's first full-time fireman. The two were friends for almost five years before admitting that they their friendship had blossomed into love. "I cried like a baby at the wedding," Middleton said.

Three years later, the couple wanted to start a family, and the first thing the doctor did was take Jill off all medicine, which meant that her muscles would return to their previous weakened state. She was told to wait three months before trying to conceive. Three months later, she was pregnant.

"She was very, very weak by then," Middleton said. "She was so weak that the muscles in her jaw wouldn't work for her to swallow. The first three months of the pregnancy were pretty normal. At four months she started to experience weight loss, in part because she couldn't chew. She was in and out of the hospital."

A physician told Jill that her life was in danger and strongly recommended an abortion. "She felt very uneasy that something bad would happen to Jill if she didn't abort," Middleton said. "She was afraid Jill would go into a myasthenia crisis, and what effects that would have on Jill were unknown. But Jill was adamant. She was not going to abort. They just wanted to make her aware that she was jeopardizing her life. Jill told them she was well aware."

Middleton remembers speaking with her at the time and hearing her say, "Susan, I'm having this baby, because I'm already a mother." I said, 'Jill, the culture is going to tell you that your life is more important, but faith is going to tell you that maybe the reason for your life is to have your baby.' I told her to trust in God."

Jill was in and out of Temple University Hospital in Philadelphia three or four times for weakness, loss of weight, and dehydration, but during this time the baby continued to grow and was doing fine. It was Jill they were worried about. Although she was due at the end of May, her weakened state found her being rushed to Temple Hospital at twenty-nine weeks. Her blood pressure was soaring and she went into contractions.

On March 20, 2004, doctors performed an emergency C-section and delivered a two-pound, eleven-ounce baby girl named Allison Patricia.

"Everything was OK for about ninety-six hours," Middleton said. "Then Jill started to feel like she couldn't breathe. She was so anxious she stayed at the nurses' station the whole night. She went to bed at 8:00 in the morning. After that point, doctors cannot agree what happened. The obstetrician thinks she had severe preeclampsia, and the pulmonologist thinks she had an amniotic embolism."

Whatever it was, it caused Jill's heart to stop beating. She went into "code."

"By the grace of God, there was a wonderful doctor on call, a pulmonologist who was ranked third in the country," Middleton said. "He stayed with Jill for four hours. He never left her side."

But even the best could not revive her. "When her parents arrived they were told she would have to be put on a heart-lung machine. She was going, maybe even gone. They could not get her to come around. She had been without oxygen and there were no brain waves."

Pat Hawkins remembers telling the whole family to join hands and "pray to God with everything you've got to save Jill." They prayed like never before.

Twenty minutes later a stunned doctor came into the room and announced, "We have a pulse." Jill was alive.

"They told Pat they were sure she had brain damage," Middleton said. "They wanted to see how much, and they were going to have to run tests. As she started to come out of it, Pat asked them to bring her a writing board, and Jill wrote, 'Am I going to die?' There was no brain damage. From that moment on, they knew they had a miracle."

Jill later revealed that she was aware of seventy-five percent of what was going on around her during the code. "The nurse asked her what she heard," Hawkins said, "and when Jill told her, her jaw hit the floor because that was exactly what happened."

Which is why she remembers that last prayerful thought, "Jesus, you have to breathe for me."

Jesus answered by returning the life this young mother was so willing to sacrifice that her child might live.

—Susan Brinkmann

Susan Brinkmann, O.C.D.S., is a correspondent for the Catholic Standard and Times *of Philadelphia and member of the Third Order of Discalced*

Carmelites. Formerly an historical fiction writer with two novels published by HarperCollins, Susan has devoted her life and talents to building up the Church and tearing down the culture of death.

She is the author of a book on Carmelite prayer, Lord, Teach Us to Pray, *as well as a book on the fraudulent research of "sex researcher" Alfred C. Kinsey,* The Kinsey Corruption *(Ascension Press, 2004). Susan has won numerous national awards, including a First Place Award for Investigative Journalism from the Catholic Press Association in 2005, the Bernadin O'Connor Award for Pro-Life Journalism in 2003 and 2004, the Eileen Egan Journalism Award from Catholic Relief Services in 2005, and the National Right to Life Excellence in Journalism Award.*

I Am a Mother

Looking at a Mother's Day advertisement, I suddenly realized that I was not cringing inside. For so long, the celebration of motherhood by others caused me great pain. It was not that I had no children; it was that I had two and lost them. Or rather, I aborted them. This reality was especially painful because I wanted those babies. But the people in my life, whom I depended on, pressured me to have the abortions. I was told it was selfish for me to think about giving birth. Both times, I felt that abortion was my only option.

It was an ugly secret that I kept even from my doctors. But through the grace of God, I experienced healing almost twenty years later. Now, I can openly say, "I *am* a mother." Through my husband's children who call me "Mom," and through my grandchildren, whom I cherish, my maternal desires have found rest. But more importantly, through facing the truth of my abortions and finding forgiveness, I have been able to experience the love I still have for my children. I love them and I am their mother.

I was just twenty years old in 1974 when my mother took me to a Planned Parenthood clinic. They confirmed that I was pregnant— unmarried and pregnant. "Aren't you lucky abortion is legal now?" the medical assistant gushed. The Supreme Court had just made it legal for women to abort their babies. The seventies were a time of liberation. It was a brave new world for women. Sitting in the clinic, I felt anything but brave. My birth control had not worked, and now I was pregnant.

Staring blankly at the medical assistant, I flatly informed her, "I'm not getting an abortion."

"We will talk about this later," my mother said curtly. My father hit the roof. He thought I should get married. The guy I was dating thought we should get married. I had started going with him on the heels of a break-up with another guy. How could

I tell him that I was not sure whose baby it was? My mother informed me that abortion was my only logical option. "You will bring shame on this whole family if you have this baby," she said. "And it's not even a baby. It's just a blob of tissue."

Although we were only occasional church-goers and there was no religious instruction at home, my father planned on becoming a deacon in the Church of Christ. "You will destroy your father's chances and humiliate your three brothers," my mother claimed. "You are being totally self-centered thinking about having this baby." Then my mother's final words ended any hope. "If you think I'm going to help you raise this child, you're wrong." Up until that point, I had looked to my mother for guidance. At twenty years old, working as a receptionist, I could not imagine trying to negotiate motherhood alone. I gave up.

We returned to the clinic for an injection to prepare my cervix for the abortion. Then, the next day, on my birthday, February 25, I lay on a table waiting for the abortion. When the doctor walked in, I desperately asked, "Can I change my mind?"

"No," the doctor told me. "It's already too late. The injection you had yesterday has already started the abortion." Years later, I learned that was not true. I lay there in a daze. Society was telling women that we now had control over our bodies, but I felt I had no control over anything. I was told the procedure would take just twenty minutes out of my life. In truth, it took more than twenty years from me. There was a jar on a table next to me. After the abortion, it was filled with my baby. I turned away and cried. There was no one to comfort me. Was this what women's rights was all about? I left with my mother through a side door. Women who had abortions were not allowed to walk back through the lobby and possibly upset the others still waiting. My mother took me to a restaurant. "Now, let's go on with your life and we don't need to discuss this further," she said matter-of-factly. I sat across the table and just stared blankly at her. A part of me had died with my baby. I no longer trusted her.

Three months later, I became involved with another young man. He treated me like a queen. We were soon engaged and married. Maybe this will be my chance for happiness, I thought. I imagined having children and living happily ever after. It was not to be. On our wedding night, when he discovered I was not a virgin, I had to lock myself in the bathroom to escape his fury. He was mentally and physically abusive from the start. Finally, after six months, I admitted to my family that the marriage was a terrible mistake.

By 1977 I moved in with another man. He was in the process of getting a divorce. He and his wife had two children, and she had two children from a previous marriage, so there were four kids at home. Although the plan was for us to get married, his divorce became bitter, so he decided he did not want the hassle of making things legal with me. Even though I still wanted children, he got a vasectomy six months after I had moved in. Two weeks later, we discovered I was pregnant. I was thrilled. He was furious. I hoped that he would get over it. I even bought a couple of maternity tops envisioning a pregnant belly that would announce to the world that I was a mother. But I was informed that if I had this child, he would deny it was his. Then, I heard the familiar threat: "If you have this baby, you are on your own. I won't help you. And anyway, you can help me raise my kids," he insisted. I did not feel strong enough to handle motherhood alone. God was not a part of my life, either. Surely, he was disgusted with me. My live-in partner dropped me off at the abortion clinic and then picked me up afterwards. From there we picked up his four kids for the weekend. It was those kids that stopped me from committing suicide after we returned home. I already felt dead inside, so I envisioned finishing the job. Standing in the bathroom, I contemplated how I could do it. Then, I realized how traumatic it would be for the children to discover my suicide. I had already hurt my own babies. I did not want to hurt anyone else's.

For thirteen years I continued to live with this man. He was verbally abusive, telling me over and over that I was stupid and ugly. I believed him. We drank and smoked a lot of marijuana. It helped dull my pain. Then, one morning, I walked into the bathroom and glanced into the mirror. I looked straight into the eyes of a skull. My heart beat through my chest and I went weak at the awful vision. I blinked back in disbelief, and then it was gone. I was stone sober that morning. The vision had given me a glimpse of where I was heading.

I made plans to leave. I left but returned for another year out of guilt after he had a heart attack. His insults continued. I left him again, only to begin a relationship with a man I worked with. His flattery was music to my ears after more than a decade of being beaten down. That relationship soon ended, however. One night, alone in my apartment, I thought about how miserable my life had been. Then, I thought about God. I did not feel worthy to talk to Him, but I had nowhere else to go. "Dear God," I cried out in desperation, "please bring someone into my life who will just love me as I am." Then, on April 1, 1990, I called a friend to ask him to the Soroptomist Ball that I had tickets for. Although Bruce and I had been friends for three years, our relationship soon turned romantic. He was a divorced combat veteran of Vietnam with two grown daughters. We shared our pain with one another.

We married on October 10, 1991. Bruce planned to have surgery to reverse his vasectomy so we could have children together. Instead, I woke up hemorrhaging one night. An ultrasound revealed a huge black mass in my uterus. I had never admitted my abortions to any doctor, although I often complained of irregular and very long periods. It was determined that my abortion seventeen years earlier had perforated my uterus. I had been slowly hemorrhaging all that time. A complete hysterectomy was necessary. Gone was my last hope of ever giving birth.

Although neither of us was practicing any particular religion, Bruce and I agreed that it was important to include God in our marriage. We started praying together and reading the Bible. When a friend asked me to go with her to check out the Catholic Church, I readily agreed. I returned by myself the following Sunday. During the consecration of the Holy Eucharist, I felt the love and forgiveness of Christ come through to me. I did not understand it all, but I made an appointment to see a priest. My fear was that the Catholic Church, known for being strongly against abortion, would reject me. Instead, the priest embraced me. He explained that the Church welcomed sinners and offered Christ's forgiveness and love. I was euphoric and told Bruce that I was going to begin instruction to become Catholic. He informed me that he did not want to get roped into this church. "That's fine," I said, trusting everything to God.

After attending my second Rite of Christian Initiation of Adults (RCIA) class, Bruce joined me. "I'm just going to see; it does not mean I'm going to Mass every Sunday," he cautioned. But Bruce did start coming with me to Mass. Then, one Sunday during the consecration, Bruce felt an immense sense of Christ's presence. On Easter Sunday in 1997, we entered the Church together. Since that time, I've accepted God's forgiveness and sought further healing from my abortions. I joined "Silent No More" and began giving public testimony as to the pain of abortion. Then, I attended a retreat through Rachel's Vineyard. This is a healing ministry for woman suffering from abortion. It was there that I gave my babies names and realized that I was still a mother. I asked forgiveness from my children and told them how much I loved them. I spiritually baptized them, and Bruce asked the children to let him be their adopted father, promising to always take care of me, their mother.

As a symbol of my love and healing, Bruce and I planted a flower garden, which we call our "Children's Garden." It is dedicated to all babies lost to miscarriages and abortion—and their mothers. There is a pond, a walkway, and a large statue of the Blessed Mother and one of an angel. A bench with a statue of a little boy and girl sits in the garden. The children are sharing a book, and a puppy leans on the boy's shoulder. I've placed a Divine Mercy bracelet on the wrist of the little girl. This statue represents Sarah Rose and Michael John—my children. The pain never completely goes away, but through the grace of God, love, and joy overcome it. My stepchildren call me mom, and they have given me four grandchildren. I was even blessed to be present at the birth of three of them. As I watched our grandson and granddaughters enter the world, there was a pang of regret that I had missed out on this experience myself. But instead of running from the pain or trying to bury it as I once had, I acknowledged it and let the excitement of new life overpower it.

While I was preparing to become Catholic, my mom was diagnosed with brain cancer. Before she died, we had a real talk for the first time since my abortion. "Please forgive me," she pleaded. "I was wrong to force you to have an abortion." The wedge that had driven us apart was removed. I realized then that my mother had also carried the guilt. Just as I knew in my heart that God had forgiven me, through His grace, I too was able to forgive my mother. Now, I hope for the day when we can all be reunited in love in the presence of Our Lord.

—Suzan Marcy

Suzan (Suzie) is the mother of Sarah and Michael. She is the second mother to her husband's daughters, Lesa and Nancy, and grandmother to Aaron, Rhiannon, Larrisa, and Aidan. Suzie and Bruce, a decorated combat veteran of Vietnam, have been married for fifteen years and are both very active with their grandchildren and church.

A Family Forever

We're going to be a family, I thought excitedly when I learned that my husband, Eric, and I were expecting our first baby. It seemed my life was perfect. I was married to the only man I had ever loved. I was sixteen and Eric was nineteen when he had stolen my heart with his deep brown eyes and generous spirit. Seven year later, we married and were soon expecting a baby girl.

While the little life growing inside me was safe and secure in my womb, I also felt safe and secure, covered with Eric's love. Together, we delighted in each new phase of our baby's development. Eric often whispered to his baby girl through my belly. It seemed that every night he came home with another book on pregnancy or parenting.

During the morning of April 7, 2003, Eric accompanied me to my prenatal appointment. Together, we listened to our baby's heartbeat for the first time. What a thrill to hear the pulse of her life. "Let's go shopping for some of the baby things," I suggested after the appointment. I could not wait to start getting ready to welcome our precious baby into the world.

As Eric pointed the car in the direction of the mall, I absent-mindedly slipped one hand under my seatbelt. It suddenly flashed through my mind that I had recently heard that expectant mothers should wear their seatbelts low in order to protect themselves but not risk injuring the baby in the event of a sudden impact. I pushed the belt just under my growing belly.

In the very next minute, a truck lost control and careened into our car. Squealing tires and shattering glass ended in a horrible silence. I was wedged into our mangled vehicle, unable to free myself. I looked over at Eric. I knew immediately that he was gone. I reached over and felt for a pulse I knew I would not find. In shock, I waited to be cut out of the vehicle and taken to the emergency room.

"Your baby is fine," the doctor told me. I had a broken ankle and dislocated a thumb. The pain did not sink in. Nothing seemed real. How could it be? How could my perfect life have ended so abruptly—without warning?

Someone asked my permission for Eric to be a tissue donor. Eric always wanted to help others. He had decided in high school to become a donor. "Yes," I tearfully agreed. "It's what he wanted."

In the following months, my body began to heal. My heart was a different matter. For the first three months, there were tears and grief, but it still did not seem like my life. One evening, while at my mother's home, we talked about my recent doctor's appointment and the upcoming delivery. It was then that reality suddenly hit full force. Eric was never coming back. He was not with me at my doctor appointments anymore, and he would not be present to embrace our baby when she entered the world.

It felt as if my life had drained out from me. How could I go on without Eric? He was my soul-mate, my husband, my baby's daddy. "I'm never going to see him again," I wept. "I'm having this baby without him. I'm all alone!" Deep sobs poured out.

My mother held me in her arms and cried with me. "We'll get through this together," she promised. After an hour, there were no more tears left. I was exhausted but somehow ready to face my world as it was now.

During the first three months, I had prayed to God for strength, but I had also lived with the unanswered question: "Why did God have to take Eric and leave me? Did I do something to deserve this? What if we had gotten into the car just a couple minutes later?"

But after my release of grief, I experienced a new level of realization. It finally hit me that, instead of just going through the motions, I had to start planning for my life. I was emotionally ready to survive without Eric now.

The pain was still there, but I accepted it and leaned on God to hold me up. Every time I felt too low to take another step forward, I called on God. Then, He gave me the strength to keep going. I felt it. There was a calming feeling knowing that God was there. And my baby was also with me. She was my reason to keep living. When Eric died, I understood how someone could die of a broken heart. If it were not for my baby, I would have preferred to die and be with Eric. But for my daughter, I wanted to take care of myself and live.

In a way, I came to understand that Eric was still alive and still with me, too. Sometimes I dreamed about him in much the way I dreamt about other things. But there were times when I was dreaming with him. Eric was really with me during those times. The first time this happened, I was walking down a long hall with rooms on each side. Eric was in one of the rooms. "You're really okay?" I asked him.

"Yes, I am," he answered and smiled at me. "Tell everyone I'm okay." Every time Eric came to me in a dream, I woke up feeling peaceful. We often had conversations about raising Erica. I could feel Eric's presence, and he helped me to move on. On the delivery table, I felt Eric with me. At a time when I could have been overwhelmed and lonely, instead, God filled me with strength and the knowledge that Eric, Erica, and I were all together at that moment as a family.

Erica is three years old now. She has a picture of her daddy in her room, and she always tells him good night. Erica once seemed to be watching something. When I asked her about it, she explained, "Daddy is here." She has also told me that she has seen him with people around him, but she did not know who they were. I asked her what those people looked like. "Kind of white and shiny," she responded.

The hardest part of my grief is behind me. I know that Eric would not want me to spend my life in mourning. I still miss him; especially when Erica passes some milestone and he's not here to share it with me. But Erica and I are not alone. God will see us through. And through His grace, we often feel that Eric is not so far away.

—Kari Barlament

Kari Barlament is involved with volunteer work in raising awareness for organ and tissue donation. She is also an assistant high school girls' basketball coach. Erica and Kari love to travel, their favorite destination being Aruba. Erica is now three and involved in dance.

Sweet Sixteen

One of my sons had come into my room, distraught. "Mom, why do you let them treat you this way?" My children, ages nine, seven, two, and one, had been willing to share their life with the six siblings that my husband, Russell, and I were planning on adopting. They had never complained about the upheaval in family life until now. But seeing Russell and me treated with disrespect was hurting them.

"These children have not known the love and security you've had all your life," I explained. "We need to embrace them for who they are. They are children of God, and He loves them just as He loves us." It was not a matter of "letting" them be disrespectful because we were doing everything we could to try and get behaviors under control. "Things will get better," I promised my son.

Later that evening, I lay on my bed, and a flood of tears poured out. I had been so sure that God wanted us to adopt this group of siblings. But now, after two months, it seemed that Russell and I and our original five children were trapped in a nightmare. Have I ruined our family? I wondered. Screaming, tantrums, fire setting, urinating on furniture, breaking things, violence … how much more could we endure?

I did not know how much more I had to give. During the entire year, I had worked hard to get those kids out of the foster-care system in California, there had been no doubt in my mind that they were ours. As I reflected on the long and determined fight, I realized that God had wanted us to be 110 percent sure that we wanted those children. They needed to be with each other, and I believed they needed us. "God, show me and teach me what I need for our kids," I prayed. "Help me to love and care for these children."

When Russell and I had married on November 25, 1988, we knew we wanted a big family. Ten years later, with four young sons, I learned I could not have more children. Yet our family did not feel complete. The next year, we adopted a beautiful six-month-old baby girl, Caitlyn, from a Chinese orphanage. Caitlyn filled our lives with love and joy, but there was room in our hearts for more.

I began looking for sibling groups in this country to adopt, since I knew they were hard to place. When a social worker called to tell me about a sibling group of six, she had my attention. The six kids, ages three to nine, had been removed from an abusive home and bounced around foster homes for three years. They were in two separate homes at the time. It was likely they would be split up further in hopes of finding them adoptive homes. Hearing about these poor, innocent children, my heart opened wide. They needed a loving home, and I believed they belonged with us.

"Six kids?" Russell gasped when I told him. "Are you crazy?" I told him about their hardships. "I feel bad, too, but we'd need a bigger house, a bigger van, even a bigger kitchen table." But he did not say no. "I need some time to think about it," he explained.

I knew that Russell and I would need to be a team. I prayed and trusted that God would lead us in the right direction—together—whichever way that would be. A few days later, Russell, who was a builder by trade, handed me a blueprint to our new house. "My buddies offered to help with the construction," he said and then added: "I guess we can always add a leaf to the table."

"We can do this!" I cried, hugging him. Then, I got on the phone with the social worker to set up a visitation to meet our children. Russell and I flew from Idaho to California in October of 2000 for a three-day visit with them. Our first visit was spent in the social work office for four hours. I had come prepared with a backpack full of games and treats to help with interaction. I was not prepared, however, for the hostility from the three oldest girls—Daisy, nine; Sandra, eight; and Rosa, seven. They had no idea a family wanted to adopt them. The girls expected to return to their original home eventually. Instead, on the drive to the office, a social worker told them they were going to meet their new parents.

Being watched by multiple social workers while we interacted with the children was exhausting but still exhilarating. Russell and I had never even seen their pictures. They were beautiful, and we fell in love with them. Our excitement overflowed. When we stopped at a grocery store on our way back to the hotel, a woman looked at us and commented, "I don't know who you two are, but you both just glow."

The next two visits were easier since we took them to a park for a picnic and games. At the end of the three days of visits, we began an uphill battle of getting through mounds of red tape. Finally, by the time the children arrived in Idaho on June 1, 2002, the media had reported on our fight for them. There were forty to fifty people at the airport with us to welcome them home.

Seven-year-old Rosa got off the plane looking confused and scared. "Rosa," I called. "Momma's here." Her eyes lit up and she ran into my open arms. I cried tears of joy and saw onlookers crying with me.

But before long, the tears that flowed were out of frustration. The three oldest girls had been told they could return to their foster home if they wanted. They tried every trick in the book to get us to kick them out. When that failed, they would pack their bags and threaten to leave, but never at the same time. One would pack and the others would talk her out of leaving. We told the girls we loved them and wanted to be their parents, but we would not force them to stay. The girls loved each other. They knew that getting adopted by us was the only way for them to stay together and to stay with their younger siblings, Francisco, six; Maricela, four; and Carmen, three. Still, they were confused and scared.

"You're not our blood!" the girls often screamed at me. Russell and I were a tag team, always backing each other up, but it was exhausting. It had been two months when I experienced my moment of doubt. But fortified by prayer, Russell and I dug our heels in and loved those children. I met them after school with homemade snacks and tucked each one into bed at night with an "I love you." Every morning and evening, we knelt as a family and prayed. Before meals and before settling a problem, we prayed, too. Still, the behavior worsened. After a lifetime of insecurity and rejection, these kids were daring us to throw them out. But after three months of security and love, they finally started to respond. The bad behavior gradually slowed down. The kids started feeling like they were home.

In December, six months after they had arrived, I knew we were finally a family. My sister had just made each of the children his or her own special blanket. When Russell and I walked downstairs to join them to watch a Christmas video, all eleven kids were mixed in together, cuddling under their new blankets, giggling and sharing popcorn. "Honey, look," I whispered. "We're a family."

Russell and I smiled at each other. "We made it," he said.

But there was still a missing piece. I learned from Daisy that there was an older brother. Since he had been separated from the rest of the family and put into institutionalized care four years earlier, the social workers had lost track of him. They originally thought I was mistaken because there was also an older half-sibling living in Mexico. After some digging, we found thirteen-year-old Victor living in a group home. He was considered unadoptable for extreme behaviors, and parental rights had never been terminated. Now that the children had all settled in, Russell and I were determined to bring Victor home, too.

We got permission to have Victor visit us for four days over Thanksgiving. He seemed to be in awe at family life, watching our every move, but unable to join in on the fun and laughter himself. He came again at Christmas. It was then that he had an emotional release that resulted in a full-blown tantrum. Victor was learning disabled, so he was having trouble processing everything. His fear and heartbreak at having been abandoned by his family when he was nine years old poured out. But now, surrounded by his family again and all our love, Victor begged us not to send him back at the end of the visit. Unfortunately, we had no choice. There were still lots of hurdles and red tape to get through. Finally, after five months of pleading his case and getting help from our governor and senators, we were able to bring him home for good.

When Victor stepped off the plane, our youngest son shouted out to him. The expression on his face went from scared to joyful. "You came!" he cried.

The social worker confided in me, "He was afraid you wouldn't really come for him." We all hugged Victor and welcomed him into our family for good.

As the years rolled by, the love deepened between us, and I often looked over my family in awe. They were growing up to be such beautiful, loving, and respectful children. I felt blessed. But at bedtime prayer, I kept feeling as if everyone was not there.

Then, out of the blue, a friend who was looking into an adoption sent me an email about four young siblings who were up for adoption. They had already been adopted out once and brought back because the family really only wanted the baby. "I think these kids are meant for you," my friend wrote. I agreed. It had been five years since we had added to our family, and in all that time, I had felt that our family was not complete yet.

I shared the email with Russell. "It's such an emotional roller coaster," he said. "I think we are done." I just prayed. I believed that this was not something I should pressure Russell about. Only God knew if we were done or not, so I put it completely in

His hands. A couple weeks later, Russell asked me why I had not mentioned that sibling group again.

"You work hard all week and I respect your feelings," I said. "If you think this is not right for us, I accept that."

"I've had a change of heart," he confessed. "I know the kids would love them, and if you think you can handle it, I can too."

There were ten other families looking at this group, but everything fell into place, and the social worker thought they belonged with us. On November 6, 2006, Samantha, seven; Selena, five; Stephanie, three; and Jaden, twenty-one months, slipped into our family as if they had always been here. There was not so much as a ruffle. They immediately moved into our hearts and found laps galore waiting to hold and love them.

It's been three years since we have been a family with sixteen kids. We moved to the outskirts of town on seven acres so that Russell could begin a natural-produce business and provide safe after-school employment for our kids. The kids share rooms, chores, love of family, and a faith in God.

As I look back at the storms we navigated and how far we've come, I'm in awe. With hindsight, I can see clearly that for every wall we backed into, God opened a door. Even during the rough times, He never abandoned us. And now, thanks to Him, no one in our family will ever need to feel abandoned again.

—Jan Walgamott

Jan Walgamott is a fun-loving woman from Gooding, Idaho. She was a computer programmer by trade but left that job for what she describes as the best job in the world—being a mother to her sixteen beautiful children and a wife to a wonderful husband.

Chapter 2
A Family's Wisdom

Let the Children Come Unto Me

Few people will ever forget the day Brenda Roundtree and her four adopted children entered the Catholic Church. It was during the Easter Vigil of 2003 at Visitation of the Blessed Virgin Mary Church in Norristown, Pennsylvania. It seemed there was not a dry eye in the church.

This story of a family's journey began a year earlier at the breakfast table. "I have to go talk to a special person," Meredith announced to her mother, Brenda. "I have to go over there. I know where to go." Brenda had no idea what her daughter was talking about. Meredith just kept insisting: "I have to go over there. I know where to go." Finally, Brenda piled everyone into the family van and headed out.

Meredith gave directions, while continuing to insist: "I know where it is."

"She told me where to turn," said Brenda. "I had never been down Trooper Road before, not ever. She led me straight to the church." That church was Visitation of the Blessed Virgin Mary, and the "special person" Meredith insisted on seeing was someone she had never met before—the pastor, Msgr. Thomas A. Murray.

"Brenda came into our office and told me that her daughter had led her there," Monsignor Murray said. Although this might seem unusual for a child, it is perhaps even more unusual in Meredith's case. At twenty-seven years of age, Meredith has

Down Syndrome and functions at a preschool level. Monsignor Murray realized that he had a very special situation on his hands. He welcomed them with open arms.

Until her husband's death a year earlier, Brenda had been raising her seven biological children in the Mormon Church. Still, she had not felt settled there and had stopped going to church. Now, with Meredith's incident, it resurrected her search for "the Church." She tried to return to the faith of her childhood, Lutheranism, but halfway through a service she felt, "This is not it, either." After the trip to Visitation, Meredith kept saying over and over, "I want to go to my church." That led Brenda to inquire about RCIA, the Rite of Christian Initiation of Adults, to enter the Church. The church, coincidentally, had a special class for children with special needs. This enabled both Brenda and four of her adopted children to receive preparation.

The first time they attended Mass, Brenda cried. "Everything was so beautiful. It made so much sense and I kept thinking, 'Finally! Finally!' I knew this was the Church. There was no question at all in my mind."

While Brenda's conversion story is remarkable, the story of how she and her husband adopted children with special needs is equally compelling.

Meredith was born twenty-eight years ago with Down Syndrome and was called a "failure to thrive" child, with no sucking reflex. She was literally thrown out with the hospital trash. Thankfully, her soon-to-be-adoptive mother, Brenda, who was active in the pro-life movement, was known in area hospitals.

"I used to go into hospitals to talk to people about how they were killing living humans. One night, I got a phone call from a hospital about a baby who had just been born and thrown away." The baby was Meredith. "She was literally thrown in the trash. They were hoping she would just die right away."

The Roundtree family was close friends with the former Surgeon General, Dr. C. Everett Koop, who had operated on their son many times. They called Dr. Koop at Children's Hospital of Philadelphia to tell him what had happened. Brenda wanted to get the child herself, but Dr. Koop told her to stay home and prepare for the arrival of her new baby. Then, he went by ambulance to the hospital and rescued the child. A few days later, Dr. Koop called Brenda. "Come down and see your daughter," he said. When she arrived at Children's Hospital, Brenda found the surgeon in a room with six bassinets. "Can you pick out the one who was so disgusting that they threw her away?" he asked. Brenda could not. They were all beautiful.

When Dr. Koop saw her inability to answer, he told her: "You're looking for the wrong thing. Look for the most beautiful little girl you've ever seen." Brenda's eyes went right to Meredith.

Not long after this, the Roundtrees were alerted to another abandoned child with Down Syndrome living in a foster home in New Jersey.

"When I got there, Cassandra was lying on her back and sucking a bottle," Brenda said. "She was over a year old and had never eaten solid food. The smell coming from her was so bad. When I picked her up, she had sores all over her back. She was so thin, but beautiful, with curly blonde hair and big glue eyes. She was breathtakingly beautiful. She's twenty-nine now and still has trouble eating."

The Roundtrees then heard abut a little girl in a New York institution for hydrocephalic children. "This was a beautiful place," Brenda said. "The ceilings were all decorated with paintings, and there was music playing. All the babies had their own cribs and a worker who stayed right next to them and talked to them. It was the ideal setting. Debbie was a year-and-a-half old and was walking all over the place. That's why they were trying to find a home for her because she was a little more advanced. But she was so tiny. Nothing moved on her except her legs. But could they ever move! She would just disappear. We ended up taking her home." Debbie is twenty-seven now and in the early stages of Alzheimer's disease.

Last came David. "We went to a social agency in Jersey to get David. When we got there, he was sitting on a deck with a runny nose and a soaking wet diaper, and his face was all broken out from allergies. No one was there. We really could not just take him, so we waited for about an hour and a half. Finally, a lady walked in and said, 'Did you come for him? Well, here he is.'"

Brenda's biological children are all grown and living on their own now. She could have been at the point in life where she could be retired, but instead, she is caring for a house full of children with special needs. "I'm spoiled with these kids," she said as if no greater blessing could befall her. She says she feels blessed the way the Lord has led her to a spiritual home for which she had searched. "The whole congregation of people there has loved us," she said. "It's the warmest, sweetest, most loving place I've ever been."

—Susan Brinkmann

Susan Brinkmann's biography appears after "A Mother's Ultimate Sacrifice" in chapter one.

Lucy's Star

Scanning the pet section of the classifieds in July of 1997, I found just the dog we were looking for—a small Yorkshire terrier. The owners were moving out of state and unable to take the dog. They had actually advertised two dogs, but the other dog was a Lab-Chessie mix, which was bigger than what we wanted.

When I arrived for the dog, another family had beaten me to it and was walking away with the little bundle of fur. As I turned to leave, the dog's owner practically begged me to take a look at the other dog. But such a large dog was not at all on my periscope that day—until, that is, she told me her story.

Star was her name. The woman and her husband had raised her from a pup and then given her to their daughter and son-in-law, who lived on a farm fifty miles away. Unfortunately, their son-in-law was abusive. A couple of months earlier, he had tried to harm their daughter and her baby in a drunken rage. Star had jumped in and received a knife wound intended for his wife. The woman was able to escape with her baby, and the dog was left to fend for itself. Eventually, the wounded dog had managed to get all the way back to Kansas City and the parents' home—a fifty-mile trek. Star had been tracking her way home for several weeks when, within blocks of the parents' house, the dog collapsed at a gas station on the interstate. As she described the scene and named the station location, my heart skipped a beat. I knew the very dog she was describing.

My husband had come home from work one evening very upset. On his route home that particular day, he had passed by that same gas station, and this was the very scene he had described to me. He had seen a badly starved and beaten black-Lab-mix dog collapse. He had stopped to try to assist the dog, but she was too frightened to let anyone approach her. Finally, a woman had come along and said she recognized it as her neighbors' missing dog. The woman called her name, and the dog allowed the woman to load her into a truck.

My husband had spoken of the dog often, worried about her fate. Now I was unbelievably being given the opportunity to save her. She had heartworms, and the couple were moving; they had no money to care for her and did not want to have to put her to sleep. I felt compelled to take her.

When I came home with this pitiful, scrawny bunch of canine fur, my husband said, "Good heavens! She looks just like the Lab I saw at the gas station." When I explained to Gene that it was the very same one, he was instantly in love.

After several rounds of treatment for her heartworms, she regained her health. In the meantime, she quickly learned that Gene was her champion. He held her and cuddled her through all the misery she had to endure with treatments. With our children all grown, Lucy filled the void in our home with love.

After a couple of weeks, Gene decided we should change her name from Star to Lucy. She wasn't responding to the name Star. He suspected the man must have used it when beating her. Sure enough, she instantly came to accept the name Lucy.

Initially, we suspected her voice box had been removed, as she never made a sound. But one day, as we were walking her, a child who ran out onto the path unexpectedly startled her, and she let out a bark. Then she cringed as though she expected a beating. Gene and I hugged and praised her. From then on, she got her doggie voice back, and she could sing like an angel on cue. Within days of finding her bark, she would prove to be a hero once more.

One night in November, she woke us by barking and growling. She jumped at the window and then ran to the front door of the house and barked some more. We turned on the lights and looked around but could not discover the reason she was so upset. The next day we discovered a burglar had broken into two houses on our block during the night. We were pretty sure Lucy had run him off from our house.

As the years went by, Lucy became as dear to us as any dog we have ever owned. She was great with our grandchildren and loved everyone.

In the summer of 2003, she began to have problems with kidney failure. Her kidneys had been damaged in her earlier years of abuse and it would finally prove irreversible, but she still managed one last heroic deed. In early October of that year, she started jumping up and licking my husband's neck. She would shiver and whine and bark. This was something Lucy had never done before. We were baffled at first, but then Gene admitted that he had a sore in his mouth and his neck hurt. I convince him to see a dentist. It turned out that had oral cancer. The cancer required extensive surgery, but thanks to Lucy, they were able to slow down the spread of the cancer.

Then, at 1:00 p.m., one day in July of 2004, Lucy's earthly light burned out. How we missed our little angel dog in those following days. We knew we had been blessed to have owned her and thought we could never possibly replace her. But once again, God had another plan for us.

By September of 2005, my husband's cancer battle was growing more difficult. He had required more surgery the previous April, and he was struggling to maintain his strength and a positive outlook. He continued to miss Lucy so much that I decided to look for another Lab. On our anniversary, I showed my husband the picture of Max and his story listed on the local animal shelter's website. Instantly Gene said: "Why, he looks just like our Lucy. Let's go get him." It was the first time in quite a while that Gene had shown any enthusiasm for life. And what a joy Max became for us in the trying days ahead.

From the moment we brought Max home, he and Gene were inseparable. Max quickly picked up on Gene's every need and his physical limitations. By December, Gene was on oxygen and heavy medications. The cancer had spread to his brain and to his lungs. During the last few days of Gene's life, he required constant care, which was difficult for me. I don't know what I would have done without Max to help.

When I needed to sleep from sheer exhaustion, Max was faithfully there beside Gene and attuned to his every need. If Gene's oxygen slipped off, Max would come and wake me up. If Gene was in pain or needed anything, Max would alert me. Having Max made it possible for us to get through the remaining time we had at home before Gene entered the hospital for the last time. On the night my beloved died, Max was there at home waiting to comfort me, and I like to think, in spirit, Lucy was, too. December 13, the day Gene died, is the Feast of St. Lucy.

—Christine Trollinger

Christine Trollinger lives in Kansas City, Missouri, and is a freelance writer. She has been published in several magazines and books of inspirational anthologies, including several previous Amazing Grace *books. Christine is a widow, mother of three, grandmother of three, and great-grandmother to Tyra Grace and Ireland Eve, who are her pride and joy.*

The Unbreakable Bond of Family

Our most basic instinct is not for survival but for family. Most of us would give our own life for the survival of a family member, yet we lead our daily life too often as if we take our family for granted.

–Paul Pearshall

The history of mankind, the history of salvation, passes by way of the family ... The family is placed at the center of the great struggle between good and evil, between life and death, between love and all that is opposed to love.

–Pope John Paul II

The first thing that a person finds in life and the last to which he holds out his hand, and the most precious that he possesses, even if he does not realize it, is family life.

–Blessed Adolph Kolping

The happiest moments of my life have been the few which I have passed at home in the bosom of my family.

–Thomas Jefferson

The family—that dear octopus from whose tentacles we never quite escape, nor, in our inmost hearts, ever quite wish to.

–Dodie Smith

What greater thing is there for human souls than to feel that they are joined for life - to be with each other in silent unspeakable memories.

–George Eliot

At the end of the day, a loving family should find everything forgivable.

–Mark V. Olsen and Will Sheffer

We are all going to heaven together. If any of you chose not to come, it will ruin everything.

–St. John Vianney

We cannot destroy kindred: our chains stretch a little sometimes, but they never break.

–Marquise de Sévigné

Other things may change us, but we start and end with the family.

–Anthony Brandt

Our House

The first house my parents owned was one they designed and built in Bloomington, Minnesota, a suburb of Minneapolis. The neighborhood grew up along with my sisters and me. In winter, we rode sleds recklessly down the many hills. We roved through the connecting back-yards with the numerous other children in the neighborhood. I helped my dad build stairs up a hill in the back-yard and helped plant trees and shrubs. My mother was in her element sewing curtains, wallpapering, and even painting the kitchen ceiling red.

Between eighth and ninth grade, we moved away farther from the sprawl of the suburbs. I left that neighborhood with fond memories. Being my first home, the address stuck in my head long after I grew up, married, and moved out of state.

Later, my wife and I returned to the area and for fun drove through my old neighborhood. A gentleman stood in the driveway, and I told him I had once lived there. On a whim I asked him if he was interested in selling. He smiled and quoted the price for which he'd be willing to sell it. Though buying the house would have been terrific, at the time I was pastoring a small church, and I could barely afford a car, much less a house.

I could see from the street that after twenty years the kitchen ceiling was still red and mom's curtains still adorned the windows.

A few more moves around the country brought us back to the Minneapolis area, and we settled in a home in a northern suburb. I began teaching several Bible studies at parishes in the Archdiocese of St. Paul-Minneapolis, and I began organizing tours to Israel. At the one of these Bible studies, I attended the year-end thank-you party for volunteer organizers. I sat at a table with several of these volunteers. When I asked if anyone was interested in joining me on a trip to Israel, a gentleman next to me wrote his address down on a tablet and handed it to me. I casually glanced at his address and then took a second look. There it was, the address I had repeated so often as a kid. "That's my house," I said, trying to remain calm. Unable to contain my amazement, I exclaimed, "You're living in the house I grew up in! My parents built that house!" The man grinned with surprise.

"I have your book and many CDs by you that my wife and I have read and listened to," he informed me.

I was so amazed. "Some of the pictures in my book, *My Life on the Rock,* were taken in that house!" I exclaimed. I told everyone around us the amazing coincidence, or as I always call these kinds of happenings, a "God-incidence." He graciously invited me and my family to come and visit them. On a pleasant summer day, my parents, two sisters and I re-gathered nearly thirty-five years later, now with my wife and my own children, to see that house of fond memories.

They had bought the house not long ago and had since finally painted the ceiling white and stripped off the black and white floral wall paper, but not before taking photos of the process, which they shared with us. I walked from room to room reliving the many snippets from the lives of all of us. I went down the hall to the room that used to be my bedroom. This was the room where I first had a desire to read the Bible on the evening of my Confirmation. Unbelievably, now in that room is a shelf with books and tapes on it which I have written and recorded. What an interesting full circle. Who would have thought that night, when I, at the age of fifteen decided reading one verse of the Bible every night would be my goal, that one day, other people would be reading my books and listening to me teach the Bible? I am so grateful to God for letting my path cross with the owners of that house. It has added another layer of memories to our first family home.

—Jeff Cavins

Jeff Cavins is co-creator of the Amazing Grace *series and an editor of* Amazing Grace for Families. *His biography appears at the end of the book.*

Pride Goeth Before a Water Ticket

Just weeks before our summer vacation, our doorbell rang at 8:30 in the morning. I peeked out to see a police officer standing on my porch. My heart sank as I thought of the possibility that one of my older sons had been in an accident, since both had already left for work that morning. I quickly opened the door. Rather than telling me bad news, the officer proceeded to ask me if I knew that I had water running down the street. "We *do?*" was my reply. I went on to politely explain to him that we have a sprinkler system that is precisely set so as to *conserve* water, not waste it, and I asked him if he was sure the water was coming from our lawn. He was not impressed with my sincerity and asked me to show him some form of ID. I was just shocked.

My youngest son kept saying, "Mom, what'd you *do?* What'd you *do,* Mom?"

Emphatically, I answered, "Nothing!" I tried very hard to remain calm—especially when he proceeded to write me up a ticket. *Surely this is just a warning,* I thought. *Surely.* Nope. It was a ticket. The officer proceeded to tell me that I would not be given the chance to pay the fine, but rather, I would have to appear in court! As he circled my court date with his pen, my mind slipped into sheer disbelief. *Wait a minute ... is this some kind of joke ... my birthday's coming up ... where are the cameras?*

No joke. He was real and so was the ticket. *This can't be happening!* I thought. *I am a law-abiding citizen. I pay my taxes and I am honest! We make our kids obey the laws...they're not allowed to drive before they are sixteen and we don't let them drink alcohol!* My thoughts went on and on with our attributes, while at the same time I pictured myself standing in line at the courthouse with all the men in the orange suits and handcuffs. I was just mortified.

After dropping my youngest off at his violin practice that morning, I cried and scolded God, "*This* is why people get discouraged! It was just a leaky gasket! I didn't even know the sprinkler system was on! Why did you let this happen?" I figured God already knew what I was thinking, so I might as well say it.

Normally, I am one of those "morning people" who some would like to clobber for being overly chipper. But because of many recent disappointments, I guess I was weary of a world wherein many times wrong is called right and right is perceived as wrong. Though I knew this was a small thing in the scheme of life, at that moment, it felt huge. Through my tears, I told God that I was sorry I yelled at Him, but in reality, I really did feel let down. If I had been speeding through a school zone and endangering lives, I would have been given a ticket and fined, but because my sprinkler system leaked, I was going to have to appear in court at 8:00 a.m. the very morning after we returned from vacation.

Later, I received notification that my court appearance had been changed to a later date. Though happy with the date change, needless to say, I was still angry at the idea of appearing in court. I even contacted a city commissioner to try and get the ordinance changed.

When my court date finally arrived, my heart felt heavy as I climbed the stone steps. The temperature that July day was about 108 degrees, and with every step I took, I felt the weight of disappointment, discouragement, and defeat. I had a brief vision of Jesus' journey to Calvary and felt shame at the comparison.

As the coolness of the courthouse swept over me, it took my eyes several moments to adjust to the much darker interior of the building. Within moments, I looked up to see a former catechism student of mine running down the stairs. She was crying and ran straight into my arms. "You came!" she cried. "You came! Did you get the message? I wanted you to be here!"

I had absolutely *no* idea what she was talking about. I had no idea she had been trying to reach me. The last I had heard, she had been living out of town. I held her; and when she calmed a bit, she explained that she was in court for a family matter involving her custody. She had previously been in foster care and was hoping to get placed permanently with her biological father. The judge had just ruled that it would take another six months before she could live with her dad. Her foster mother had been trying to reach me, but to no avail.

A combination of humility, shame, and wonder all washed over me as I realized that if it weren't for the infamous ticket and the change in the court date, I wouldn't have been there for this young girl, who had gone through some very hard times. After all, it wasn't as though I ran into her at the grocery store or at Wal-Mart. I *never* go to the courthouse for anything.

I assured her that God was aware of all things, both great and small, and told her how I had come to be there at that moment in time. We laughed together when I told her the story. Her laughter quickly replaced her tears. We then prayed that the judge would change his mind, or that the delay would go quicker than expected. I promised to keep her in my prayers.

After she left, I walked around the nearest corner and wept. This young woman was special to me. When I had first met her, I sensed that she was struggling, and I tried very hard to show her extra love and attention. If I hadn't been there at the courthouse that day, I may never have seen her again.

Upon returning home, I received a phone call from the girl's foster mother. The judge had unexpectedly given the girl a month with her father after all. She now happily lives with him permanently.

To this day, I am still humbled at how many times we do not see God's hand, holding us, changing us, shaping us, protecting us, refining us. Through every storm, through every trial, great or small, He is there.

—Elizabeth Schmeidler

Elizabeth Schmeidler's biography appears after her story "Just Do It!" in chapter one.

The Tree

Sunday mornings at our house were always my favorite day. From the earliest years of our marriage, my husband John would get up very early in the morning and make breakfast for the whole family. It was usually a feast of sausage, bacon, eggs, home-made biscuits, and gravy. He would turn on a Christian radio station and fill the house with music. Everyone could smell the food and hear the music as they crawled out of bed, all eleven children. They clustered around the kitchen table and then proceeded to bring me breakfast in bed. This is the way it happened for many years.

We always attended the noon Mass. That gave us a space of about two hours between breakfast and departure time. While I was up and about and the children were dressing for church, John would sneak in a little nap.

One Sunday morning in February, as I sat in the kitchen relaxing with a cup of tea, I gazed out the window into our back yard. My attention was drawn to an old, stately tree at the very back of our lot. There were many trees on our lot, but this was the biggest. The former residents of the house had tied a long fire hose up on one of the high branches. Our children, along with a lot of the neighborhood children, dubbed it the "Tarzan tree" and spent many hours swinging from that hose. Lately, it had begun to give me a bad feeling. The tree was so old. I just didn't trust it anymore.

The three youngest children were in the kitchen with me: Andrew, age eight; Linda, seven; and Michael, five. Looking out the window, I remarked, "I don't want you kids to swing on that tree anymore." The kids said they had just been swinging on it the day before. "I don't know why, but I just don't want you on it any more. We'll just put it in the hands of God," I remarked. I knew that with a houseful of kids and all the neighborhood kids, the tree's presence might still pose a threat in spite of my ruling to ban them from it.

About a half hour later my daughter Linda screamed from the kitchen, "Mom! Mom! Come quick!" I ran quickly from the next room to the sound of her alarm. "Look!", she announced and pointed out the back window. The Tarzan tree was lying flat. Nobody had even heard a thunderous roar of the tree falling to the ground. The massive trunk crowned with branches was just lying there. It took my breath away to see our giant tree— the one I had seen standing in our yard only moments before— completely still on the ground. It gave me an eerie feeling. We threw on our coats and went outside to have a closer look. The tree had not been uprooted. My impression was that the hand of God had gently bent it over and lay it on the ground.

There was something about that tree and the conversation that preceded its falling that left our family in awe. The kids called it "Mom's tree miracle." Did I have a premonition of the tree not being strong enough to hold up the children anymore? Had my desire to put the situation into God's hands lead him to put the old tree safely to rest?

In the early spring we delighted in looking at the tree sprawled across the back-yard with new leaves sprouting from its branches. The "Tarzan" tree continued to live all through that summer until we finally decided it was time to remove it. Yet even after the tree was gone, it still cast a big shadow on our family.

—Margaret Williams

Margaret Williams and her husband, John, were married for forty-eight years until he passed away in 2005. She has eleven children, twenty grandchildren, and two great-grandchildren. In 1995, Margaret was selected by Right to Life-Lifespan as Mother of the Year for her inspiration, patience, and boundless energy.

Loving Blindly

"Where's that great little buddy of mine?"

The Secret of Sanctity

Jack Hines was a normal guy living an average life. Born and raised Catholic in the coal-mining town of Pittston, Pennsylvania, Jack's childhood was filled with touch-football games and altar serving. There was a time when he thought he might have a vocation, but then he met and married Joni Orloski from nearby Scranton. They both came from a family of ten; Jack was the oldest; Joni, the youngest.

The couple was blessed with two sons, John III and Mark, and moved to the Archdiocese of Philadelphia in 1986. Jack worked for various food markets while raising his family. It was a job that kept him on the road calling on hundreds of convenience stores in five states.

On the surface, Jack Hines could be any man. He cut the lawn, raked the leaves, fixed the car, and carried his sleeping sons to bed after long car trips. But there was something very different about Jack Hines, something that didn't come from the outside but from somewhere deep within him. It was holiness.

Everyone who knew this "average" man says the same thing about Jack Hines—God was always first in his life. At first glance, this might not sound like such a big deal, but it was this quality that made an impact on every life he touched.

Jack's son Mark, a doctor who resides in North Carolina, described his father as a "priestly" man who did nothing to draw attention to himself. In a letter he recently wrote to his father, Mark said, "I never understood why you never did anything to please yourself. You always spent your effort and time helping us or others, encouraging our fulfillment, not your own. I always felt sad for you. You never seemed to get the rewards you deserved. How foolish I was. You understood what so few others ever had or will. You knew . . . you have always known the greatest gift to ourselves is giving happiness to others."

He was one of those people you could count on to listen even after everyone else was tired of hearing it. No matter what was going on in his life, he would rather talk about you than himself.

"He always listened," said son Jack. "He would sit down and talk for hours with people because he was truly interested in everything you had to say."

With twenty aunts and uncles in the family, Jack and Mark have in excess of thirty first cousins. "He knew everything that was going on about all of them at all times, because he would ask," Jack said.

Even though his devotion to God was not something he wore on his sleeve, almost everyone sensed it. "That's what makes it even more inspiring," Mark said. "He wasn't trying to show how good a Catholic he was. He just was. He was never direct about doing the rosary in front of everyone, but he'd pray it all the time ... in his pocket while he was walking down the street ... in the privacy of his room ... He wasn't doing it for show; he was doing it for himself and his relationship with God."

In fact, the reason he loved his job so much was not because of the pay, the benefits, or the hours. It was because "he could pray the Rosary in the car all day," his wife, Joni, said. Jack's holiness was imbedded in all the tiny details of his life, from the way he loved his wife and kids to the prayers he whispered while driving down the interstate to work.

But never was it more apparent than on that dark day in June, 2004, when a doctor told him the results of an MRI on his brain. "It happened so quickly," Joni said. "We had just had a fun-filled Father's Day weekend, and he was fine. He woke up on Monday, June 21, with a headache. On Tuesday it was worse. He went to the doctor later that day. They sent him for an MRI on Wednesday and found nine tumors on the brain. They had to find the primary source of the cancer, and it turned out to be cancer of the esophagus."

When the doctors told him he could no longer drive due to the possibility of seizures, the first thing he said was, "How am I going to get to my holy hour?" He didn't ask, "Am I going to die?" or "Is my hair going to fall out?" or "How sick am I going to get?" Even at a devastating moment like that, Jack's heart remained with his treasure—God.

Treatment began with radiation to the brain and then to the chest area, but the cancer had already spread to his bones and lungs. "The day they were done with radiation the doctor told him there was no point in starting chemotherapy because it would only be twenty percent effective," Joni said. "It was senseless to put him through that."

His brother, Father William Hines of St. Mary's Parish in Landover Hills, Maryland, said that the day he received that diagnosis, Jack said, "'Bill, if God wants me to do something, I'll get through this. But if this is it, I'm ready to go.'"

It was an attitude that never left him, Father Hines said. "The Sunday before he died, I asked him, 'Jack, what are you going to say to Jesus when you meet Him?' Jack's face illumined and he said, 'The first thing I'm going to do is thank him for everything—*everything*. Then I'm going to ask him to explain everything about himself from the beginning.' Only my brother Jack would have an agenda for heaven."

One day, close to the end of his life, Jack asked him, "How will I know if God's calling me?"

"The question just floored me," Father Hines said. "I told him that I didn't know how to answer that question, except that he would just know. Two weeks later, he said, 'Bill, God's calling me. He's been calling me for about the last four days. I have to answer Him.'"

He asked for his beloved wife of thirty-nine years and told her that God was calling him and it was time to go. Then he asked for his pastor at St. Mary's Parish in Schwenksville, Father Charles McElroy, because "he taught me how to love God." Two days later, on September 1, 2004, after sixty-three years of life, Jack Hines followed his heart out of this world and into the arms of his Treasure.

"Jack's was the most beautiful funeral I have ever been to," said Mary Kay Bushey, Head Coordinator of the Perpetual Adoration Program where Jack Hines adored every Tuesday afternoon. "There was just something so special about that man."

Jack's sister explained it perfectly when she said, "Jack taught us how to live, and he taught us how to die." And he reminds us all that the flower of holiness can bloom wherever God plants it.

—Susan Brinkmann

Susan Brinkmann's biography appears after "A Mother's Ultimate Sacrifice" in chapter one.

Words from Blessed Teresa of Calcutta

Everybody today seems to be in such a terrible rush, anxious for greater developments and greater riches and so on, so that children have very little time for their parents. Parents have very little time for each other. And in the home begins the disruption of peace of the world.

Keep the joy of loving God in your heart and share this joy with all you meet, especially your family.

Yesterday is gone. Tomorrow is not yet come. We have only today. Let us begin.

I am not sure exactly what Heaven will be like. But I do know that when we die and it comes the time for God to judge us, He will not ask, "How many good things have you done in your life?" Rather He will ask, "How much love did you put into what you did?"

Be faithful in small things because it is in them that your strength lies.

God doesn't look at how much we do, but with how much love we do it.

I know God will not give me anything I can't handle. I just wish that He didn't trust me so much.

It is easy to love the people far away. It is not always easy to love those close to us. It is easier to give a cup of rice to relieve hunger than to relieve the loneliness and pain of someone unloved in our own home. Bring love into your home for this is where our love for each other must start.

If we have no peace, it is because we have forgotten that we belong to each other.

Intense love does not measure, it just gives.

We, the unwilling, led by the unknowing, are doing the impossible for the ungrateful. We have done so much, for so long, with so little, we are now qualified to do anything with nothing.

The family that prays together stays together, and if they stay together they will love one another as God has loved each one of them. And works of love are always works of peace.

The child is God's gift to the family.

Letting Go

Maybe I should have kept better track of time, appreciating the drooling, screaming, pulling-down-underwear-in-the-middle-of-Mass years. I feel as if one night I changed my son's diaper, went to bed, and then woke up the next morning trying to figure out how to fill out his high school class schedule. I struggle to remember the sound of his toddler laugh—the same one, at the time, I deemed so infectious, adorable, and unforgettable.

I vaguely remember the blur of the past—kitchen sink baths, mud pies, bugs, giggles, lost glasses, fresh school supplies, old friends, new friends, hurt feelings, burying hamsters and dogs, moving, emergency rooms, scrapes, stitches, tears, hugs and kisses, Christmas awe, Easter egg hunts, snuggling and tiny weenie Nike high-top tennis shoes that fit in the palm of my hand.

But on the morning I had to drive him to a weekend young men's retreat, even though I tripped over his tennis shoes the size of Nebraska, I decided I was not ready for my son to leave home.

I certainly wasn't ready for the car ride that followed. The tears started flowing with my turn of the key. I don't know why it hit me so hard—he'd been away from home before.

"Did you pack enough underwear?"

"Yesssss!"

"What about a jacket? Is that sweatshirt going to be enough?"

"Yes, Mom. I'll be fine."

I knew this would be a great experience for him; so why couldn't I stop weeping? Was it out of pure joy that he finally acted so responsibly? That he remembered underwear and socks without me reminding him? Hadn't this been my training goal for the last fourteen years? Surely it wasn't because he was going to spend a long weekend in prayer and contemplation, seeking guidance on the direction that the rest of his life should take. Which of course would mean that, one day, he'd actually grow up enough to move out.

I reached behind me. "Here, take this. But don't tell anyone I let you use my secret ashtray stash of dental floss."

"Mom, I already packed floss."

"You did? How about your retainers?"

"Yes."

"Toothbrush?"

"Yes."

"Dress shoes, blazer, tie, belt, shampoo, hat?"

"Yes. Yes. Yes, already!"

"How much money do you have with you? Are you stopping for lunch?"

What happened to the boy who used to do his homework and then stuff it under his mattress? What happened to the boy who left his brand-new $200 glasses on top of the car before driving out of town for Thanksgiving? What happened to the boy who walked out into the freezing cold in short sleeves or ran around the muddy back yard in his new white socks?

We pulled into the church parking lot and Morgan gave me a discreet kiss and "Love you" behind the safety of the van door, and then ran off to find his friends.

My little boy was growing up ... leaving town to contemplate life decisions ... and he was so responsible about the whole thing. He didn't need his mommy to remember a single thing for him.

Then, he returned to the car: "Hey, Mom, do you have a rosary in the car? I forgot we needed to bring one." Score! He still needed me!

Our pastor then gathered us for prayer, and the boys loaded the van and drove away.

I turned away so no one saw my tears, only to face my dear mother-figure friend Ann.

She had already been there. She understood all the unspoken words, fears, and joys my tears expressed. She alone knew there was only one thing he really needed from me at that moment— wings—with my heart firmly fixed on their tips.

—Karen Rinehart

Karen Rinehart, creator of The Bus Stop Mommies trademark, is an award winning syndicated newspaper columnist, author and speaker. Her column is featured weekly on the Catholicexchange.com Humor Channel. Contact Karen and read more at www.busstopmommies.com.

Beatitudes for Parents

Blessed are those parents who make their peace with spilled milk and with mud, for of such is the kingdom of childhood.

Blessed is the parent who engages not in the comparison of his child with others, for precious unto each is the rhythm of his own growth.

Blessed are the fathers and mothers who have learned laughter, for it is the music of the child's world.

Blessed and wise are those parents who understand the goodness of time, for they make it not a sword that kills growth but a shield to protect.

Blessed and mature are they who without anger can say "no," for comforting to the child is the security of firm decisions.

Blessed is the gift of consistency, for it is heart's-ease in childhood.

Blessed are they who accept the awkwardness of growth, for they are aware of the choice between marred furnishings and damaged personalities.

Blessed are the teachable, for knowledge brings understanding, and understanding brings love.

Blessed are the men and women who in the midst of the unpromising mundane, give love, for they bestow the greatest of all gifts to each other, to their children, and—in an ever-widening circle—to their fellow men.

—Marion E. Kinneman (1895–1985)

Marion Kinneman wrote this piece specifically for her two daughters to assist them in the raising of her six grandsons. First published in Family Circle *magazine, and has been reprinted numerous times since.*

Torn Between Two Loves

I hung up the phone and swallowed hard. Never had I felt so rejected. I thought that my mother would understand and comfort me, but instead she was just like all the others: "Kim, do you know what you are doing?"

I was traveling with a group of students through Greece and Italy. During this trip, my journey to God was growing as I embraced my Catholic faith. But it became clear through emails with my fiancé, Brian, that I could not be fully Catholic and marry him. I had to choose. My family thought I had gone mad. "He is Christian; isn't that good enough?" my mom asked.

No, it was not enough. I did not fully understand what was happening to me because my family and I had not even been religious before. So, why now, on the cusp of a promising future with a wonderful man, was I letting Catholic teachings stand in my way?

The trouble began completely out of the blue one Friday night. It was homecoming weekend, and I was a senior at Concordia College in Minnesota. It had been my habit to spend weekends partying with fellow track and cross-country runners. But this night something inside me felt empty. My fiancé, Brian, had just insisted on getting married in his Protestant church. It surprised me how much it bothered me. Even though I had long ago ceased to be a true Catholic, I had harbored little-girl fantasies of getting married in my hometown parish.

I felt like the loneliest girl on campus. A huge bonfire roared behind me, intermingled with laughter and school cheers. I looked down at the diamond rock on my finger and felt cold inside. I had every girl's dream—a handsome man to marry and a family who loved my fiancé, but I suddenly felt empty inside.

I wandered into the athletics building and noticed a friend, Jason, on duty at the desk. He was a recent convert to Catholicism. "Hi. How's it going?" he greeted me.

"I'm sick of partying," I blurted out.

He looked at me thoughtfully and said, "Why don't you go to confession?"

Confession? If I had not been so down, I might have laughed. I did not even remember how to go it had been so long. "Right," I answered sarcastically, rolling my eyes and walking away.

Jason was not deterred. "Tomorrow night at seven. The Newman Center. See you there."

The next day, sitting in the library with my books scattered on the table, I tried to focus on homework, but the idea of confession kept distracting me. Out of frustration, I began scribbling down all my sins. All day I walked around with that paper in my back pocket. And all day I couldn't focus on anything else. It seemed the only way to get confession off my mind would be to go to it. That night I stood in the confessional line literally shaking. *What will the priest think when he hears my sins,* I thought. *I don't even remember what I'm supposed to say.*

When it was my turn, I blurted out that I could not remember how to confess. To my surprise, the priest calmly responded: "That's okay; I'll help you." This was the beginning of my journey to the Church. On one level, I stuffed this experience away, but just for a while. The seed had been planted.

Two months later, I was on a plane to Athens, Greece, to spend my final semester of college studying abroad. Brian, my fiancé, was reluctant to see me leave, but supportive of my opportunity. I cried, he cried, my family cried, and then I boarded the plane, already missing everyone yet excited for the adventure before me.

I was immediately enthralled by Greece, but then, on the third day, a taxi in Athens hit me during a morning jog. Afterwards, I couldn't walk without severe pain in my knee, so for a few days I stayed at the hotel while the rest of the group went sight seeing. I finally rejoined the group on a bus trip to the ruins of Mycenae. Instead of climbing all over the ruins, however,

I simply had to sit at the gates and wait for them to return. I limped over to a stone wall facing the sunset and slumped down, resting my head against the rock. My friend Jason, who also on this trip, walked by and threw his stack of prayer cards to me: "Why don't you make yourself useful?"

I threw the cards down next to me. Maybe I'd look at them later. It was a beautiful evening, and the setting sun was casting golden rays over the countryside. I thought of Brian while gazing at the vineyards in the distance. During our week apart, I had time to consider our unresolved differences. We had talked by phone earlier that day. I was learning more about the Catholic Church and finding deep meaning in her teachings. I wanted to share all this with Brian, but he was unenthused. He especially did not understand the Church's teaching on contraception. At the time, I was still on the birth-control pill, so he could not accept that I was suddenly making an issue out of this. We loved one another, and we were going to get married, but we were not ready to have children—end of story, for him. Neither of us had a true understanding of love as sacrifice. To us, the physical union of a man and woman was nothing more than expressing one's emotions.

During this trip, I began to question our understanding of contraception and of love and opened my eyes to see the beauty of the Church's teachings. I wanted to say yes to God, but it was complicated. Sitting on the mountainside with my painful knee and mulling over my relationship, I felt depressed. As a cross-country runner, I longed to release some of my frustrations with an exhilarating run. My knee started to throb.

It then occurred to me at that moment to pray. I flipped through the prayer cards and stopped on St. Raphael the Archangel, the patron saint of healing and of marriages. I prayed the prayer on the back. Then I closed my eyes, let out a sigh, and imagined God's presence in the warm sunlight, right there, on that mountainside. St. Raphael seemed to be sitting right next to me.

After a few moments, the group began to climb down the ruins, heading back to the bus. I stood up and began to make my way back, too. To my surprise, the pain in my knee had disappeared. I couldn't believe it! Nothing like this had ever happened to me before. I could walk without pain. God must have healed me. I couldn't wait to share this amazing event with Brian.

That night, I called him, but his reaction doused my enthusiasm. "The saints are just dead humans," he scoffed. "They can't help anyone." I was crushed. Brian was always on the attack, and I was always on the defensive, which was especially difficult for me because I was still only learning about Catholicism myself.

Still, he could not stop my growing love for the Church. As it happened, both professors leading our group were Catholic. One was a Benedictine sister and the other a Catholic convert. Between these two, Jason, and extensive reading, I was learning a lot in a short period of time. When I learned about Natural Family Planning as a completely natural way for couples to understand their fertility and embrace its cycle in union with God's natural plan, I instantly quit taking birth control and began praying the Rosary. Brian was baffled. In an email he wrote, "Recently, it seems to me, that whatever the Catholic Church says, you believe and live out simply because it has a Catholic endorsement stamped on it. This is very, very scary for me ... I might be wrong, but I am beginning to feel that you think that the Catholic Church is correct on all matters."

Precisely! I was falling in love with the Catholic Church, but I loved Brian, too. My two loves were opposed to one another. I wanted to give myself fully to both of them but felt ripped apart. Every night, I soaked my pillow with tears. All the other students on the trip were enjoying themselves, but I was confronting the challenge of my life.

We traveled to Italy, and while we were in Rome, I received another email from Brian. This time he made it clear that if we were to remain together, I would have to take birth control because he believed there was no other way. According to him, this trip was "the worst thing that ever happened to him."

As I read that email, my stomach tightened and tears poured down my face. My soul was yearning for God, but my heart was breaking for Brian. My perfect little world of a beautiful wedding gown, a lake house, and new cars was slipping from my grasp. How could I hang on to something that would pull me from God? I had to let go of one, and it was not going to be God.

Calling my mom that evening only brought more pain. I cried myself to sleep. A few days later, Brian and I talked again. We both remained unmovable on all our decisions related to religion—where we would be married, which religion we would raise our children in, and on birth control. When I hung up that day, I realized that it was probably over.

A friend found me in the hotel bathroom crying so hard that it hurt. She sought to comfort me, but she only increased my pain. "It's too hard to be that strict of a Catholic, Kim," she tried to reason with me. "Nobody is like that except maybe Jason."

That night, I lay awake still crying. My mom called around 1:30 a.m., and she was crying, too. My parents thought I had gone crazy. "Kim, life is too short to act this way," my mom warned. "Brian is a good man. If you walk away from him, you may never find anyone else."

Her words stabbed at my heart. *What if she's right*, I feared. But the final six weeks in Greece strengthened my resolve. I devoured Catholic literature and sought answers to all my questions. Reading the diary of St. Faustina helped me understand the value of suffering when we make the choices God calls us to make. When I returned home for a couple weeks to finish schoolwork for my degree, my relationship with my parents was very awkward. They did not understand what had happened to me. I threw out all my music and immodest clothing and gave away many of my possessions to strive for a simpler life. My mother cried daily and pleaded with me to patch things up with Brian. After a couple weeks, she finally accepted that I would not change my mind.

Although my family did not understand my conversion, they began to ask questions. The result was that little by little my mom and dad, brother, and sister all came to embrace the Catholic Church. My sister soon ended a bad relationship and found a good Catholic husband. My brother had just graduated from high school at this time. I felt compelled to talk to him about saving himself for marriage. With tears in his eyes, he thanked me. We've been very close since then and can talk about anything now. My mom began asking me a lot of questions. I shared my devotion to St. Thérèse of Lisieux with her. My mom had never talked to a saint or asked for intercession before, but at this time, she tried it out. While four-wheeling with a group of friends in a barren area of Montana, my mom wondered if my dad really loved her. She prayed and talked to St. Thérèse. Suddenly, she came upon a wild rose-bush. Since St. Thérèse is said to send roses from heaven as a sign of her intercession to prayer, my mother stopped in awe of the roses that seemed to appear out of nowhere. Just then, my dad came up from behind her: "I love you!" At that time, it was totally uncharacteristic of him to make such an announcement. My mother was instantly sold on the value of petitioning our brothers and sisters in heaven.

I had decided to get a master's degree in Catholic studies at the University of St. Thomas in Minnesota. That summer, I met Shawn, a recent graduate from college who was just returning to the Catholic faith. We immediately hit if off and talked until dawn. "You need to go to confession," I advised when I learned he had not gone in many years. I expected never to hear from him again.

Instead, the following week he called. "I went to confession. Can I come over and see you now?" I laughed, and we got together for a few casual dates. As it became clear that we were quickly getting serious, I gave him a copy of *Good News about Sex and Marriage*, by Christopher West, which outlines the Catholic teaching, derived from Scripture, on the role of sex in marriage.

"If you want to seriously date, I need to know if you agree with everything in this book," I told him. Two days later he had read the book cover to cover. "Okay, when can we start dating?" he asked.

Shawn and I married a year and a half later. Soon after, our daughter Maria Karen was born—Maria after Mary and Karen after my mother, two women who mean the most to me.

I was willing to give up everything to follow God, but instead, God has blessed me more than I could have ever imagined.

—Kimberly Heilman

Kimberly Heilman holds a BA in art history and English literature from Concordia College and an MA in Catholic studies from the University of St. Thomas in St. Paul. She teaches an Old Testament class to sophomores at St. Mary's High School in Bismarck, North Dakota. Shawn works as an electrical engineer.

Chapter 3
A Family's Hope

A Time to Grieve

Dinner was ready. I was about to call everyone in to eat, but hearing the laughter outside my kitchen window, I turned the burner down low. Dinner could keep. Four-year-old Matthew had waited all day to go sledding with his brothers.

It was March 1, and in North Dakota that meant there was still plenty of winter left. This particular winter of 1993–94 had been one for the record books, with deep snowdrifts still burying much of the fence around our farm. The crisp blue sky had been calling to Matthew all day. "Come sledding with me, Mommy," he had begged. Once in a while my husband, Joe, or I would sled with Matthew, knowing he was lonely for his brothers. As the youngest of seven boys, he thrived on the activity of a large household. Jim, at eighteen, was the first to leave the nest for college that year in Jamestown, North Dakota, two hours away.

Every morning, after the frantic routine of getting everyone out the door for the school bus, Joe usually tended to the farm, while Matthew and I had our own special time. He always pulled his stool next to my chair so that the two of us could eat our breakfast, side by side. We would leisurely visit before the tasks of the day began, with Matthew tagging along to help. Sometimes, when the weather warmed, he joined his dad outside. Matthew especially loved to sit in the tractor, riding high in a special seat Joe had installed for him.

Looking down at Matthew's pleading eyes on this day, I told him to wait until his brothers came home to go sledding. I knew he would have more fun with them, and it seemed I had a lot to do that day. As usual, as the afternoon wore on, Matthew frequently peeked out the window and asked how much longer until the boys came home. Finally, the bus arrived and deposited its precious cargo—his brothers. "They're here!" he squealed. Sam, in tenth grade, had gone into Bismarck for a basketball tournament. Steve, thirteen, and Bob, nine, got busy around the house, but Tom, eleven, and Neal, seven, were more than happy to sled with Matthew.

Their sled hill was actually our driveway. The snow was packed down hard now to make for a slick coast down, just the way they loved it. Joe was out working, and the boys were having so much fun that I decided to let them stay outside as long as there was still daylight. But we never would sit down together to that dinner. The happy shouts and laughter suddenly stopped. Neal and Tom burst into the house screaming and crying, "Matthew's dead! Matthew's dead!"

Oh no, I thought, bracing myself. On a farm with seven active boys, it seemed that something or someone was always getting hurt. I ran outside without a coat, fearing something serious but never imagining that the boys could possibly really mean what they said. I looked down the hill and saw Joe kneeling beside Matthew, who lay face down in the snow, just behind the tractor. Joe had told the boys to stop sledding while he drove the tractor down the driveway. Tom had headed to the shop to start working on the snowmobile, while Neal and Matthew had waited and watched as the tractor descended. But then, without warning, Matthew flopped down on his sled and took off, sliding directly under the tractor. Tom looked over his shoulder at that instant and took off after him. But there was not enough time for anyone to react. Matthew was run over by the back wheel in an instant.

Steve immediately called for an ambulance, but we could not wait. The hospital in Linton was fifteen miles away from our house in Hazelton. Joe drove while I sat in the backseat where Matthew lay. His snowsuit and hood covered all but his face, so I could not detect what his injuries were. Nothing in life had prepared me for such a moment. I could not think. My heart raced, and I felt like I was suffocating. Joe and I wept and prayed the Rosary out loud as he drove. It was all we could do now.

The ambulance met us five miles from the hospital. Relief flooded through me. Finally, my son would get some help. An emergency medical technician jumped out and flung open our car door. She immediately checked Matthew's vital signs and then stopped.

"We don't need to take him in the ambulance," she said solemnly and then paused to take a breath. "He's already dead." I heard the words, but I could not believe. I numbly sat back in my seat and moved my arm away, afraid to touch Matthew now. I desperately wanted to be with my little son, but I realized in horror that he was not with me anymore.

The EMT moved into the driver's seat and drove us to the hospital. Matthew was taken in by stretcher. Our pastor, Fr. Jeff Zwack, met us at the door. "We'll make it through," he said quietly. "God will help us." He sat silently with us in the waiting room. Then, the doctor asked us to come to say good-bye to Matthew. Joe and I followed the doctor and looked at Matthew lying still on the bed. We were instructed to hold Matthew's hands and touch him and talk to him. Joe held him and cried and told him how much he loved him.

I stood there blankly, still afraid to touch him. I looked down and noticed some of the blue dye from his gloves had come off onto his hands. "Pat, you need to touch him and talk to him," Joe said. I did not want to. If I touched him, it would make his death real to me. I cautiously held his hand in mine and felt it already growing cold. My body trembled as I sobbed and poured out my love for my son. I could not accept that he was never coming home again.

I called Jim before we left the hospital. Whenever Jim came home from college, Matthew would wait for him to arrive with such anticipation that he seemed to be willing him home. Matthew was Jim's pet, and one of their favorite pastimes was to sing songs together.

Shaking, I took a deep breath and pushed out the words: "Jim, Matthew's dead. You've got to come home."

Jim paused. "You mean he's hurt?" he asked.

"No, he's dead," I sobbed and then explained it all.

Fr. Jeff returned to the farmhouse with us. It was filled with close friends and my sister. Other relatives lived farther away and still needed to be called. We hugged the boys and cried together. Fr. Jeff led us in prayers to comfort and strengthen our family. Jim walked in crying and hugged us all.

Sam had not returned from the basketball tournament yet. Since none of us had cell phones at that time and we did not know how to reach him, we decided that all we could do was wait for him to come home. When his car pulled into the drive, Fr. Jeff ran outside to tell him what had happened. "I didn't get to say good-bye to Matthew," he cried to me. "I was not even here."

"Sam, none of us got to say good-bye," I choked through tears. Sam did not want to be with anyone, so he ran to his room and shut the door.

Family and friends came to help with work and funeral arrangements. Matthew would be buried at the cemetery in Hazelton next to Joe's dad. Joe received permission to dig Matthew's grave himself. It was the last earthly thing he could do for his son. Over the course of two days, other farmers and friends came by and silently dug alongside Joe.

The prayer service was held Thursday evening in the church where the funeral would be the next morning. After the service,

I was waiting for Jim to come back home with us. "I can't leave Matthew here all alone," Jim said. "I'm going to stay with him." Jim sat beside Matthew's little coffin through the night, talking to him and singing all their favorite songs they used to sing together.

The next morning, I decided there was no way I was going to the funeral. I could not accept that God had taken my child. "Why, God? Why did you take Matthew?" I cried out in anger. "I take care of my kids. I feed and bathe them and teach them their prayers. Why did you have to take one of mine?"

I told God they would need to have the funeral without me. But finally, I just got up and got dressed. I was numb and could not even pray for myself or for my family. My mind could not focus.

Life had to go on. Our family went to Sunday Mass the next day, and the kids climbed the school bus on Monday morning. Nothing would ever be the same, but we had to get back into the routine of life. I tried not to cry in front of the kids. My other kids still needed a mother, so I forced myself out of bed every morning to care for them. After they left, I could not bear to sit at the table without Matthew at my side. I went through the motions of my tasks but often had to stop and cry. Sometimes, I went to Matthew's room and pulled out one of his shirts to hold onto and rock in the chair where I used to hold him. For months, I often woke up in the middle of the night and thought it all had to be some terrible nightmare. I would get up to check on Matthew only to realize again and again that he was really was gone. Joe and I often grieved differently. I depended on a grief support group. Joe did not understand why I needed it, preferring to spend time at Matthew's gravesite. I never blamed Joe for what happened, but sometimes I got angry when our grief seemed to drive us apart instead of closer together.

People had told me time would heal our pain. I did not believe them but that proved to be true—time and prayer. Even when we felt like we were just going through the motions, we all knew we still needed God. Prayer was the glue that kept us together and pulled us through.

Fr. Jeff had told me to talk to Mary, our Blessed Mother, because she understood how I felt. She had held Jesus in her arms just as I had held my son. Over time, I felt Mary had softened my heart. Then, one day, I had a picture in my mind of Jesus at the bottom of the hill with his arms opened wide. Matthew had taken off to be with him. I began to accept that Matthew was happy with God instead of being with us. Also, I had two dreams in which I held Matthew. They were so vivid that I could feel his arms around me and smell his hair. I truly believe that Matthew was really with me again during those dreams. One day, one of my boys told me, "Mom, I'm not afraid of dying anymore." He was only in sixth grade, but I understood the significance of his statement. Now that his brother had gone before him, death did not seem scary anymore. Matthew would one day greet him in heaven.

Still, my empty arms often ached to hold him. I began asking God to please send us another child. At forty-four, I feared that menopause had already begun, but I kept hoping and praying. In March of the following year, the same month in which Matthew died, I became pregnant. It would actually take me two more months to realize it since I had not had a period for a year and never would again.

For the first time since we lost Matthew, I felt true joy again. Our family now had something to soften our loss—another baby was coming. Maria Elizabeth, our first girl, was born on December 20, 1995. Jim, who had begun studying for the priesthood at Catholic University in Washington, D.C., was home for Christmas break. He was the one who named her. That Christmas, we had the joy and excitement of welcoming both the Christ Child into our hearts and a new baby into our family.

Maria recently turned eleven. She has a special affinity for the brother she never knew. Maria keeps track of how old Matthew would be and what grade he would be in. She often asks about him, wanting to know everything she can. Maria has filled a hole and made it easer to remember Matthew fondly without the pain. The time to grieve is over. Matthew was only meant to be here a little while. Through God's grace, I have come to accept that he is in the best place he could be—a place so glorious that he would not want to leave. Just as he once waited by the window for his brothers to come home, I believe he is waiting patiently for his family to come home, where we will all be reunited in God's house.

— Pat Shea

Pat and Joe Shea still live on the family farm with Maria, who is a sixth grader. Tom and his wife, Adriann, and their young son, Jacob, also live on the farm and raise beef cattle. Pat drives the local school bus in between keeping track of her large family, who are spread across the country and England and Germany.

You Owe Me Two

"OK, that's it," I said as I dropped off bags of my maternity clothes to be taken to a home for unwed mothers. I was trying to cheer myself up about moving into a new phase of my life. Getting back in the car, I turned to check car seats before moving on. *You look so much like Sean*, I thought to myself as I gazed at my little boy Connor, who was now four years old. It had been nineteen years since my first child, Sean, was born, and now Connor was to be my last.

Connor was an answer to prayer. Five years earlier, from a medical standpoint, it looked like I would not be having any more children. God had blessed my husband, Mark, and me with nine beautiful children, and yet I continued to pray, asking God to bless us with just one more. Sean had left a few years earlier for an apostolic school. It was hard to let him go, and yet after much prayer we felt it was God's will for him, and we let him go. When Connor was born, I could see he looked just like him. God had given me a little boy that would always remind me of Sean.

When Connor was two, I was pregnant once again with our eleventh child, Joseph Michael. God took him to heaven, however, long before he was big enough to hold in my arms. Two more years went by, and I was sure my time of having children was over. Yet I continued to pray. Fully aware that God owes me nothing, I said, "You know, God, now you owe me two. Twins would be beautiful." My daughter Laura had left home to prepare for life as a lay missionary, and my son, Brendan, feeling called to the priesthood, had followed his brother into the minor seminary school. I figured that if God gave me Connor when Sean left, then he was two babies behind with Laura and Brendan gone.

One day I asked my doctor, "What are the chances of me having twins?" She said that the chance of twins was greater at my age if I should become pregnant because I could ovulate twice in one month. It was a glimmer of hope, but the possibility still seemed too far out of reach. Having left the last traces of maternity with my friend Judy in two very large black trash bags, I headed home.

Sixty-eight hours later my head started to explode with the familiar pain of a migraine. Just to be sure before taking my medication, I took a pregnancy test. I knew I could only be a little over three weeks, but I wanted to be sure. My hand started to shake, and tears of joy filled my eyes as the second pink line became darker and darker. God was blessing us with one more child, or so I thought.

Soon, I started experiencing unusual, sharp pain, and my HCG blood levels were checked to make sure it was not ectopic. In less then forty-eight hours, the levels had not doubled like they are supposed to. They had tripled. The doctor said, "I think it's twins." A short while later, it was confirmed with an ultrasound. To my surprise, though, it was not the way my doctor had expected it might happen. I was not pregnant with fraternal twins from having ovulated twice in one month. There on the screen we could see one sack and two heartbeats. They were identical twins from one egg that had split. There is no scientific explanation for why it happens. It's another beautiful miracle from God.

Needless to say, I was in shock, but nothing like my husband, Mark. He knew how much I wanted and prayed for another child, but he didn't know I was secretly praying for twins behind his back. Mark has always been open to any new life God wanted to bless us with. Over the years he has seen how God has always provided, and yet the concern for two more little ones was heavy on his heart. This was compounded with fear for my health because he knew I did not handle pregnancy well and would likely be on bed rest for many months with complications.

My concerns were different. Within a short period of time the shock, joy, gratitude and awe that filled my heart became overshadowed with fear and anguish. It wasn't from all the complications I read about on the internet. I knew the babies were in God's hands, His precious gift to me. What filled me with fear was the kind words from well meaning friends like, "You are such a good mother that God decided to give you two more," or "Obviously, God knew you deserve them." I knew that what they said could not be further from the truth. I knew my sinfulness, and I also knew that I did not deserve these precious little ones.

In my mind I could see only one possible solution. God would realize that I was not worthy of such a gift, and He would take them back to Himself just like my little Joseph. In other words, God just needed to realize He had made a mistake. I started to plead with Him. I will try to do better; just let me keep them. Then while pouring my fear out to God in prayer, I heard this in my heart, "You are right. You don't deserve them. You don't deserve any of your children. They are pure gifts of My love from all time according to My will." I was overcome with joy. The fear was lifted. Now I knew that the lives of my babies did not depend on my holiness, but on the will of God.

Over time I came to realize that God had never even taken Sean, Laura, or Brendan away. Physically we are apart, but when we let them go, God gave them back to Mark and me in a spiritual way that is far more beautiful than we could have ever imagined.

As I write these words, two identical little boys, Johnny and Tommy, are taking my kitchen apart, and I couldn't be happier. They are identical to most of the world, but I think Johnny resembles Laura, and Tommy looks very much like Brendan. But, that's just me. As I watch them toddle about, in my heart I hear the words, "You owe me two." I answer with great joy, "Yes, Lord, I do. These little ones are yours. Thank you."

—Elizabeth Matthews

Elizabeth Matthews is the author of Precious Treasure: The Story of Patrick *and, with her husband, Mark,* A Place for Me. *The Matthews are founders of Chelsea Shire Communications, a publishing and speaking apostolate—www. chelseashire.com. A "retired" nurse, she and her husband are the homeschooling parents of twelve children and reside in Indiana.*

Second-Time Love

While sweeping my front porch, I lifted my thoughts to God in prayer. My ex-husband of almost seven years came to mind. "And Lord," I prayed. "Please send Michael a good Christian wife—one that will be good to our two boys and get along with me."

A year earlier, it was unthinkable that I would have sent up such a prayer. It had nothing to do with my ex-husband, but everything to do with me. I simply did not pray. The closest I came to prayer was complaining—"Why me, God?"—when things got tough. I was so full of myself, that there was no room for God. Our marriage did not survive because everything was about "me," not about "us."

The trouble started long before our wedding vows. Back when I was just eight years old, my dad died and our family stopped going to church. At a time I really needed God in my life, no one ever explained that I had a loving Father in Heaven to whom I could pray. Without God, I would forever be searching for something to fill the void. When Michael and I married in 1991 at twenty-two and nineteen years of age, respectively, I believed he would fill the void. I felt grown-up, and it was romantic to walk down the aisle on the arm of an adoring and handsome man. Johnny was born two years into our marriage, and Cameron came twenty-two months later. My little sons were beautiful, and I was so proud to be their mother. But soon the glow of romance and motherhood settled into monotony. Michael worked full-time as a computer programmer and attended college for a degree to better care for our family. I felt neglected and tired of housework and childcare. Most nights, I sat in front of the TV eating to stave off boredom. My weight ballooned up over two hundred pounds.

"You need to get out of the house," friends advised. "Get a part-time job." It made sense to me. I found a part-time bank teller job and rather quickly lost seventy pounds. I started feeling better about myself. Michael had accepted me no matter how I looked, but now I began enjoying the admiring glances of other men when I went out with a group of co-workers and friends for "Ladies Night Out." I was having so much fun, it turned from once a month into once a week and then twice a week to take advantage of the traditional "Ladies Night" specials at bars on Wednesdays. I had started working full-time to earn more money for clothes and fun. There was no time for cooking or housework, so Michael picked up the slack. I loved my boys, but I also wanted to party. Michael began putting his foot down. He expected me to be a more attentive wife and mother. Michael, who had originally attracted me because of his calm, responsible nature, became a boring, papa-warden holding me back from having fun. Our arguments grew heated as he tried to keep me home. In the end, I always went out, happy to get away from him.

I craved the same freedom my single and divorced friends enjoyed and became increasingly irritable around Michael. During this time, he left town on a business trip. I reveled in my freedom. When he called me to say he loved me, dread came over me. "I don't care anymore," I admitted. "I want a divorce." We separated in spite of Michael's pleas for counseling. I felt a little guilty about leaving the boys, but I decided my happiness was more important.

A year later, our divorce was final. The boys were two and four. Michael had primary custody of them while I got on my feet financially, but this eventually changed into every other week. In the meantime, I set out to find a man, looking for romance to fill the void in my life. Over the next few years, I had a series of short-term relationship, and also went through a string of jobs.

During this time, my original group of friends split up. One lady, I learned later, had spread a vicious lie about me, which turned others against me. I hooked up with another group of people in highly regarded professions who introduced me to marijuana, which I began to use regularly. Nights out had grown stale, and the stress of trying to keep up with bills and motherhood led me to overeating again. Everything I lost and more piled back on. Michael and I were cordial to each other in front of the kids, but there was a lot of hurt and resentment between us. If the kids were not around, our hostility came out.

When Cameron was in kindergarten, we discovered he had a very serious disease, Pertches, in which the hip bone deteriorates. Fortunately, early treatment can minimize the effects. For three years, Cameron needed to be in a leg brace and wheelchair and receive treatments four times a year at a hospital two hours away. "God, am I that bad that this has to happen to me?" I thought indignantly. Michael and I both wanted to take him, so we drove together to save gas and were forced to spend half the day together. During these drives, I was irritated to be stuck hearing the Christian music Michael started listening to. I even had the audacity to ask God to save me from those songs. I knew that Michael had begun taking the children to church on Sundays. "It's no concern of mine," I thought.

A couple years into Cameron's treatment, I began yet another new job. There was a group of women in the office, very different from my partying friends or co-workers from the past. These women were cheerful and kind. When I asked one of them what she did for fun, her answer surprised me: "The most exciting thing in my life is my church. It really changed my life." The lady sitting next to her agreed.

Oh, brother, I thought. But the urge for something more meaningful in my life began to nag at me. I had been unhappy for so long that I had even contemplated suicide once. The women at work took me under their wings. For instance, when I complained about not being able to lose weight, one woman very gently pointed out that eating two Big Macs, fries and a shake was not the way to lose weight. She helped me see that the diet fads I tried in the past were not as effective as healthy eating. I also started going for walks at her suggestion. The pounds melted, and I began feeling good about myself. My co-workers also encouraged me to go to church. Monday mornings, the women would ask me if I had been to church on Sunday. It was getting harder and harder to say "no" each week.

During this time, I took an extra part-time job to help out an elderly woman. Ironically, she wanted to go to church, so I took her. I was there physically, but I kept my guard up. Then, one of the women at work told me I should be taking my sons. "If you don't take those boys of yours to church, they're going to grow up to be hoodlums and come and get us," she kidded me with a twinkle in her eye.

The first Sunday I took the boys, I nervously clutched their hands and slipped into the back row. As I listened to the sermon about Jesus' love for me and his death on the Cross, my heart opened wide. I was ready to accept that I needed Christ in my life. After the service, I knelt down and took the only money I had in my wallet—five dollars. "Here, God," I said, tearfully. "This is all I have and I'm giving it to you. No one loves me. I don't even love myself. Do whatever you can to take this pain away. I want to feel loved." I dropped the money on the pew where I was praying; I was giving it to God. Now I had no money to go to the Wendy's across the street. But suddenly, it did not matter to me. I had prayed sincerely for the first time in my life, and a burden had lifted. I realized I had been angry for so long.

I walked out of church and started introducing myself. People were friendly in return. It felt good. I kept going back to church every Sunday and started participating in church activities and making friends. Prayer and reading the Bible also became a part of my life.

I was living with a guy at the time but came to realize the Lord would not want this, so I had him move out. I was on my own again, working at a good company and filling myself up with God rather than partying. As my love for God grew, I saw how selfish I had been and how much pain I had caused my family—especially Michael, who was really a good man. Once I had prayed for him, I kept it up. He really deserved a good wife. I never considered him ever being interested in me again. Too much hurt had come between us.

But the boys began telling Michael that they were going to church with me. Michael also took notice of the changes in my life. I was no longer so angry. Once, when he came to pick up the boys, he looked around my house in surprise. The shiny floors and tidy rooms were not what he had come to expect from me. One day, Michael asked me questions about my faith. I did not realize what he was after. He had been praying for a good woman—"…but please God, don't let it be Michelle." He really did not want anything to do with me after all I had put him through. After questioning me about my faith, he could see that I had really let God into my life and was different now.

Soon Michael asked if I would be willing to attend counseling with him at his church. I agreed, thinking that it would be good for us to get past all the old resentments. We also began going on family dates with the boys to things like plays and sporting events. As we worked through the past, my feelings for Michael began to grow. He was still the same strong, even-tempered and reliable man I had fallen in love with so many years before. Our pastor had us pray together before each counseling session. This was humbling for me because I had never prayed out loud with anyone before. Through counseling, I began to understand where we had gone astray in our marriage.

One of our last counseling assignments was to make a list of all the things we were grateful for in the other person. We were told to read them to each other and then to pray together. When Michael arrived at my place for our next date, he walked cautiously inside, holding his letter. The boys sat on the sofa while I sat on the floor. Michael sat down across from me. I volunteered to go first. "Dear Michael," I read. " I'm so thankful for you. You're doing an excellent job raising our sons. I don't know how long I have on this earth, but however long, I want to spend it with you."

Michael did not respond but opened his letter and began reading. "Dear Michelle, You're the only woman I've ever loved…" When he finished, he took my hands in his for the first time since our divorce. "Lord, we want to do what you want us to," he prayed. "Just help us understand what that is." At that moment, Johnny and Cameron came over and laid their hands on ours. Michael took a deep breath. "Michelle, will you marry me? Again?" he asked.

Tears came to my eyes. "Yes," I said. "Yes, I will."

This time, I knew it would be different. I understood that life was not about making myself happy but about loving and serving others. Selfishness had led to self-destruction. We remarried on June 8, 2003. Surprisingly, the boys had mixed emotions at first. With us split up, they had been able to play one against the other and get away with murder with me. I was indulgent because I felt so guilty. With Michael and me working as a team, there was no more manipulating. But in the end, they have thrived under the care of two loving and united parents. The boys, fourteen and twelve, are more relaxed and affectionate now and very happy to be a family again.

I understand now that marriage is about giving and not taking, because in the end, the more we give of ourselves, the more we get back. I feel that mine is truly a Cinderella story. Growing up, I was always told about Prince Charming. Little did I know, my Prince would be the Prince of Peace, Jesus and through him, all my dreams would come true.

— Michelle Stewart

Michelle Stewart is from Claremont, North Carolina. She believes her calling is helping her husband, Michael, in homeschooling their sons, Johnny and Cameron. Visit www.marriedagain.blogspot.com for more information.

A Heavenly Smoke

My father-in-law, "J.D.," died unexpectedly in his favorite easy chair early one morning. His worn and tattered Bible was at his side. The man who had been the backbone for his family was suddenly gone forever.

Although he was in his seventies, no one was prepared for this. J.D. was still active and at the center of everything. He was a retired university professor and avid golfer, and had just begun a stint as a math teacher at a local school. Over the years, J.D. had managed to rear four children (with my wife, Judy, being the eldest), run a business, coach Little League, commute to a university in a neighboring state for a Ph.D., and be actively involved in a wide variety of political, charitable, and social organizations.

J.D. was a lifelong Baptist who, only months before his death, converted to the Catholic faith, much to the delight of his wife, Jessie, and the rest of the family. His faith was constant as evidenced by his ever-present Bible.

J.D.'s other devotion was cigars. My father-in-law was never without a cigar for much of the time I knew him, though he did stop smoking them a couple years before his death. Anyone who knows a smoker, especially a cigar smoker, can testify to the aroma that permeates everything. J.D. smoked the same brand as long as I knew him, and, other than at mealtime, his teeth clenched a cigar wherever he went. Even after he quit smoking, the aroma stayed, having settled into the nooks and crannies of his life.

My wife and her dad shared more than just a father-daughter bond; they were best friends. They were the other's most ardent supporter, but also harshest critic when the need arose. Both earned doctorates in education; both were educational administrators, headstrong and compassionate, and devout in their beliefs. They conversed almost every day and visited most weekends.

J.D. immediately adopted me into the family after I married his daughter. Weekends, holidays, and special events were always held with J.D. in attendance and frequently as ringleader for whatever went on. He was the center of attention but not because he sought or demanded it. People were drawn to him. And if there was trouble, J.D. always offered to help.

Losing my father-in-law was like losing the hub of a wheel with the spokes having nothing to support them. In spite of Judy's life-long Catholic faith, this sudden and unexpected loss shook her concept of a living, loving God. In spite of our own close relationship with each other, the hole left by her father seemed bottomless.

Judy struggled to make sense of it all. She prayed novenas, cried, grieved, and spoke with our parish priest. We tried not to let our children's lives be disrupted, but it was a struggle.

Several weeks after his death, our son Thomas, then five years old, proclaimed matter-of-factly that he knew "PawPaw" was okay because he had seen him in the corner of the room the night before. His older sister, Katie, and younger sisters Ashley and Kristen seemed to derive solace from his revelation. I am certain that young children often have a unique ability to sense the divine, so I wasn't going to discount the vision. But knowing that Thomas really wanted to see and believe that J.D. was safe in heaven, I just was not convinced his claim was real. I was a little ashamed for my lack of faith, but found myself trying to explain and rationalize Thomas' vision to myself.

Several months went by, and Judy's sorrow was compounded somewhat by a difficult situation at work. A variety of professional dilemmas at work were a source of intense personal conflict. The loss of J.D.'s advice and guidance was painfully felt.

During this time, while returning home from Katelyn's sixth-grade basketball game one evening with our four children bundled up in the van, Judy and I talked about her work. Neither of us felt confident that we had arrived at a correct decision. We were stopped at a red light when suddenly, the smell hit me—cigar smoke. Not just any cigar, but the same exact smell that came from the brand J.D. smoked! I looked at Judy, and her eyes were as large as saucers, and her mouth open. We were both speechless. My brain kicked in to high gear, and the scientist in me took over. I looked at all of the cars around me (there were only a couple), and there was no evidence of any smoke or cigars anywhere. There were no embers on the ground and nothing in the air, no open windows … nothing. Suddenly, the quiet mini-van came alive with the chatter of my children's voices exclaiming "PawPaw" in unison.

What could I say? Better yet, what needed to be said? In an instant our family was transformed. We hurt a bit less, felt less tired, felt less sorrow, and grief's vacuum was filled with love. For the first time since J.D.'s death, Judy and I experienced a warm, relaxing peace that we had been in such need of. It was an affirmation that God was there and J.D. was too. We knew then that we would be fine, and things would get better.

To this day, I don't have a logical explanation for what happened. Well, on second thought, maybe I do. It was a God moment, one of those events when the only explanation is God's amazing grace.

—Thomas "Tim" Armstrong

Dr. Thomas "Tim" Armstrong is a native of Baton Rouge, where his parents, Dr. and Mrs. Paulsen Armstrong, also reside. He is the father of four children— Katelyn, Thomas, Kristen, and Ashley, and is married to Judy Hickman. He enjoys watching the sporting and school events of his children, hunting, fishing, and practicing veterinary medicine at his clinic, Armstrong Veterinary Hospital.

My Grandmother

I have this great photograph of my grandmother on my desk. Wearing a mischievous smile and a flower-print dress, she's grabbing a handful of cookie dough from the mixing bowl and—for once, totally unrepentant—is about to snarf it down. The picture represents everything I knew and loved about my grandmother. She was prim and pious yet could be wonderfully playful and fun. That was my grandmother.

She passed away in the summer of 1996. I was a year out of college at the time but still just a kid in a lot of ways, and I took the news hard. My grandmother was really gone. At the funeral home, as various members of the family stood up to say nice things about her, I sat glued to my seat, too choked up to say anything, too insecure to let anyone see my sadness. My silence at that moment is something I still regret.

If I had had the nerve that day, I would have waxed poetic about that kind old woman. I would have recalled the simple moments: eating sandwiches and playing board games at her house after school. I would have mentioned her quirks: She was the only one I knew, besides Winnie the Pooh, who used the phrase, "Oh, bother." And I would have proclaimed her a saint—an honest-to-goodness saint—who spent innumerable hours in the last pew of St. Ann Church fingering her rosary beads, whispering the Hail Mary and meditating on her God. Those were my memories: rose-colored and reassuring. But, as it turns out, I had only half the story.

In recent years, during long talks and long walks with my mom, I discovered a different side to my grandmother. As sure as she was a saint, she was also a sinner. Living a dream life with six beautiful children and an immensely successful husband, my grandmother's fortunes took a fateful turn in 1951. On vacation together in Buck Hill Falls, Pennsylvania, my grandmother's husband—the grandfather I never knew—took ill with stomach pains. A day later, he was dead, the victim of bleeding ulcers. Although there was nothing my grandmother could have done to save him, she blamed herself for his death and dedicated the rest of her life to making it up to him. She started, ironically, by disobeying his orders. He had told her that if anything were to happen to him, she was to immediately sell the business— one of the first Buick dealerships in northeast Ohio—and use the profits to take care of the family. Instead, my grandmother mustered up her courage and entered the male-dominated world of motorcars, ruffling feathers along the way as a pioneering businesswoman.

Despite her best efforts and glowing praise from local newspapers (one called her "three remarkable persons wrapped in one—mother, father, and business manager"), she eventually realized that she couldn't do it all. Sales dwindled and, over the course of several years, so did the family's bank account and esteem in the community. Then came a devastating blow. Her eldest son was diagnosed with cancer. He died at age sixteen. A family that had so much suddenly became keenly aware of what they were missing. In her despair, my grandmother dealt with things the only way she knew how: through substance abuse. She drank too much. She became dependent on prescription drugs and became painfully thin. She became a pain to her family. That, too, was my grandmother.

Sometimes I wonder why I'm looking for more detail about my grandmother's life, why I continue to ask my mom about her. Why tarnish the saintly image of the sober, contented woman she became in her later years? Recently, the answer has become clear. These stories make my grandmother more real, more complex, more human, and no less lovable. Amazingly, through each of her trials, she maintained an unwavering faith in God. Examining her life has allowed me to think about these questions: What makes you a "good Christian"? What makes you a believer? What makes people love God while living with tremendous sorrow? In the end, my grandmother, gone for over a dozen years, continues to teach me this lesson: All of us go through a process over and over again during our lives. We sin, we repent, and we believe—we've gotta believe—in redemption and resurrection. If life is full of deaths, both little and big, then it must be full of resurrections.

— Brian Kantz

Brian Kantz is a Buffalo-based writer and editor. His work has appeared in dozens of newspapers and magazines across the country, including the Christian Science Monitor *and* National Catholic Reporter. *His column, "The Newbie Dad," appears regularly in* Western New York Family *magazine and details his life as a husband and stay-at-home dad. Visit Brian online at www.briankantz.com.*

A Child Gives Life

"How could I have been so stupid?" Norrie asked herself in tears. Once again, her husband John was out on the town, likely on his fifth or sixth drink by now. She looked at her precious baby, Noah, and cried. What kind of a life would he have with a drunk for a father? Norrie knew the answer full well. Her own father had been an alcoholic.

Norrie's dad was a likable guy when he was sober. In business for himself, his customers thought of him as Mr. Charisma. But when he got home, after several drinks, her poor mother became the object of mental abuse and anger. Norrie had always loved her dad, but it blended with fear and anxiety, making for a conflicted childhood. Not until she was an adult did her father finally stop drinking.

When Norrie first met John, an immigrant from Ireland, he swept her off her feet with his Irish charm and natural intelligence. He seemed to have all the good qualities that Norrie had admired in her father. They were married in 1981.

Since John seemed able to handle his liquor and became all the more charming after a couple drinks, Norrie's guard had been down. Just two years after their wedding vows, however, John's drinking became all-consuming. An occasional night on the town with buddies after work became habitual. Missed dinners and drunken staggering through the house upon his return became the routine.

In two short years, John had become a stranger to her. Because Norrie believed her Catholic marriage was forever, she could see no way out except to beg for God's mercy. *"Please, Lord,"* she often prayed, *"deliver John from his drinking. I beg of you to help save our marriage."*

When Noah, was born shortly after their two-year anniversary, he brought peace into their lives—for a time. The joy of a beautiful son and the hope of a peaceful life, buoyed

Norrie with hope. But after a few short months, the pattern began anew. Fishing-drinking trips and all-night bouts at the bar, kept John away from home. Typically, after she had put Noah to bed at night, Norrie often prayed and cried herself to sleep. *Where had the love gone?* She wondered. *Why does John never want to be with me or our son?*

John was a puzzle. He seemed to avoid the love Norrie and Noah had to give. It was at this time that John's aunt filled Norrie in on some of the missing pieces of his life. John's father had deserted him, his mother, and two siblings when he was just five years old. Due to a strong resemblance to his father, his mother took out her resentments on John. Now, Norrie understood why John avoided talking about his childhood. This realization helped take away the feeling that she was somehow to blame for John's aloofness. She understood that the abandonment from his father and harshness of his mother had handicapped him emotionally. Norrie had a new focus for her prayers. *Dear God, help heal the wounds of his childhood and give him the strength to be a good father and husband.*

For a time, it seemed her prayers were answered. A new job brought satisfaction and fewer nights out. But when the company went bankrupt and John was out of a job, their world collapsed. At his next job, things got even worse. John's boss became his drinking buddy. Norrie felt abandoned by booze and when John came home drunk, he often was full of verbal abuse for his wife.

The cycle of pain, hope, and more disappointment was unbearable for Norrie. When Noah was three years old, John became worse than ever. Her pleas to God seemed to go unanswered. Divorce was unthinkable in her family. For the first time in her life, Norrie considered the unthinkable—suicide. Death had to be easier than the living hell she was in. Although her Catholic faith had always taught suicide was never an option, the emotional pain dulled her thinking.

With increasing frequency, after a heated argument or often alone with the baby, Norrie thought of how she could kill herself. She imagined John coming home drunk, finding her, and finally understanding how horrible he had been. There was an element of satisfaction in envisioning his shock and the guilt he would surely feel at realizing he had driven her to her death. She would no longer exist to be taunted or abandoned. Norrie's pain clouded the reality that death would be final. She did not think about the abandonment of her little son and facing God upon taking her own life. She only thought of escape.

Finally, very late one night, Norrie determined that she would stop thinking about suicide and go ahead and do it. With a determination that pushed out any rational thought, she got up from the sofa and went to the hall closet. Reaching to the high shelf, Norrie pulled down John's hunting rifle. She proceeded to load it. Suddenly, the horror of her next planned move scared her. She forced the rifle back onto the shelf and ran to the sofa. Throwing herself down, she began to weep uncontrollably.

It was past midnight, and Noah had been asleep in bed hours earlier. But suddenly, Norrie felt the warm hand of her toddler son on her face as he lifted her head to look at him. In his other hand was a small dusty Bible he had taken off the bookshelf. He laid it on his mommy's lap and smiled innocently at her, seemingly oblivious to her distress. Norrie's tears stopped. She looked at her precious son and then down at the book she had neglected for so long. She fell to her knees, knowing this was the "Amazing Grace" she had always heard about. Norrie began to sing the familiar song with intensity, not born of despair but with a deep joy she could not have imagined only moments earlier.

Noah then put his chubby little arms around his mother's neck and tenderly said: "I love you Mommy!" Norrie knew God was speaking to her through her little angel.

From that time on, Norrie found the strength she needed. There were trials ahead, and Norrie even left John for a time. But slowly John noticed the spiritual change in Norrie. He steadily drew closer to his family and his faith in God, until one day he made an announcement: "I'm going to take instruction to become Catholic!" By then, John had stopped drinking completely. Together, Norrie and John began building a marriage based on true love of each other and God.

The couple recently celebrated their twenty-ninth wedding anniversary. Those early years are but a distant memory, but always a reminder of the power of God's amazing grace.

—Nellie Edwards

Nellie Edwards is a successful artist, sculptor, speaker, and occasional writer. She and her husband, Chrys, have eight children. Nellie was active in the pro-life movement for many years in the state of Washington and twice went to trial for sidewalk counseling. Her website is www.mo8designs.com, and she may be contacted via email: mo8@srt.com. Her family also has a tiling business, www.edwardstiling.com.

Odyssey of Faith

All my life, I dreamed of being a wife and mother, and everything I did pointed in that direction—from asking Santa for a baby doll when I was ten to deciding against medical school in my junior year of college. As the oldest of five healthy children, I just assumed that once I married, the babies would come as easily for me as they did for my mom. My husband, Bill, and I were introduced to Natural Family Planning (NFP) during our Pre-Cana preparation in 1991. I studied it enthusiastically and carefully in the weeks leading up to our wedding, and as a couple we fully embraced it in our married life.

I became pregnant rather quickly, but miscarried at ten weeks in October 1992. We grieved terribly, but using NFP made us confident we would be able to conceive again promptly. That was not to be the case. Following the miscarriage, we endured a two-and-a-half-year odyssey of doctor visits, lab tests, and a diagnosis of endometriosis that required six months of drug treatment. After all that, we were hopeful to be blessed with a pregnancy. When we passed that milestone, feelings of despair began to creep in. While we tried to remain faithful in the Lord, each month's disappointment opened the door a bit wider to the fear that perhaps we might never conceive a child.

During all that time, faithful, wonderful family members and friends had been lifting us up in prayer. In late January 1995, my mother (a confirmed chocolate lover) felt led to give up all chocolate as a fasting sacrifice until I conceived. Then, in the early spring of that year, my parents attended a healing Mass in North Carolina. My mother stood in for me when the celebrating priest prayed over her.

In the meantime, my brother John took a pilgrimage to Israel. He and a friend offered prayers at many holy places for Bill and me, and family and friends continued to pray — as did we. By the early spring of 1995, my parents and my sister Julie and her husband told me they had been led to pray in thanksgiving for the child we would conceive. They felt the Lord had told them there was no need to "ask" anymore, that it would be done. I could only hope they were right.

In April 1995, Bill and I were very excited, then terribly disappointed, when I was a week "late." A reevaluation by my physician resulted in a referral to a fertility specialist— something I had long avoided. We cried out to the Lord in a new way for faith and strength. Emotionally and spiritually, this had been one of the most confusing and frustrating struggles either of us had ever endured. All the praying and dashed hopes seemed to lead nowhere.

On May 3, another healing priest anointed and prayed over Bill and me. On May 5, we attended a healing Mass, after which I planned to ask the priest to pray over me for complete healing of the infertility. The Mass was beautiful, and the presence of the Lord was very strong. (I should mention that every May 5, we have offered special prayers for the baby we lost in miscarriage, as May 5, was the baby's estimated due date.)

On the way to receive Communion, Bill was praying—not thinking about babies or infertility—when an amazing thing happened. He felt the Lord speak directly to him, telling him that I was already pregnant. Just like that. Anyone who knows Bill knows he's not one to jump to conclusions without being certain. When he told me, right away I knew it was true. Crying, we began to praise and thank God for His goodness and the precious life He had formed in me. Based on signs and symptoms of ovulation, conception had to have occurred within twenty-four hours of this revelation. No lab test in the world could confirm a pregnancy that early, so we waited. Then, on May 19, my home pregnancy test was positive. A visit to the doctor confirmed it. Matthew arrived on January 21, 1996. In fewer than six years, he was followed by his brothers and sister, Will, Michael and Sarah.

Those years of infertility sometimes seemed like eternity, but the Lord used that time to teach us many things: to trust Him, to pray in the face of hopelessness, and to seek His will—all of which are easier said than done. In addition, our experience has given us real sensitivity to couples who struggle with infertility. It is our sincere wish that this story of the power of prayer, God's faithfulness to His people, and the wisdom of His timing, will give new hope to all who struggle with the cross of infertility.

—Cassie McCullers

Cassie McCullers is a parishioner at Mary, Mother of the Redeemer Parish in North Wales, Pennsylvania.

A Knock at the Door

Long country days filled my youth where I lived on a farm in Salem, Oregon, with my parents and two brothers. Although my dad often picked up a variety of odd jobs, he was primarily a farmer. Just prior to the Great Depression, one of the jobs Dad took on was selling automobiles. This was a job of his that I particularly enjoyed. When Mom went into town to do shopping, she would leave my youngest brother and me at the automobile business with dad. We thought it was great fun to play hide-and-seek amid the rows of cars.

As a family, we often prayed the Rosary but during Advent and Lent we made a point to pray it nightly. While I was a teenager, I recall one particular week not attached to those seasons when we were on our knees every night praying the Rosary. With the onset of the Great Depression, there was no money for even the necessities. Mom was a professional seamstress and sewed miles of fabric to make vestments for the priests and cassocks for the altar boys. But Dad was not able to keep his automobile business, so he began selling horses and later sheep for an income.

During this week, every night after supper, we prayed together, storming heaven for help. Unless a miracle happened, we would be turned out of our home. My parents had been unable to come up with the mortgage payments. They had simply exhausted all measures to scrape up enough money. The night before the bank was to come to foreclose on our home, we continued our nightly prayer. Although we were still kids, my brothers and I could see the worry in Mom's and Dad's faces. We prayed hard. We had no idea how God could arrange to save our home, but we knew He was our only hope.

On the last day, our Rosary was not quite finished when there was a knock at the door. I got up to answer it. There was a man I did not know who stood before me. "Is your dad at home?" he asked.

"Yes, I'll go get him," I answered.

My dad got up, looking curious as to what this could be about. "Yes?" he asked. "What can I do for you?"

"I bought a car from you many years ago," the man began. "I still owe you ten dollars on that car. I would like to pay for it now."

What joy filled our home when Dad held up the ten dollars to show us all. That money was enough to keep us from losing our home. Times eventually got better, but had it not been for that money in the nick of time, we would have faced foreclosure. When we prayed for help, it was through the faith of our parents that we believed that God could come up with something. And He did.

—William A. Trumm

As told to Karen Cecile Trumm Hunt. Karen Trumm Hunt and her husband, Stuart, have four children and seven grandchildren. She works as a computer technician for Clackamas Community College. Karen lives only a mile from her parents, who have been married for sixty-one years. Karen says she thanks God daily for placing her into the arms of Bill and Marie Trumm, where she learned her faith and the power of prayer.

A Rose from Heaven

It was another perfect day in a Southern California spring. I sat grading papers in my classroom at Temecula Valley High School, where I taught freshman English and junior American literature. I looked up to see one of my freshman students, Jessica, walk into my room carrying a freshly cut yellow rose wrapped with tin foil at the stem.

"Hi, Mr. Matthews," Jessica began. "I was walking through my yard this morning, and something told me to cut this rose for you." She offered it silently, awaiting my reaction. Perhaps she knew, as I certainly did, that high school students simply don't bring fresh cut flowers to their English teachers.

A wide smile came to my face, and I answered, "Jessica, you have no idea what this means to me. Thank you!" What did it mean to me? It meant an answered prayer, plain and simple. What Jessica could not know was that my wife, Beth, and I had begun a novena, a period of nine days of prayer, just that morning. It was a novena asking for the intercession of St. Thérèse of Lisieux, a Carmelite sister from the late nineteenth century, who promised to spend her eternity in heaven doing good works on earth. Many believe that if God answers this intercessory prayer, it will be answered, in part, with the gift of an unexpected rose. As Jessica left my classroom, I prayed a silent prayer of thanksgiving and gave Beth a call.

"Beth, our prayer has been answered. You're not going to believe this, but I know I've got a job back in Indianapolis," for that had been the intention of our prayer. Beth and I had moved to California the previous year with our three children, Sean, Laura, and Patrick. Her parents had moved from Indiana to San Diego, and since Beth's family was so close-knit, we decided to follow. I had been offered a job teaching English and coaching girls' basketball in one of San Diego's northern suburbs, and Beth worked as a registered nurse at Hemet Valley Hospital on the weekends. We spent a very enjoyable time living and working in the beautiful, sunny climate. Yet, after nearly a year, our house back in Indiana hadn't sold. With Beth expecting our fourth child, Brendan, in a few months, we knew we couldn't continue to make both a mortgage payment on our home and a rent payment for our California apartment. We had given ourselves, and God, a deadline of April 1 to sell our home in Indiana as we prayed, "Lord, if it is Your will, please allow our home to sell. If not, please provide me with a job that would let us return to it." The deadline passed with no offers on the house, and so our novena began.

It was no coincidence that we turned to St. Thérèse for intercession. We had prayed for her help several times both before our marriage and after. The Little Flower of Jesus, as she is known, never failed us. We had received answered prayers and roses in many ways over the years, and were confident that, if it were God's will, she would help us again. We prayed, "Holy Trinity, God the Father, God the Son, and God the Holy Ghost, I thank Thee for all the blessings and favors Thou hast showered upon the soul of Thy servant Theresa of the Child Jesus, during the twenty-four years she spent here on earth, and in consideration of the merits of this Thy most beloved Saint, I beseech Thee to grant me this favor, if it is in accordance with Thy most Holy Will and is not an obstacle to my salvation."

When my student handed me her rose, I was completely confident that our prayer was answered. We continued the nine days of prayer, nonetheless, and another student brought me a rose on the fifth day. In six years of teaching, it had never happened once, and now it had occurred twice in five days. Near the end of the Novena, as Beth was wheeling a dismissed patient to his vehicle, he reached across his tray and presented her a rose that a friend had sent. "You've been a really good nurse. I want you to have this," he simply said. St. Thérèse must have been beaming her smile upon us each time.

Two months later, we packed a U-Haul to drive back across the country, returning to the same home we had left the year before. I still hadn't been offered a job, but we knew that God wasn't going to abandon us. Before we had even unpacked all the boxes, I had a successful job interview that resulted in an offer for a teaching and coaching position that was perfect for me. Brendan was born just before the new job began, and we were, thanks be to God, with an assist from St. Thérèse, "Back Home Again in Indiana."

—Mark Matthews

Mark Matthews is a teacher and coach in Carmel, Indiana where he lives with his wife, Elizabeth, and their twelve children. Mark is co-author with Elizabeth of A Place for Me: Patrick's Journey Home, *a book about their experience with their autistic son. The Matthews are founders of Chelsea Shire Communications, a publishing and speaking apostolate. Mark is a frequent speaker on family and education issues. For more information, please visit www. chelseashire.com.*

Sadie's Rose Petals

On a glorious morning in June of 1999, I sat on my small patio admiring God's amazing handiwork and daydreaming about the warm summer days ahead. Roses and all the glorious summer flowers were just bursting into bloom. Pictures of family gatherings and outdoor summer BBQ's danced in my head.

The ringing of the telephone interrupted my thoughts and brought news of a very different sort of summer than the one I imagined. I strolled into the kitchen to catch the phone. Immediately, I knew by the sound of my Aunt Dorie's voice that something was very wrong. She quickly explained that her daughter (my cousin Terry) was on the way to a trauma hospital. Her sixteen-year-old son Kelly had been in a terrible car accident. He had flat lined several times on the way to the first hospital they took him to. It was touch and go as to whether Kelly would survive.

In the days and weeks following, Kelly remained in serious condition. In July, Kelly was still in a coma. Terry and Dwaine (Kelly's parents) had a large support base to help out with Kelly's care and the hospital visits. Terry's sister Pam and her family were a large part of the support team caring for Kelly. Pam's little daughter Sadie was the littlest prayer warrior for her cousin Kelly. She and Kelly were very close. Even though Sadie was only six, Kelly had always been her hero.

Through all the weeks of Kelly's coma, Sadie made it her project to pray to for the intercession of St. Thérèse, the Little Flower. Sadie was adamant that Saint Thérèse would gain a miracle for Kelly. She knew her cousin would be well again, because she said, "St Thérèse told me so." In return, Sadie had promised God that she, too, would help the missions, just like Thérèse had always wanted to. We were all touched by her mission fervor and her unwavering faith.

Sadie's words came true. In late July, Kelly came out of the coma and made remarkable progress. By the last week of September, Kelly was in rehab and progressing quite well at home. During this tense time, no one gave much thought to the minor surgery coming up for Sadie. It was just a routine tonsillectomy after all. We giggled at how Sadie was so brave and said St. Thérèse was going to make sure she could eat french fries when she got home from the hospital. She was not very happy, later when she was told "no french fries," until the doctor said it was OK. But she did like the fact she got ice cream whenever she wanted it. The surgery was on Monday morning and she was home by that afternoon. Sadie had always been an easy-going child. She could entertain herself for hours talking to her imaginary friends, especially to Saint Thérèse and to Jesus.

The following Friday began with a check-up at the doctor's office. After that, Pam and the girls (Sadie and her sister Laney) went shopping. Pam and the girls kept finding rose petals on every aisle they turned into in the store. No one seemed to know where they came from. Sadie was sure St. Thérèse had sent her rose petals for being such a good patient and dutifully not eating any french fries when they had stopped for lunch before going back home.

Friday night, the girls played until bedtime in their playroom. Sadie drew pictures for her mommy and daddy. At bedtime, Glenn and Pam listened to the girls say their nighttime prayers and everyone dutifully let Sadie say her favorite prayers to Saint Theresa and to her guardian angel. All in all, the day had been quite ordinary, except for the mysterious rose petals.

At the time, I was in Marytown, Illinois, at the retreat center. I was on a pilgrimage to offer our thanksgiving for God's marvelous mercy and answer to our prayers that summer. From place to place in my travels I also kept finding mysterious rose petals. On the Feast of St. Thérèse, I attended a special memorial Mass in honor of her feast day. I was allowed to take a picture of the statue. It is very old and precious, so cameras are not usually permitted. As I snapped the picture, I found a shower of rose petals at my feet once again. I decided it must be a picture meant for Sadie.

Just as I came in the door from the airport on Sunday morning, my husband told me I needed to call my Aunt Dorie. By the way he quickly turned away with tears in his eyes, I knew something was very wrong. With my heart in my throat, I quickly dialed the number, thinking Kelly must have had another crisis. Instead, my aunt delivered the shocking news that our little prayer warrior, Sadie, had died. Sadie's scab had come off during the night, and she had hemorrhaged to death. Pam found her on Saturday morning when she went to wake her up for breakfast.

Through the days that followed, we all clung to Sadie's beloved St. Thérèse to give us comfort. Losing a child is a nightmare beyond belief. Losing a child so unexpectedly was even worse. For the first week Pam and Glenn were not allowed to make arrangements to bury Sadie. The police cordoned off the house as though it were a crime scene. It took an autopsy and the doctor's surgical records to get the body released for burial. The doctor had accidentally cut the carotid artery during surgery and lasered it shut, along with the normal wound of a tonsillectomy. The doctor never mentioned the mistake that she had made during surgery. It was mistake that would take my family to our knees once more in prayers of anguish and heartbreak. We had no ability to even ask "Why God? Why Sadie?"—although I know we all must have thought it from time to time.

Sadie, ever the faithful prayer warrior would not have been pleased if we had.

As if to punctuate Sadie's happiness and trust in God, my aunt found a seemingly heaven-sent sign while cleaning up the playroom before the funeral. There on the play table was Sadie's last drawing she did of herself. She drew herself with angel wings. It was covered with those same mysterious rose petals and it was signed, "Sadie—I am so happy. Jesus Loves Me!"

In the end, we have grieved and we have mourned, but we know, nonetheless, that Sadie is enjoying the vision she seemed to see on earth. As Pam and Glenn testified at the Rosary vigil the night before the funeral, "She was ours but for a little while. God gave her to us on loan. He gave us a beautiful child to return to Him as a saint, when she was finished with her mission." Sadie's mission in this life has blessed us all. We are the family of one of God's "littlest Saints."

—Christine Trollinger

Christine Trollinger's biography appears after her story "Lucy's Star" in chapter two.

Chapter 4

A Family's Humor

Playing by the Rules

Some professional educators believe setting clear student behavior expectations is valuable. I'd estimate the value at $29. At least, that's what the rules at my kids' school have cost me so far this year.

Every September, we are required to go over the student handbook with our children. This year, we began with the general "obey-your-teacher" ordinances and quickly progressed to more specific regulations.

"It is against the rules to sell cigarettes at school," I told my seven-year-old boy. It was a formality to go over such a rule because I'm sure the thought never crossed his mind. But, being the entrepreneur that he is, he started to crunch the numbers.

"If I can't sell cigarettes at school, what things *am* I allowed to sell?"

"The handbook doesn't elaborate," I answered.

"I'll be right back," he said, running from the room.

I didn't have time to catch him because my daughter launched into an explanation of the fourth-grade discipline policy.

"Starting this year, we use the blue-card system..." she began.

I shouldn't have asked how the system worked. It was like listening to an accountant explain changes in the tax code.

"It's a multi-tiered point scheme with rewards for positive behavior, penalties for negative behavior and bonus points for special behaviors," she said. "At the end of each week, we can trade in out points for old Happy Meal prizes and pieces of candy."

I hate Happy Meal prizes. My daughter didn't know it, but her good behavior was going to fill our recycling bin.

"What are the 'special behaviors'?" I asked.

"Book covers this week," she said. "I need you to buy three book covers for me, so I can get six bonus points. Then, I get a piece of candy."

The designer, stretch-to-fit book covers my daughter wanted were $2 each. She was asking me to pay $6 so she could get a piece of candy worth a nickel.

"Why don't I give you two pieces of candy to leave your books uncovered?" I suggested.

She was aghast that I—a parent—would suggest such outrageous, antisocial behavior.

Just then, my son ran back into the room with a knapsack full of baseball cards and year-old Halloween candy.

"I'm going to make a fortune selling this stuff at school," he said.

I told him he couldn't sell things at school, but he quickly pointed out that the student handbook didn't outlaw any retail transactions besides cigarettes. Then, he offered a compromise.

"If you bought all this stuff from me now, I wouldn't be able to sell it at school," he persuaded.

I wrote him a check for $23. Combined with the book cover purchase, I was out $29.

When I was a kid, I had a friend who routinely signed his parents' names on notes sent home from school. Next year, I'm signing my kids' names to the student handbook behavior agreement. It might cost them not to know the rules, but it will be much cheaper for me.

—Tim Bete

Tim Bete is a former newspaper columnist and author of two books, In the Beginning...There Were No Diapers *(Sorin Books, 2005) and* Guide to Pirate

Parenting *(Cold Tree Press, 2007). He is married with four children and has nineteen combined years as a dad—133 in dog years—which makes him an expert at answering the questions, "Are we there yet?" "Why?" and "What's that smell?" Tim's parenting advice has been published in dozens of newspapers, magazines and Web sites, including* The Christian Science Monitor, Atlanta Parent, Big Apple Parent, Northwest Family, *FathersWorld.com, and ParentingHumor.com. He is currently the director of the University of Dayton's Erma Bombeck Writer's Workshop.*

It's All Good

I just read an article that said it's actually good for children to grow up with a few germs and a little dust because they'll develop stronger antibodies that way. Well, my children are surely developing the immune systems of Hercules.

It's not that I *will* to be such a "relaxed housekeeper"; I just can't get a grip on the laundry that never gets put away and seems to breed in the laundry baskets. I earnestly desire that all my socks would remain happily married to their mates, and I fervently desire to weed through my closet for the next St. Vincent DePaul clothing drive. Somehow, I just can never make it happen. I know that my role as heart of the home is a dignified and respectable one. I want to bring up my children in holiness and peace. It's important that they say their prayers, get plenty of rest, eat their vegetables, and brush their teeth.

They should be well fed before Mass so they're not spilling Cheerios all over the freshly vacuumed church carpet during the consecration. I realize that I should set out their clothes the night before so that we don't experience mayhem when even St. Anthony can't locate the lost loafers. Yet, try as I may to get out the door on time with peace, joy and everyone's sippy cup, I find myself invariably dealing with the unexpected poopy diaper that throws the whole universe off-kilter.

But "I do not understand my own actions. For I do not do what I want, but I do the very thing I hate" (Romans 7: 15). In every way God reveals to me my weaknesses that He may be revealed as my strength. "God chose what is foolish in the world to shame the wise, God chose what is weak in the world to shame the strong" (1 Corinthians 1:27).

Having no basement or garage provides a daily opportunity for heartfelt prayer: "Jesus mercy; Mary help." Besides, I have the awesome privilege of possessing both Jewish and Catholic guilt. My mother, who was immaculate from her conception (not to be confused with the Blessed Mother, who is the Immaculate Conception), is from the school of "If you just clean the shower doors every time you get out of the shower, you'll never have to deal with that nasty build-up." So when my house gets out of control, so does my mind. Instead of it just being an issue of making some slight revisions in my life to facilitate a change (i.e., just tackle a little laundry at a time), it becomes a moral issue in my mind, as if I *am* the sum total of the dusty nightstand.

What does all this have to do with holiness? Everything. It's the day in, day out, awful and awesome, stupid and stupendous things in our lives that God uses to perfect us. In the words of evangelist Father John Corapi, "We are all called to be great saints."

Did you ever have one of those drunken moments with the Lord? I don't mean after consuming a bottle of chardonnay by yourself. I mean one of those times where you truly give yourself—heart, mind, body, and soul—to God. You're loving Him so much and you're palpably feeling just how much He loves you, too. Then you wake up the next morning, to a mess.

If "Jesus, Son though He was, learned obedience through what He suffered," how much more do we need to learn the lesson at the College of the Cross. No servant is greater than his master. We are given an awesome and wonderful opportunity to "make up for what is lacking in the suffering of the body of Christ" (Colossians 1:24).

As we abandon ourselves to Christ we find that God's power is greater than our lack of power and His function is greater than our dysfunction. Ultimately we find that "all is grace."

The path to holiness is an incredible journey we make carried on the wings of God's love. It is in the midst of the mess that He will make us holy, not in spite of it. Face it: we are all going to suffer. So the question is, Will it be redemptive? Will it produce the fruit of holiness within us? Holiness is a by-product of living life for God. Do His will, embrace your daily crosses and He will do all the rest within you, making you into the saint that He calls you to be.

God calls us to complete and total abandonment. "It's all good" because it comes from our Father, and "Father knows best."

—Cindy Burdett

Cindy Burdett lives near Philadelphia with her husband, Paul, and their three children, Tereze, Noah, and Moses. She is a convert to the Catholic faith from Judaism. Her "Kosher to Catholic" conversion story has delighted audiences around the country. Cindy is available to present her conversion story to groups or parishes. Contact her via email at koshertocatholic@yahoo.com.

How Compatible Are You?

If you want your family to run smoothly, it helps if you are compatible with your spouse. Married couples encompass a whole spectrum of relationship styles. There's the syrupy sweet twosome that are as much fun to be around as getting a root canal. The only advantage of breathing the same air with them for an evening is the fact that they can provide an example to your spouse of how *he/she* should be treating *you*. Then there's the other extreme; you know, the Edith and Archie Bunker sort. Again, there is a silver lining to including them in your social sphere. A feuding, nagging, or irritating twosome can make you feel like a couple of lovebirds.

If you and your spouse had to place yourself on a the spectrum of married couples, with "10" being madly in love and ecstatically happy and "0" being, well, a zero, where would you land? To find out, take this quiz which reveals your spousal IQ, and then add up your score.

1. Your spouse wants to communicate with you on an issue he/she feels is very important. Your reaction is:

    A. I'm all ears, honey. But remember, whatever makes you happy, makes me happy.
    B. OK, let's clear some time and talk about it.
    C. Didn't we already have one of these discussions last year?

2. Where do you put your toenail clippings?

    A. Not an issue; I have pedicures.
    B. In the bathroom wastebasket.
    C. Wherever they flew and landed.

3. How do you feel about a spouse who does not order dessert at a restaurant but ends up tasting half of yours?

    A. It's my pleasure to share.
    B. No big deal.
    C. Order your own darn dessert and I'll "taste" what you don't finish.

4. Books, papers, clothes, dishes, and shoes are stacking up in a room. How do you feel about this?

    A. No big deal; I'll clean it up.
    B. Time to both pitch in.
    C. I probably would not notice, but if I did, I would simply find a cleaner room to sit in.

5. How do you feel about a spouse who snores?

    A. I don't sweat the small stuff.
    B. Between earplugs and the living room couch, we can work it out.
    C. There's an empty corner in the garage to set up a cot in.

6. Your mother-in-law is interfering in your marriage, you:

    A. Invite her out to lunch and try to smooth things out.
    B. Talk to your spouse so he/she will handle things as diplomatically as possible.
    C. Move and leave her no forwarding address.

7. There's a loud neighborhood party going on next door, making it impossible to sleep. How would you handle it?

    A. We would find a nice hotel and enjoy the evening.
    B. If it's that loud, I'd call and ask them to keep it down or perhaps call the police and ask them to tell the neighbors they are disturbing the peace.

    C. I'd blow up a few fire crackers, turn on their sprinklers, and set off their car alarms. If they called asking if I knew anything about it, I'd blame the whole thing on my spouse.

8. The in-laws regularly visit from out of town for overnight stays—without calling ahead. What would you do?

    A. It would make me happy that they felt so comfortable in our home.

    B. Either my spouse or I would tell them to please call ahead the next time to see if it is convenient for us.

    C. The next time they visit, I'd announce that the guest quarters are scheduled to be fumigated for the stinging bugs that are nesting there and the doctor informed me just today that I'll will be highly contagious for at least another three days.

9. It's your wedding anniversary. How will you spend it?

    A. Dressed up in our wedding outfits, while we renew our vows.

    B. If we can find a sitter, in a quiet, romantic restaurant for dinner.

    C. Apologizing to my spouse for forgetting what day it was.

10. You are at a party where your spouse knows most everyone, but you don't know a soul. Where will he/she spend most of the evening?

    A. Glued to my side.

    B. Initially at my side, but as I meet a few people, he/she may drift back and forth.

    C. I likely won't be able to locate him/her until people start asking where the lampshade went and I hear someone loudly singing, "Roll Out the Barrel."

11. Imagine you've been married for fifty years. As you walk down memory lane with your spouse, what will be your fondest memory?

    A. Since each moment gets better and better, this activity would have to be the best.
    B. Probably the birth of our children along with any milestones we conquered together.
    C. Things like his/her helping me fish my wedding ring out of the toilet after I hurled it across the room to make a point.

12. Your spouse shares with you that he/she would really like to hear you say "I love you" more often.

    A. Since I already say it throughout the day, I will happily go the extra mile and put up a billboard with the message.
    B. I can see that it will bring us closer and will make an effort to express my love more often.
    C. I'd remind my spouse that I said, "I love you" when we married, and if I change my mind, I'll let him/her know.

Scoring:

Give yourself two points for each time you answered "A," one point for each "B" answer, and a zero for every "C" answer.

24 points: A perfect score! Since you obviously are not married yet, wait until after the honeymoon to take the test again, and then see how well you do.

20-23 points: Please do your friends a favor and do not go out as a couple. Yes, you are the sort that nauseates your companions. Don't feel bad, however. You are very happy together, and that's apparently all you really need.

13-20 points: You are a considerate, loving, and mostly happy couple. You tend to get along well with each other and don't make others want to puke when they spend time with the two of you. Good job!

7-12 points: Not bad, but a little shaky. Try being a little nicer at home, or you'll slide into Edith and Archie status.

0-7 points: You either need some serious help, a miracle, or your own TV sitcom.

—Patti Maguire Armstrong

Patti Maguire Armstrong is one of the editors of Amazing Grace for Families. *Her biography appears at the end of the book.*

Humorous Shorts

The Healing Power of Holy Water?

One morning a man came into the church on crutches. He stopped in front of the holy water, put some on both legs, and then threw off his crutches. An altar boy witnessed the scene and then rushed home to tell his dad.

"Son, you've just witnessed a miracle!" his dad said. "Tell me, where is this man now?"

"Flat on his back over by the holy water!" the boy informed him.

Divorcing After Forty-Five Years

An elderly man in Phoenix calls his son in New York and says, "I hate to ruin your day, but I have to tell you that your mother and I are divorcing; forty-five years of misery is enough."

"Pop, what are you talking about?" the son screams.

"We can't stand the sight of each other any longer," the old man says. "We're sick of each other, and I'm sick of talking about this, so you call your sister in Chicago and tell her," and he hangs up.

Frantic, the son calls his sister, who explodes on the phone. "Like heck, they're getting divorced," she shouts. "I'll take care of this."

She calls Phoenix immediately and tells the old man, "You are NOT getting divorced. Don't do a single thing until I get there. I'm calling my brother back, and we'll both be there tomorrow. Until then, don't do a thing. DO YOU HEAR ME?" and hangs up.

The old man hangs up his phone and turns to his wife. "OK," he says, "They're coming for Thanksgiving and paying their own fares ... Now what do we do to get them here for Christmas?"

Missing Jesus

It was Palm Sunday, and the family's six-year-old son had to stay home from church because of strep throat. When the rest of the family returned home carrying palm branches, the little boy asked what they were for. His father explained, "People held them over Jesus' head as he walked by."

"Wouldn't you know it," the boy fumed. "The one Sunday I don't go to church, and Jesus shows up!"

Where Is God?

A couple had two little boys who were always getting into trouble. Their parents knew that if any mischief occurred in their village, their sons were probably involved.

The boys' mother heard that an elder in town had been successful in disciplining children, so she asked if he would speak with her sons. The elder agreed, but asked to see them separately.

So the mother sent her youngest son first, in the morning. The elder, a huge man with a booming voice, sat the boy down and asked him sternly, "Where is God?" The boy's mouth dropped open, but he made no response. So the elder repeated the question in an even sterner tone, "Where is God!!?" Again the wide-eyed boy made no attempt to answer.

The elder raised his voice and bellowed, "WHERE IS GOD!?" The boy screamed and bolted from the room, ran directly home and dove into a closet, slamming the door behind him.

When his older brother found him hiding, he asked, "What happened?"

The younger brother, gasping for breath, replied, "We are in BIG trouble this time. God is missing, and they think WE did it!"

The Man Who Orders Three Beers

An Irishman by the name of Paul McLean moved into a tiny hamlet in County Kerry, walked into the pub, and promptly ordered three beers. The bartender raised his eyebrows but served the man three beers, which he drank quietly at a table, alone.

An hour later, the man finished the three beers and ordered three more. This happened yet again. The next evening the man again ordered and drank three beers at a time, several times. Soon the entire town was whispering about the Man Who Orders Three Beers.

Finally, a week later, the bartender broached the subject on behalf of the town. "I don't mean to pry, but folks around here are wondering why you always order three beers."

"'Tis odd, isn't it?" the man replied. "You see, I have two brothers, and one went to America, and the other to Australia. We promised each other that we would always order an extra two beers whenever we drank as a way of keeping up the family bond."

The bartender and the whole town was pleased with this answer, and soon the Man Who Orders Three Beers became a local celebrity and source of pride to the hamlet, even to the extent that out-of-towners would come to watch him drink.

Then, one day, the man came in and ordered only two beers. The bartender poured them with a heavy heart. This continued for the rest of the evening. Word flew around town. Prayers were offered for the soul of one of the brothers.

The next day, the bartender said to the man, "Folks around here, me first of all, want to offer condolences to you for the death of your brother. You know—the two beers and all."

The man pondered this for a moment and then replied, "My two brothers are alive and well. It's just that I myself have decided to give up drinking for Lent."

Salvation by Annoyance

An exasperated mother whose son was always getting into mischief finally asked him, "How do you expect to get into Heaven?"

The boy thought it over and said, "Well, I'll run in and out and in and out and keep slamming the door until St. Peter says, 'For Heaven's sake, Dylan, come in or stay out!'"

An Atheist's Hell

A young lady came home from a date looking rather sad. She told her mother, "Arthur proposed to me an hour ago."

"Then why are you so sad?" her mother asked.

"Because he also told me he was an atheist. Mom, he doesn't even believe there's a hell."

Her mother replied, "Marry him anyway. Between the two of us, we'll show him how wrong he is."

Don't Cry Over Burnt Toast ... or Chicken

My kids aren't particularly talented at hiding their bad behavior. The other morning, my seven-year-old son, Paul, stopped me at the top of the stairs and shouted, "Don't come down, Dad!"

Perhaps I would have fallen for his ruse if all the smoke alarms in our house hadn't been blaring.

It seems Paul had an idea. Most of Paul's ideas end in smoke, broken glass, crashing sounds, and/or screaming siblings. Luckily, there was no damage—just a lot of noise and some smoke.

After making toast, Paul had decided to pre-heat an empty toaster—not one but four times in a row. By the fourth time, the toaster was more than a tad warm.

Paul didn't tell me why he was pre-heating the toaster, and I didn't ask. I'm not fond of explanations. If Paul gives any defense after an incident, it's usually, "I was just trying something." Ironically, that's the same thing I said to my wife when the gas grill on our deck burst into flames. You'll be happy to know I didn't try it again.

While I didn't ask, I wondered about Paul's thought process. Paul and his older sister had already made their own toast. Paul isn't thoughtful enough to have been pre-heating the toaster for my wife or me. I can only assume he thought the toaster would make a nice tanning bed for Barbie. Barbie is probably so grateful for smoke alarms, she'll be the next spokesperson for National Fire Prevention Week. I can hear her now: "Only you can prevent toaster fires."

Paul isn't the first person in our family to try to cover his tracks by asking a parent to look the other way. His great uncle Vince had an even more magnificent disaster when he was five.

Vince had the job of gathering the eggs from the henhouse each day. One morning, the hens kept pecking at Vince's hands as he tried to reach under them to get the eggs. But Vince had a brainstorm that was one hundred times greater than pre-heating a toaster.

Vince ran to the house and found a box of matches. He soon proved his hypothesis that setting fire to a hen's nest will get the hen to stop pecking you. He also discovered that henhouses make great kindling.

But, like Paul, Vince knew just what to do. He ran back inside the house and shouted, "Mom, don't look out the window!"

Vince can't explain why he thought telling his mother not to look would help. Perhaps he imagined his mother wouldn't notice the charred remains of the henhouse as she strolled through the yard later in the day. But, she did look out the window. It was then Vince decided being pecked by chickens wasn't nearly as painful as dealing with a mother whose henhouse has gone up in flames.

—Tim Bete

Tim Bete's biography appears after his story "Playing By the Rules" earlier in this chapter.

Boy Genius

"If he's such a genius, how come he couldn't
talk his parents out of having to take violin lessons?"

Happy Anniversary, Handsome Stranger!

This year, I celebrated an important anniversary. Not the day I married my husband (seventeen years ago) or a milestone birthday (forty-four). No, the balmy breezes of summer will usher in the first anniversary of that momentous occasion: The Day a Handsome Stranger Hit on Me While My Husband and Four Children Stood Nearby.

It's an event I'll never forget.

We were downtown at the music festival listening to a Cajun band. The accordion was fired up, the fiddle hot, and the lead singer played a mean triangle. They were singing in French, mostly, so who knows what they' were saying? They had roughly three hundred people dancing under a tent, generating some heat to make up for the unseasonably cool temperature on that summer night.

My husband and our two younger kids had staked out a spot several feet behind me, where the chances of dripping ice cream on strangers were minimized. They perched on a curb for a better view. The older girls were with me, just behind the last row of chairs that surround the dance floor.

I'm not one to let a good beat go unnoticed, so I bounced to the music, which also helped me keep warm. Bopping in place to the music with my wedding ring hidden under the sleeve that doubled as a mitten, I must have looked like I was itching to join the dancers. On about the third song of the set, a tall, attractive, thirtyish guy came over to me and said, "Would you like to dance?"

Dance? Me? With you? A good looking thirtyish guy who isn't the father of my four children, who are now all watching you and wondering what you've just said to their mother?

"No thanks," I smiled, "I brought my regular dance partner." I nodded back toward my husband. The tall, attractive guy said something gracious and walked away.

I turned to my spouse, who gave me a wink and a look that said, "You've still got it, babe!" And that was that.

But not quite.

Next, the children weighed in. The younger ones were confused: "Who was that? Do we know him? Why did he talk to you?"

The older girls were livid. "How dare he come up and ask you to dance! What kind of woman does he think you are? And just what did you do to get his attention?"

Mostly, they were so embarrassed they wanted to vaporize. How *could* I interact with a man who's not their father in a conversation about *dancing*?

One daughter stalked off to stand on the curb with her dad. The other one looked at me like I was a Jezebel and plopped down in an empty seat several rows from where I was standing. Clearly, this encounter seemed disloyal to them.

But they did not get that I had just impressed the only man on planet Earth who matters to me.

I don't expect this will happen again in my lifetime, so I've decided to create an anniversary out of The Day Someone Reminded My Husband He Is The Lucky Man Who Got the Girl.

These days, lots of young men ogle us, but they aren't looking at me. They're checking out our eldest daughter. Needless to say, my husband's response is less enthusiastic.

I mean, a handsome stranger hitting on his wife is one thing. But his fourteen-year-old high school freshman? Don't even think about it.

—Marybeth Hicks

Marybeth Hicks is a weekly columnist for The Washington Times. *She is an award-winning writer, speaker, radio personality, and the author of* The Perfect World Inside My Minivan: One Mom's Journey Through the Streets of Suburbia, *a collection of her columns. Her second book,* Bringing Up Geeks: How to Raise Happily Uncool Kids, *will be published in early 2008.*

Marybeth began her career in the White House, where she scribed special correspondence and talking points for President Ronald Reagan. She lives in the Midwest with her husband of twenty years and their four children. Her website is www.marybethhicks.com.

Out of the Mouths of Babes

One Good Turn Deserves Another

When I went to the hospital to have my fifth baby, my sister offered to stay with my four other children. The youngest one was nearly potty trained but still had accidents. He messed his pants one day, while I was still away. My sister scolded my son and told him she did not want to have to clean up his mess. He listened until she was done and then told her: "That's OK, Auntie. When I get big and you get little and mess your pants, I'll change yours for you."

—Ginny Dolojak

An Unusual Suspect

Soon after Easter my daughters went to the neighbors to compare what the Easter bunny had brought in their baskets. Upon their return, one daughter said with concern, "Mom, Rosie asked me if I knew who the Easter bunny really was, but she wasn't allowed to tell me because her mom said she couldn't."

Trying to be diplomatic about this I responded, "Who do you think it is?"

I expected her to guess the truth as she shook her head and replied, "I don't know who he really is, but I think he stole my wallet!"

—Jeff Cavins

Bloopers

I had to laugh when my grandson Christopher explained to me that the angel "Gatorade" appeared to Mary. Then, my granddaughter Carrie told me about Jesus' special friends—the "twelve impossibles."

Perhaps they were onto something. After all, the Angel Gabriel can surely be considered an athlete of sorts with all his long-distance travel. And if not for the grace of God, those twelve apostles would certainly have been on a mission impossible.

—Jim Horvath

Communion Cookies

My godchild Natalie was a bit precocious as a small child. On the occasion of the Confirmation of her cousin Tara, her mom, Cindy, went to the bishop's Communion line with Natalie in tow. As Cindy headed back to the pew, she turned around to see Natalie, standing in front of the Bishop, staring him dead in the eye, hands on her hips. Natalie exclaimed loudly: "How come everyone else got a cookie, and all I got was a pat on the head?"

Not only did Bishop Curtis begin to laugh loudly, but so did the entire congregation. It was heard loud and clear since the Bishop's microphone was still on.

—Christine Trollinger

Laughs for Our Lady

After a long journey to get to Lourdes, France, our family (including Kyle, age nine; Zachary, age seven; and Spencer, age five) finally arrived at the beautiful grotto where Our Blessed Mother appeared to Saint Bernadette. It was a beautiful sunny day in July, and there were thousands of people at the Shrine and hundreds of people kneeling in prayer outside the grotto. Our little family knelt down and began to "quietly" pray the Rosary as best we could with three young boys. I told Kyle and Zachary to go slightly forward and silently pray the rest of the Rosary by themselves. After less than a minute, Zachary said, "Mommy, I'm done."

"Zachary, how can you be finished with your rosary already?" I asked.

He replied, "I am, Mommy. I prayed the joyful AND the terrible mysteries!"

—Lynn Mishky

Nap Time?

When my husband was ordained to the permanent diaconate, family members came to participate in the liturgy for this wonderful occasion. It was deeply touching, especially the part in which the deacon's prostrate themselves before the altar during the litany.

At the reception afterwards, my young nephew Charles said he liked church but this one was sure long. I agreed it did take longer than a regular Mass. He then said: "Is that why Uncle Rex and those other two men laid down on the floor to take a nap while everyone else was praying?"

—Joyce McDowall

Something Special

My daughter, Marcelene, loves going to church. When she was four, she explained what made the services so special to her. "Mom, they're saying my name! They said, 'Christ have Marci on us.'"

—Terri Pilcher

The Power of Baptism

When two of my kids, Davis and Becka, were little, they played "church" sometimes. On one occasion, Becka brought her doll to the priest (Davis) to be baptized. As Becka held her little doll, Davis piously poured water over its head. Then, the two of them looked down at the doll in surprise and broke up into laughter. Instead of removing original sin, this particular baptism had removed the doll's eyelashes.

—Betty Heidrich

Only Say the Word

I was rounding up John Michael, my three-year-old, and his two-year-old brother David for naps. I asked John Michael if he was ready for a nap. He replied to me, "No, I am not ready for a nap but only say the word and I shall be healed."

I got a big chuckle out of that and related the story to our priest, Fr. Joel.

"I wish words could heal him from his aversion to naps," I laughed.

Father suggested, "Behold the nap of John. Blessed are they who nap until supper."

—Mary Klopcic

Fruit and Cheeses

When my daughters were about four and six, my sister-in-law, Nancy, died a tragic death from cancer at age thirty-nine. My daughters had never been to a funeral or a Rosary service and were quiet and respectful throughout. When we got in the car, all silent and quietly weeping, my daughter in the back seat suddenly piped up, "OK, tell me about the fruit and the cheeses."

I asked, "What do you mean?"

She said, "During the prayer, they kept talking about the fruit and the cheeses. Tell me about that." It took me a while to figure out that she was hearing, "blessed is the FRUIT of thy womb CHEESES."

—Maureen Jabour Nurmikko

Wine Tasting

The wine region in southern Spain where we lived is famous for its sherry. The priest of our parish took advantage of this fact by doing wine tastings for the perfect wine for consecration and purchased large quantities from a local *bodega* or winery. After two years, we moved our family back to the United States. One day after receiving Holy Eucharist, I returned to the pew and began to pray. Our Zachary, then age eight, returned to the pew after me. After a few seconds, he leaned over to me and said, "Mommy, the Blood is much better in Spain."

—Lynn Mishky

Career Choices

Before my daughter Shannon turned three, she informed me that she was going to be an inventor. She took her career choice very seriously and was always full of creative ideas. One summer, she even turned our driveway into a ski hill of sorts. Not until I heard my neighbor scream and saw her feet in the air, did I realize that Shannon had not taken out the dish soap to wash our car. A thin film of soap had knocked down two neighbors before I learned that she had invented a way to ski without snow.

During first grade, however, another potential career caught her attention. She loved religion class at St. Elizabeth's and enjoyed learning about the saints. One day, she brought me a book on the lives of the saints to read with her. "Mom, maybe I don't want to be an inventor," she said thoughtfully. "Is it possible to be a saint for a career choice? What would I have to do to become a saint?"

"Well, for starters, you could sit still in church," I suggested.

Without missing a beat, she responded, "Oh, then I guess I'll just stick to being an inventor."

—Mariann Petersen

An Early Calling

When our youngest son was almost four, I found him walking through the house with a big wooden crucifix. His expression was so somber that it actually looked funny and made me chuckle. He looked up at me when I laughed, and I said, "What are you doing with that cross? Are you going to be a priest when you grow up?"

He looked at me, shrugged his shoulders, and just as serious as could be, said, "I guess I have to ... you said you were sending me to priest school (pre-school)."

—Elizabeth Schmeidler

A Test for Sisters

Are you and your sister almost like identical twins with separate birthdays in different years? Or are the two of you as repellent as oil and water with the cat scratches to prove it?

There's nothing like the closeness of a sister or the friction when the two don't mix.

Which sort of relationship do you have with your sister? Take the quiz below to find out. Read the pairs of statements below and circle either A or B for the situation that best describes you and your sister. You will then score your relationship at the end.

1.   A.   You and your sister often end up owning the same
          types of pets.
     B.   When one sister buys a pet, the other one buys something
          that will eat it.

2.   A.   When your sister was pregnant, you found yourself
          experiencing weird food cravings.
     B.   When your sister was pregnant, you often told her
          she looked like she was expecting triplets.

3.   A.   You and your sister are so close, that when she eats two
          desserts, you are the one that gains the weight.
     B.   When one sister is dieting, the other usually feels a
          sudden urge to bake a pan of brownies to share.

4.   A.   Your sister and you often finish each other's sentences
          to the point that it seems that only one person is talking
          instead of two.
     B.   You and your sister usually interrupt each other and
          find the volume gets loud enough to shake glass
          since one must scream to be heard over the other.

5. A. When your sister walked down the aisle to get
       married, you found yourself wanting to shout,
       "Sisters forever" when the priest asked if there was
       any reason "why these two should not be wed?"
    B. Just before your sister walked down the aisle, you
       told her the color white makes her look heavy.

6. A. You often pick up the phone and say hello before it rings
       and discover your sister is on the line.
    B. When you check caller ID and see your sister's
       number, you run into the shower.

7. A. Your children's names all start with the same letter
       of the alphabet or rhyme, (i.e., Timmy, Jimmy, and
       Kimmy, or Betty, Bob, Belinda, Boris, etc.)
    B. Your children don't know they have cousins.

8. A. When you were younger, the two of you giggled and
       told stories so late that your parents had to come
       to your bedroom and warn you two to quiet down
       or else...
    B. All your girlish pillow fights resulted in broken
       furniture and bones.

9. A. You and your sister sometimes have the same dream,
    B. In your nightmares, the scary monster always bears
       a striking resemblance to your sister.

10. A. You and your sister are very affectionate, often
       linking arms and hugging.
    B. Whenever you are around your sister, she frequently
       helps you up off the floor and apologizes for
       having her foot out too far—once again.

Scoring:

Give yourself +1 for each "A" answer and -1 for each "B."

Ten points: You and your sister might as well be conjoined twins. Your husbands feel that the two of you are closer to each other than to them. You probably use baby talk with each other and nauseate those around you.

Seven to nine points: The two of you often wear identical outfits and have no other friends but each other, but neither of you cares.

One to six points: Now we are getting into the normal, healthy range. you can have fun and feel close to your sister, but there are still those times where you disagree or get on one another's nerves.

Zero to minus six points: It's best to wear long sleeves around your sister to avoid the cat scratches. Also, be advised to bring your own food when dining at your sister's house.

Minus seven to minus ten points: You need restraining orders on each other.

—Patti Maguire Armstrong

Patti Maguire Armstrong is one of the editors of Amazing Grace for Families. *Her biography appears at the end of the book.*

A Test for Brothers

There's nothing like a brother, right? I have three myself and my own eight sons can all claim seven brothers. My husband has two. Given that the emotional makeup of men is a few notches lower than women, the brother relationship is usually less complicated than with sisters. Still, even the most easy-going guy has limits. To test what kind of brotherly relationship you have, answer the questions below and see how you and your brother(s) rate.

1. When it comes to competitive sports you and your brother:
    A. Have a lot of laughs and it never really matters who wins.
    B. Refuse to quit until there's blood.

2. Whenever playing a board game such as Monopoly or Trivial Pursuit, you two:
    A. Have fun but half the time don't even get around to finishing the game.
    B. Refuse to quit until there's blood.

3. As kids, when it came to borrowing each other's clothing:
    A. We pretty much shared to the point that we forgot whose clothes were whose.
    B. We had a rule: any unauthorized clothing was confiscated it on the spot—yes, even in church.

4. If your parents teamed you up to do some outside yard work:
    A. We worked twice as fast.
    B. Rakes and shovels became weapons.

5. As boys, when you got together with friends to play ball game:
    A. You two always played on the same side.
    B. One of you inevitably became the ball.

6. When the older one had friends over, the younger one:
    A. Was invited to join big brother and friends
    B. Was locked in a closet.

7. When the younger one had friends over, the older one:
    A. Typically served as a mentor and helped with projects or played games with them.
    B. Locked the visitors in the closet.

8. The younger brother:
    A. Idolized his big brother.
    B. Tormented his big brother then tattled when the finally big brother punched him in.

9. The older brother:
    A. Lovingly looked out and guided his little brother.
    B. Tried to sell his little brother to the neighbors—at a very good price.

10. Now that you are married with children of your own, your kids:
    A. Are closely bonded with their cousins
    B. Have never met.

11. At you brother's wedding:
    A. You were "best man."
    B. You were not invited.

12. Your parents:
    A. Treated you both equally
    B. Frequently wondered out loud if they came home
       from the hospital with someone else's baby.

13. When it comes to politics you:
    A. Always vote the same
    B. Never vote because your brother locks you in the
       closet on election day.

14. When you brought a date home to meet the family:
    A. You always trusted your brother's opinions
       regarding the girls you introduced him to.
    B. Your brother would only walk into the room when
       he had to burp.

15. You and your brother's careers are:
    A. In the same field so you have a lot to talk about.
    B. Diametrically opposed, such as oil field developer
       vs. environmentalist or big game hunter vs. animal
       rights activist.

16. When it comes to showing feelings and emotions you
    and your brother:
    A. Feel comfortable giving each other a hug.
    B. Affectionately wrestle each other to the ground.

Scoring:

Give yourself +1 for each "A" answer and -1 for each "B."

Sixteen points: You and your brother are more like sisters.

Ten to fifteen points: The two of you probably have nicknames for each other like Wally and Beaver. You are the brothers of every parents dream and the model for other parents to say: "Why can't you two act more like Wally and Beaver?"

One to nine points: Now we are getting into the normal, healthy range. You can have fun and feel close to your brother, but there are times that you get competitive or egg each other on.

Zero to minus ten: You two probably don't communicate much because it could lead to bloodshed.

Minus eleven to minus sixteen: You should wear football pads and helmets at all family get-togethers.

—Patti Maguire Armstrong

Patti Maguire Armstrong is one of the editors of Amazing Grace for Families. *Her biography appears at the end of the book.*

And the Winner Is ...

Last week I ran a 5K race. It was the first race I had run in twenty years. It wasn't my choice to run the race. My nine-year-old daughter needed someone to run with her.

I wouldn't say that I'm out of shape, but my shape is closer to the Stay Puff Marshmallow Man than Mr. Universe. There was a single reason my daughter wanted to run the race: All kids nine and under would get an award. All they had to do was participate.

When I was a kid, there were no awards simply for participating. Woody Allen once said, "Eighty percent of success in life is just showing up." In today's youth sports, it seems 100 percent of success is just showing up.

We finished the race in an unimpressive time, and I was thankful I didn't cross the finish line in the back of an ambulance. Awards for the fastest runners were given out in dozens of categories: men age forty to forty-five; men age forty-six to fifty; men age fifty-one to fifty-five...born in May...on a Tuesday...before noon.

Many awards that should have been awarded were omitted. Hundreds of parents ran with their kids, which is a little like doing the high jump while carrying three bags of groceries. My brother-in-law's time would have been faster had he not had to escort his daughter to the Port–o-John during the race. His wife had to slow down because their son had a cramp. Once the finish line was in sight, however, he flew ahead, beat his mom, and proceeded to taunt her for losing.

During the children's awards ceremony, I had a brilliant idea. The kids had been motivated to run for miles in return for a small, inexpensive plastic trophy. Surely our kids would be thrilled to win similar awards. If I acquired a few cases of trophies, I might be able to get our kids to participate in the activities I'd like them to do...like cleaning their rooms and sweeping the kitchen floor.

"Hey kids!" I'd announce. "Tonight we'll be holding the First-Annual Oscar Madison Memorial Room Cleaning Marathon. All children under the age of nine will receive a stunning three-inch plastic bowling trophy for just participating!"

The kids might wonder why I was offering a bowling trophy for room cleaning. I'd have to confess that I got them cheap at an estate auction. My daughter would think it was gross to get a trophy that belonged to a dead guy with the nickname Rocko, who had a 190 average. My son would think it was cool and brag about it to his friends. But they'd both be willing to work tirelessly to earn such a distinctive award.

Which proves it isn't whether you win or lose. It's whether you get a trophy.

—Tim Bete

Tim Bete's biography appears after his story "Playing By the Rules" earlier in this chapter.

Culinary Critic

"Does this stuff have all the vitamins and
minerals I need, or will I like it?"

All in a Name

As a first grader at St. Alphonsus School, I was excited to learn that our parish priest would be coming to the classroom to visit and teach us about the Mass. Our teacher, Sr. Catherine Paul, made sure we had all the papers picked up off the floor and that our desks were in nice neat rows.

When Father entered the classroom, we all stood up and in unison announced, "Good morning, Father" in the sing-song sort of way kids do when speaking together. Father was animated and friendly, telling us a little about himself along with explaining that during the Mass, God is present to us and we come together as a community to spend time with Him. After his brief teaching session, he opened it up to questions.

I was just a little nervous but excited to have a chance to ask Father a question. I kept my hand up until finally he pointed to me. "Yes," he said, kindly. "What would you like to ask?"

I stood and began to speak, but before I could get my question out, the classroom erupted into laughter. Even Father and Sister were laughing. I was confused. It could not be that my question was silly, because I had not even gotten it all out. I wondered if there was something on my face or my hair was sticking up. Finally, Sister cleared things up for me.

"Brian," she said still chuckling, "His name is Father Mahoney, not Father Baloney."

—Brian Maguire

Brian Maguire grew up in Dearborn, Michigan. He now lives in Portland, Oregon, where he and his wife are raising their two boys, Matthew and Dylan.

The Eyes Have It

My wife and I recently celebrated our fifteenth wedding anniversary, and we did what all romantic couples do on such an auspicious occasion. We got our eyes examined.

I hadn't been to the eye doctor since before we were dating. But after performing poorly on an eye test to renew my driver's license, my wife encouraged me to consider glasses. She needed a new pair, too.

As a kid, the eye test was pretty basic: Cover one eye while reading a chart on the wall. Now there was a long line of sophisticated machines to put me through my paces. After having my peripheral and color vision tested, I gazed into the eye pieces of the third machine.

"What do you see?" asked the doctor.

"I see a waste basket," I said.

"Is it full or empty?" she asked.

"Full," I said, feeling quite confident in my ability.

"That's good ... but surprising," said the doctor. "Your wife told me you can walk right past an overflowing waste basket without seeing it or bothering to take it out to the trash."

'What else did my wife tell you?" I asked.

"She said you have trouble seeing things her way," said the doctor.

It was clear my wife was looking for more than my vision to be corrected.

After I was through with the doctor, I met my wife where the eyeglass frames were displayed. The doctor had dilated my eyes and I was having trouble focusing.

"I'll need you to tell me which frames I look best in," I said to my wife. "Do these frames make me appear sophisticated?"

"Have your eyebrows always been different sizes?" she countered.

I took that as a "no," and proceeded to try on dozens of frames during the next ten minutes.

"Your eyes are still blurry from the dilation, aren't they?" my wife asked.

"Yes, how did you know?" I asked.

"Because those aren't eyeglass frames," she said. "You just picked up a pair of pencils and put them behind your ears."

"That would explain why they felt so wooden," I said.

After I found the perfect pair of frames, which I was convinced made me look like Robert Redford, it was my wife's turn. Her face is small, and most adult frames are too large for her. So, she tried the section with children's eye glasses.

My wife would have been the talk of the town in the glow-in-the-dark Sponge Bob Squarepants frames. But, she finally settled on a simple pair of gray frames. Without lenses in them, she couldn't read the small red print on the side of the frames. Who would have guessed Nintendo even made eye wear?

After waiting an hour for our glasses to be made, I tried mine on. The world around me snapped to attention, and I discovered fifteen years of marriage hadn't made my wife blurry after all.

My wife liked her new glasses, too, but I'm not sure she needs them. Even without corrective lenses, she's always been able to see right through me.

—Tim Bete

Tim Bete's biography appears after his story "Playing By the Rules" earlier in this chapter.

Pursuing Peace

With three sisters, my second-born boy had his work of sister-harassment cut out for him. By the time he was in middle school, he was a pro. He was also the frequent target of my motherly counsel based on the Bible verse 1 Peter 3:11, "Seek peace and pursue it."

Since his older sister, already in high school, and his two younger ones, still in elementary school, arrived home before he did, the girls were calmly settled into their afternoon snacks and homework before Aaron arrived. As I went about my housework on the second floor, I could hear him make his way through the house by the screams and shrieks of his sisters.

"A-a-a-ron! Leave me alone!" from one; seconds later, I heard: "Stop it! I'm telling. M-o-m!"

I hollered down from upstairs, "Son, are you pursuing peace?"

I didn't even have to see the impish grin to know that it was plastered on his face, "Yes, I am, Mother. I am chasing it right out of the house."

—Mary Kohan

Mary Kohan is a senior editor for Catholic Exchange.com. She was raised as a third-generation Jehovah's Witness, worked her way "backwards" through the Protestant Reformation, and entered the Catholic Church on Trinity Sunday, 1996. She is a writer, speaker, and counselor on religious cults. To arrange for Mary to speak at your event, contact her at mkochan@catholicexchange.com.

Bad Hearing

One Sunday there was a visiting missionary priest to say the Mass at our church. During his homily, he kept referring to himself as a "married old priest." Every time he said it, I laughed loudly. I did not think it was all that funny, but I thought he was making an attempt at humor, so I went along with it. I wondered why others were not at least making a polite attempt to laugh.

Each time I laughed, my husband shot me a quizzical look. It was not until after Mass was over that I learned the priest was a Maryknoll missionary. Although I am a lifelong Catholic, I had never heard of this group before. I realized in horror that the missionary had been referring to himself as a "Maryknoll priest," not a "married old priest." Ah, the humility.

—Michelle Webster

Michelle Webster is the wife of Daniel and the mother of Gabriel, eight, Olivia, six, and Teddy, five. She is a nurse-turned-homeschooler. The family lives in Bel Air, Maryland, and belong to St. Joan of Arc Parish.

Playing Chicken

"Son, what did your mother tell you
about playing with your food?"

Special Guest at the Hyatt

My mother had an opportunity to come to Baltimore for a medical conference. I was excited as she had not yet had a chance to visit us there since our move. Her time was short, however, so we had to make due with a lunch date at the hotel where she was staying. Our oldest daughter, Maggie, three years old, went with me. We had a great visit with a big kiss and hug good-bye.

The next Sunday during the opening prayers and songs at Mass, Maggie began to fervently tug at my skirt hem and call me, "Momma, Momma." I tried to shush her, but she would not be put off. I looked down at her.

"Momma, was God there?"

"What?" I asked. "Was God there?" Totally misunderstanding her, I began to tell her what I had many times before. "God is everywhere, honey; you know that. We just can't see him."

Rolling her eyes at me, she spoke more firmly. "No! Was God there with Gramma?"

Becoming frustrated myself, I repeated, "Yes, God is always with Gramma," and turned my attention back to the altar. Maggie, however, was not done.

Tugging at my skirt again, she demanded, "Momma, if God was with Gramma, why didn't we go see Him?" I looked at her, confused. "At the hotel with Gramma, why didn't we go see God?" she asked again.

Finally, I gave her my full attention and bent down to her level. "Maggie, what are you asking about?"

Taking a deep breath, she asked, "Momma, when we went to Gramma at the hotel why didn't we go see God?"

"Maggie, we couldn't have SEEN God at the hotel, God is invisible." She shook her head at me in disagreement, "Yes, we could have. We just sang it: Glory to God at the Hyatt!"

—Rachel Watkins

Rachel Watkins' biography appears after her story "It Takes a Village" in chapter six.

Parenting Is a Lot of Work

The federal government's *Dictionary of Occupational Titles* provides descriptions for more than 12,000 jobs—everything from "Able Seaman" to "Zoologist." You might expect to find "parent" between "Parcel Post Clerk" (Wraps, inspects, weighs, and affixes postage to parcel-post packages) and "Parimutuel Ticket Cashier" (Cashes winning parimutuel tickets for patrons at race track). Unfortunately, "parent" is not one of the 12,000 occupations listed.

Being a parent is the second job most adults—whether they are chef, hazardous waste management specialist, or wardrobe supervisor—go home to after a hard day's work. For stay-at-home parents, it's the job with continuous twenty-four-hour shifts.

My son and his second grade classmates recently drew pictures of their parents' occupations. As I looked at the art exhibit, I overheard one boy tell his dad, "You and Billy's dad are like a team: he starts fires and you put them out." You probably guessed that the boy's dad was a firefighter. You might not have suspected that Billy's dad is an electrician, not an arsonist. The firefighter's son heard his dad say that most fires are electrical fires and assumed that's what electricians do—start fires.

After reviewing the children's pictures, it became clear that most of their parents' jobs were pretty boring (except perhaps the guy who starts fires) and weren't nearly as cool as the Dictionary of Occupational Title's definition of "cheese sprayer" (Tends equipment that coats popcorn or similar food product with melted cheese) or "Mortuary Beautician" (Prepares embalmed bodies for interment: Manicures nails, using files and nail polish and performs other grooming tasks).

According to the artwork, the most common occupation for dads is sitting in a chair. Coincidentally, that is also their most common activity at home. Pictures of moms indicated that sweeping is a common occupation. When my oldest daughter was in second grade, her picture showed my wife screaming, "You're driving me crazy," while a child clung to her leg. That job description isn't going to attract too many applicants.

You might think the vagueness of the pictures is support for "take your child to work day" so that kids can learn what we really do to put bread on the table. On the contrary: I think it's time for "take your parents to school day." That's just the ticket parents need to get a twenty-four-hour break from their typical job routines.

Instead of writing memos, we could pass notes. Instead of serving customers, we could eagerly anticipate gym class, recess and lunch period. Instead of sitting in a dazed stupor during hour-long meetings listening to co-workers drone on about profits and losses, we could sit in a dazed stupor in hour-long classes listening to teachers drone on about the history of ancient civilization. Hey, at least it would be a change of pace.

But at the end of the day, when we went home from school, we'd still hold the title of chef and hazardous waste management specialist and wardrobe specialist—just not of the paid variety.

—Tim Bete

Tim Bete's biography appears after his story "Playing By the Rules" earlier in this chapter.

Household Skulduggery

I apologize to the rest of you if archaeologists in the distant future ever stumble onto my home in an excavation site. Such a discovery could inspire these scholars to write book-length studies claiming that all family groups from our culture shared the same peculiar habits.

"Why," the future archaeologists would wonder, "did inhabitants of late twentieth-century North America hide old birthday cards in their underwear drawers? And why did they stuff bags of outdated newspapers in their closets?"

Digging a little further, they would unearth a decade's worth of scenic wall calendars from behind the microwave. Then they'd locate the ticket stubs and programs from family outings stuck between place mats in the linen closet.

In case *you're* wondering, the answer is simple: it was vital to do these things to preserve the peaceful coexistence of the particular North Americans who resided at my address. That's because my home is ruled by the housekeeping equivalent of Jekyll and Hyde.

My husband, Mark, is a highly organized neat freak, the Jekyll role in our domestic partnership. When he walks through the living room, magazines jump up off the floor and arrange themselves tastefully (by issue date) on the coffee table. Encyclopaedias re-alphabetize themselves. Dust balls roll out from under the sofa and march single file to the trash can.

Then there's me, a bit absentminded and downright comfortable with clutter. Just call me Hyde. When I walk through the room, magazines hurl themselves off end tables (kamikaze-style) onto the carpet. Dirty socks leap from the laundry basket and scurry underneath the recliner. And those dust bunnies, they run and hide for cover, which is not much of a challenge for them where I am concerned.

Mark loves vacant counter-tops and uncluttered desks. Any item not specifically required for sustaining life in the next fifteen minutes he deems unnecessary and throws away.

I live to be organized, too, but not today. I plan to be organized tomorrow. I have never encountered an "unnecessary item" in my life. Any objects that wander in the front door, from broken-handled brooms to single-bladed scissors, appear to me somehow useful. And I get nervous when my counter tops are showing.

How have two such opposite-minded people managed sixteen years of happy marriage? It has a lot to do with deep, abiding love and the calculated use of clutter concealment. I simply hide all my important stuff where Mark can't find it.

Hence the underwear drawer full of old birthday cards (which I will one day organize in a scrapbook); the closets full of newspapers (containing articles I will one day clip and organize in a scrapbook); the scenic wall calendars (full of attractive pictures I will one day mount on construction paper and organize in a scrapbook); and a linen closet full of family-outing keepsakes (which I will one day sort and—but you've heard this before).

Before you judge me too harshly, consider how you might feel if you found yourself chasing the end of your garden hose across the lawn because your obsessively organized mate was around the corner rolling it up before you could finish dousing the petunias. Or how might you react if the clean clothes you laid out in the morning were routinely rounded up and placed in the laundry hamper before you could even get out of the shower?

The really frightening part is that our children have begun copying our behavior. Lately, when I've opened the piano bench to stash some cereal box tops (I'm saving up for a *Hits from the Seventies* CD), I've encountered preschool craft items and crayon drawings that I didn't hide there. Our five-year-old son had a simple answer: "I didn't want Dad to throw them away."

And my daughter, eleven years old and savvy to her mother's Hyde-like habits, is careful to keep her library books secured in her room, where they can't be carried off to one of my infamous piles, never to be seen again.

But I'm not the only parent who makes her nervous. She's equally careful to keep her homework off the kitchen counter, where her father may collect it in one of his frequent "clean sweeps" through the area and throw it away before she has a chance to hand it in.

I doubt that archaeologists excavating our home will ever understand how domestic cohabitation spawned elaborate household rituals like math papers hidden under cookbooks, completely empty boxes sealed and stacked in the basement, and preschool craft items stuffed in the piano bench. But there's nothing I can do about it. We're happy—now that we've learned to live together in an atmosphere of peace and good-natured skulduggery.

—Renae Bottom

Renae Bottom is a writer, newspaper reporter and school teacher. She and her family live in Imperial, Nebraska.

Editors' Note: *This story originally appeared in* Marriage Partnership *magazine.*

Chapter 5
A Family's Faithfulness

What Does It Mean to Be a Christian?

After six months of wedded bliss, my husband, Mike, and I rejoiced upon learning that we were going to be parents. The thrill of embarking on this new stage of life cast an exciting glow on everything we did. We read about the developing baby, anticipated each phase, and talked endlessly about names and what it would be like to really be parents. At sixteen weeks, our doctor offered to do an alpha feta protein test on our developing baby. Mike and I wanted to do everything we could regarding the pregnancy, so we agreed. When the nurse called and said everything was fine, we continued on our merry way. Life was good.

In the midst of all the excitement, however, there was a missing piece—God. He was there, but I did not know really where he fit in. During this time, Mike and I attended a funeral. That night, as I thought about life and death, I especially cherished the new life growing within me. But I felt an urgency for God to be a bigger part of our lives than just paying lip service at Mass on Sundays. Mike and I talked about it, but we had no real answers. "Dear God," I prayed that night, "help me to know what it means to be a Christian. Please lead us to you."

The next evening, while I was at work doing a haircut, the receptionist told me I had a phone call. It was Mike. The doctor had called to inform us that he had read the test incorrectly and something might be wrong. He wanted us in the office the next day to do another ultrasound. My heart sank, and I felt sick with fear. *Everything just has to be OK*, I thought. "Dear God, please let everything be all right," I instinctively prayed.

The next morning, during the ultrasound the nurse looked at the screen and sighed, "There's that lemon-shaped head we didn't want to see." My stomach tightened. *There really is something wrong with our baby.* Mike and I looked at one another but said nothing.

The doctor came in to talk with us. He looked from Mike to me and then explained: "The baby has spina bifida." The rest became a blur of shock and disbelief. We were told not to ever expect our baby to walk, and she would likely be mentally challenged. Mike and I broke down and held each other as we wept. We had envisioned a future of guiding our child in her first wobbly steps, reading books and singing songs, playing games, and all the other joys of parenting. *How can this be happening to us?* I wondered.

Suddenly, it seemed that our happy life had just been an illusion. My pregnancy became a heartbreaking burden, not a joy. People sent flowers and offered sympathy as if there had been a death. Now, seeing healthy babies and young children with their parents poured salt into our fresh wound. They had something we were going to be denied.

Our doctor referred us to the Mayo Clinic in Rochester, Minnesota, for a second opinion. Although there was a part of us hoping for better news, it only got worse. There was no discernable brain. Instead, her head was filled with fluid. The expectation was that our daughter would be a vegetable requiring institutional care. After the specialists contacted our primary physician, he strongly recommended terminating the pregnancy. "If you were to contact ten of the best doctors in the world, they would all suggest ending this pregnancy," he stated.

As twenty-six-year-old newlyweds the thought of becoming parents to such a child filled us with horror. We wanted out and the sooner, the better. Our doctor informed us that the two

Bismarck hospitals would not terminate this pregnancy through inducing labor. We were scheduled to be induced in Fargo the next day.

In our fear, our minds had not truly sorted through the decision we had frantically made. When my mother asked me if the Catholic Church would allow us to have a funeral for the baby, it caught me off guard. We were thinking only about ourselves. After all, what was there to think about this baby who did not even seem to be fully human to me? My mother's question perplexed me. I called our parish but was unable to reach the priest, so I called my cousin, Fr. Austin Vetter. When he learned of our plan, he came over to see us right away.

"Melody, you are talking about having an abortion," he stated, looking me firmly in the eye. "You know better than that." Anger welled up within me. He was putting it in such harsh terms. The way I looked at it, my labor would be induced, and then the baby would be born but would not survive. What kind of a life would it have, anyway? This was the best choice for everyone. My doctor thought so and, according to him, so would every other medical expert.

"You have no idea what we are going through," I cried. "It's easy for you because your life will go on, but ours will stop. Who is going to help us raise this child? You won't, yet you are trying to tell us what to do."

Fr. Austin talked about God being the giver of life and He alone had the right to end it. He said we would all be praying for a miracle, but, either way, our baby should live or die according to God's will and not because of our choice.

Father Austin's caring and reasoned words cut through our fear. We cancelled our appointment in Fargo, less than twenty-four hours before our baby's life was scheduled to end. With our decision to hand everything over to God, we gave Him not just our unborn baby, but our entire beings. Mike and I suddenly understood our complete helplessness and total dependence on

God.   Although it did not occur to me at the time, God was answering my prayer for him to become a central part of our lives.

That evening, Fr. Austin said Mass at our apartment with other family members present, too. Surrounded by our loving, faith-filled family, a spiritual aura of peace and strength covered us. We were put on prayer chains and lifted up by the prayers of many.

Yet the medical news continued getting worse. The fluid in her head kept increasing, and there was no brain to be seen. Ultrasounds showed that she had a foot growing out of the side of her leg. I imagined that my baby must be suffering very much. "Dear God, she is in your hands. Please just take her and end her suffering," I prayed.

At twenty-five weeks, all movement ceased. *She must be gone now*, I thought. When I called the doctor, he was not surprised. It was the weekend, so we were told to come in on Monday so I could be induced. Mike and I had mixed emotions. Part of us was relieved that it was over. Our daughter would not suffer, she was with God, and it had been His decision, not ours. There was another part of us that felt guilty that the death of our own daughter would bring us relief.

On Monday, Mike came with me to be induced. Together, we would see our poor little daughter for the first time, to bring her into this world only to say good-bye. During the preliminary exam, however, there was a surprise. Her little heartbeat came through loud and clear on the heart monitor. She had kicked herself into a position she could not get out of because her feet were paralyzed. It was as if our daughter had been raised from the dead. We were filled with wonder, and, in spite of an element of confusion and fear, our love for the little girl we thought was gone was growing. We had felt guilty for not loving her enough, but now, we had a second chance. Still, there was fear of what lay ahead for us.

In the weeks ahead, we met with a neonatalogist, and a neurosurgeon who would be present at the birth. Then, we switched over to Fargo to get a second opinion from another doctor. This doctor had a disabled child and said it was not a big deal, that they had a good life. He also told us that children with spina bifida usually do very well. He gave us a feeling of hope.

At this point, I told God that if He healed her of either her mental handicaps or her physical handicaps, I would share our testimony with as many people as I could. It was not a deal in an attempt to force God's hand, but it felt more like an inspiration of what I wanted to do for God. I was praying for a healing, but I was also accepting God's will, whatever that meant. I gave my life to God to use as He wanted. I thought of Mary, who said "yes" to God's plan when the angel Gabriel appeared to her saying she was chosen to be the mother of God's son. Her situation seemed less than perfect at the time, but God had a plan. I trusted that he had a plan for me, too.

After giving myself completely over to Him, I abandoned my fear and was filled with trust. I was ready to be a mother now. The initial glow that once filled me, returned. We were going to have a baby! Mike, too, caught the excitement. We bought a crib and painted her room. Finally, we named our daughter, Hailey Christina. Although I had switched to the doctor in Fargo, my water broke in the middle of a treacherous snowstorm. The Bismarck hospital was not expecting us anymore, but in we came. As I was readied for a C-section, the doctors prepared me for what I was about to see. My daughter's head would look like a basketball. She had a foot growing out of the side of her leg, we would see through her head like a light-bulb, and she had only a ten percent chance of living. Lying on the surgical table, I turned to Mike, who was sitting on a stool just behind me. His hands were folded close to his chest, his eyes closed, praying for his daughter to live. Very quickly, the incision was made, and Hailey was lifted up. Mike hurried behind the doctors and nurses as they wisked her into another room. Half an hour later, Mike came in and told me that our daughter was beautiful. She did have an opening in her back, but it was nothing like anyone expected. I was wheeled to the nursery and heard her beautiful cries—the ones we were told she would be unable to make.

Hailey was quickly baptized and then taken into a four-hour surgery to close the hole. It was uncertain what her brain development was. At that point, Mike and I loved her so much, we wanted her no matter what they discovered. A week later, a shunt was placed in her head to remove the fluid. The following week, our precious baby came home.

One night while I was rocking Hailey, God spoke clearly to my heart. He let me know that Hailey was healed according to His plan. Her spina bifida was a blessing on our family that would keep us close to God. Mike and I would thank Him for each milestone in Hailey's life rather than take them for granted, and we would remain aware of our dependence on our Heavenly Father.

When Hailey was only one year old, she began walking with crutches. She started talking and reaching developmental milestones at the expected ages. Now, at the age of thirteen, she attends St. Anne School and is a light for all to see. Each day we realize how blessed we are to be the parents of this beautiful, faith-filled girl.

I kept my promise to God and often give my testimony before groups and also give comfort and hope to new moms coping with a child's disabilities. God answered my prayers more completely than I had ever imagined. I am so thankful that God has given us Hailey to teach us what it means to be a Christian by leading us to give God our lives and to put our trust in Him.

—Melody Haider

Melody and Mike Haider live in Bismarck, North Dakota. They have two children, Hailey, thirteen, and Jayden, ten, who attend St. Anne School. They enjoy camping and spending time together. Melody is involved in Moms in Touch, a ministry to pray for school children. She can be emailed at m.haider@ bis.net.com

A Family Converts

If there was ever a family far from hope of coming to Christ, it was mine. My father was a fallen-away Catholic; my mother had no religion at all. We never attended church, not even for Christmas and Easter. I was not baptized. My father's mother, devoutly Catholic, wrote to let us know that she was praying for us, even enrolling us in Masses from the Blue Army of Fatima. My father dismissed this communication with open ridicule.

The earliest memory I have about religion is when, at age five, I asked my father if there was a God. My father, in a quite matter-of-fact way, explained to me that there was no God. This was a tough world, and people liked the idea of a "big daddy in the sky" to make themselves feel better. I accepted this without further question, and spent the rest of my childhood as an atheist. Christianity was no more credible than the volumes of Greek mythology that I enjoyed reading. By age twelve, I was reading books such as Mark Twain's *Letters from the Earth,* which made Christianity look irrational, even ridiculous.

My father was raised Catholic, but fell away from the faith in college—at a Catholic college, no less. He later finished his schooling at the University of California at Berkeley, receiving a doctorate in anthropology in 1967. My father became involved in many social causes—labor organizing, civil rights, and socialism. Indeed, my father was a founding member and first state president of the American Civil Liberties Union in the state of Alaska.

My mother grew up with a vague, unchurched Protestant Christianity. Years later, I discovered that my grandfather helped to build the first church in Delta Junction, Alaska. He and my grandmother were pioneer Alaskans and homesteaders. When their four children grew older, my grandparents wanted them baptized in the church they helped build. My grandparents offered to barter homegrown chickens in place of the mandatory stipend, but the pastor refused. Humiliated, my grandparents never went to church again. "You don't have to go to church to be close to God," my grandmother would tell my mother. "But," my mother added, reflecting years later, "you have to do *something*, and we as a family did nothing."

At fifteen, I discovered the writings of Ayn Rand, author of *The Fountainnhead* and *Atlas Shrugged*. Rand's theme of the "brave individual defying conformist society" appealed to my budding intellectual pride. Rand's celebration of the "virtue of selfishness" resonated with my adolescent, self-absorbed mindset. From this unpromising beginning, I became interested in philosophy.

A year later, PBS ran the series *Six Great Ideas* with Mortimer Adler. Adler introduced me to the "Great Books." Adler mentioned, at some point, that Thomas Aquinas had proofs for the existence of God. Pulling down volume nineteen, I read the article "Does God Exist?" and discovered, to my astonishment, that Thomas Aquinas had real arguments for God's existence. I could see that St. Thomas was not appealing to faith or emotion—these were arguments based on evidence in the natural world, with logical connections. This was the beginning of the end of my atheism. By sixteen, I would have described myself as an agnostic and by seventeen, a deist.

While I was beginning to question my atheism, my father was having intellectual challenges as well. By my teenage years, he was part of a conservative men's discussion group, the "Wednesday Night Club," which met on Thursday ("to fool the liberals," they said). The discussions often divided between economic conservatives (libertarians such as my father), and social conservatives, mostly Catholics and Evangelicals.

The social conservatives maintained that society needed a moral standard, a moral standard supported by religion. The economic conservatives for their part maintained that civil law and respect for individual rights was enough for a good society.

Over time, my father became more and more uneasy about this stance. The social conservatives started sending books home with him, which at first he accepted from politeness.

Thoughtlessly perhaps, my father left these books around the house, and I started reading them myself. Many of them were works of Francis Schaeffer, a theologian and Christian apologist. I found Schaeffer's arguments devastating to my preconceived ideas. I had always assumed that the Christian religion had gone hand in hand with superstition, irrationality, and ignorance. I found to my horror that all of these traits more accurately described the modern society that rejected the Christian faith.

Other books came my way and helped me further down the path. I read C. S. Lewis's *Mere Christianity* and a Catholic catechism called *The Question Box*. Despite my reading of Schaeffer and Lewis, I had no inclination to join a Protestant Church. I had read too much history to find "Bible Christianity" appealing.

After weeks of reading and thinking, I had to go one way or the other. I was wrestling with Schaeffer's account of the philosophy of Friedrich Nietzsche. If there is no God, Nietzsche argued, there is no moral law. One creates one's own "values." If I did not accept the Christian God, that seemed the logical alternative. Could I accept this? No rules, no limitations. If I denied God, I could give free reign to my will.

But in an inspired moment it all vanished. I realized that I had always acted as if there was a right and wrong. If there was a moral law, there had to be a lawgiver. I rejected Nietzsche, and I accepted Christ. The next day, I told my father that I was going to start attending Catholic Mass. This was early January of 1984.

When I had asked my dad to borrow his car so I could go to church, he silently tossed me the keys. We talked about many things, but while he was rethinking his longtime atheism, we never discussed religion. On my own, I began instruction into the Catholic faith and continued attending Mass. One Sunday as I prepared to leave for church, Dad commented, "If I had the gift of faith, I'd be Catholic, too."

Shortly after this comment, my dad informed me he had gone to confession after thirty years away from this sacrament. We began attending Sunday Mass together. Dad could not receive Holy Communion until he had his marriage validated, but he had set the process in motion. By the time I received the sacraments of initiation in March of 1984, my little sister and brother, ages nine and four, came with my father and me to Mass. Soon they were baptized, too.

Now, only my mother remained at home on Sunday mornings. It seemed her family had gone from atheists to Catholics in the blink of an eye. She knew very little about this faith and was unsure what to make of it. My mom did, however, knew of Mother Teresa. She began reading about this little nun and learned more about her extraordinary life. Through Mother Teresa's selfless example and simple, love-filled teachings, my mother, too, was drawn to the Catholic faith. She entered the church a year after I did.

One of the men who had been working on my father became my godfather. He prepared me for my reception into the Church with a series of audio tapes by Archbishop Fulton Sheen. He also guided me to apply to Thomas Aquinas College, a small, Catholic liberal arts school in southern California that helped enormously to solidify my faith. Contrary to the experience of many who attend Catholic colleges, my college friends introduced me to the Brown Scapular, devotion to the Sacred Heart, Montfort's true devotion to Mary, and countless other means for sanctification in ordinary life.

My grandmother had died six months after we opened her Mass card. At the time, converting our family looked unlikely, if not impossible. But within a year of her death, all five of us had converted to the Catholic Church. By contrast, it was not

until after my conversion that I realized that some of my friends
were Christian. I never knew but it would have meant a lot had
I known during my journey.

St. Paul exhorts us, "How are they to believe in him of whom
they have never heard? And how are they to hear without a
preacher?" (Romans 10:14) As a college and high school teacher,
I encourage people to share their faith with others. If God is at
the center of one's life, it should be kept secret. At times when
sharing with an unbeliever seems futile, remember my family
and know that God's grace can change everything.

—Arthur Hippler

*Dr. Arthur Hippler teaches religion in the Upper School at Providence Academy.
Since 2001, he has been an adjunct professor with the Institute for Pastoral
Theology of Ave Maria University. Before coming to Providence Academy, he
served the Diocese of La Crosse, Wisconsin, teaching moral theology and social
ethics in the diocesan programs for lay formation and continuing education for
teachers. He is the author of* Citizens of the Heavenly City: A Catechism of
Catholic Social Teaching, *published by Borromeo Books. He holds a bachelor's
degree in liberal arts from Thomas Aquinas College and his doctorate in
philosophy from Boston College*

The Blessed Mother in Kuwait

As a little girl, I often noticed my father fingering a string of pretty beads. I would wonder why he played with those beads so often. When I was six years old, my dad explained the power of Mary's intercession to her Son through the Rosary. He taught me how to say this very special prayer.

I have prayed it ever since. Mary has not only helped me throughout my own life, but I believe she helped save my son's life as well as the lives of his buddies during a difficult time. My youngest son, Randy, was stationed in Kuwait during Desert Storm. Like any mother would be, I was greatly concerned about his safety with so much combat all around him. It was a terrible feeling of helplessness to know that Randy was surrounded by danger and there was nothing I could do to protect him— nothing, that is, except to pray. In my helplessness, I knew that I had to put my son in our Lord's hands and trust in Him.

During this time, I attended the Diocesan Convention of Catholic Women in San Angelo, Texas. I spoke with Monsignor Rabroker, who is a friend. When he realized my son was stationed in Kuwait, he decided we needed to have the Rosary said on my son's behalf. I should add that Monsignor often invited me to pray the Rosary with him if he felt that someone needed prayer.

Several other women agreed to join us. We started the Rosary at eleven p.m. and prayed until about four a.m. the next morning. I prayed in earnest to the Mother of Jesus. She knew my pain. I trusted her with my prayers, knowing she would take my intention to her Son. Two weeks later, I received a letter from Randy. He wrote:

"At two a.m. there were bullets flying over me and my buddies. I could hear them whizzing by. I was scared and started praying. A calmness came over me and I realized that

I was going to be all right. Some person told me I would be all right. It was a voice from the sky."

My heart warmed as I read those words. It was the same day and time that Monsignor and I were praying the Rosary. I was certain that it was our Blessed Mother who spoke those words and comforted my son for me. I took the letter to Monsignor, and he read it out loud at our next meeting of Catholic Women. Among this room full of women of faith, it seemed everyone was filled with awe. We all believed in the power of the Rosary, but what a blessing it was to be witnesses to this power in such a concrete way.

—Veronica M. Hairgrove

Veronica Hairgrove is a seventy-nine-year-old cradle Catholic. She is originally from Burlington, Vermont, and currently resides in Texas. She and her late husband, Marion, a former Navy telegrapher and electronics technician, had seven children. Today, she has six grandchildren and eight great-grandchildren.

Walking Paths I Never Dreamed Of

As many of my clients strove to overcome their addictions to drugs or alcohol, I always suggested they tap into a powerful source for recovery—God. Sure, some people did it without Him, but not most. God could pick them up where they were and carry them through the pain and struggles all addicts must work through. However, it became harder and harder to send people to Narcotics and Alcoholics Anonymous meetings without feeling like a hypocrite. *What of my own spiritual recovery?*

Although I worked as an addiction educator and counselor, my own lifestyle left me restless and seeking. With a failed marriage behind me, I unfortunately kept seeking love in all the wrong places while I lived life for myself. Looking out for "number one" was my mantra, but my soul ultimately rebelled. Happiness eluded me. I Although I had been raised in the Methodist and Presbyterian churches, by my late twenties, I had turned completely away from God. I had even been married for a time, but that failed. Yet I had seen so many of my clients move from pain to joy, from emptiness to fullness through Christ.

It was my turn. A friend gave me a verse that challenged me: "Delight in the Lord, and He will give you the desires of your heart." I was tired of running from God, for that is what I was really doing by shutting him out. I began praying every day while I ran—a bit symbolic now that I was running toward God and not away. If I woke up in the middle of the night, I prayed. I started going to the Presbyterian church, where I was counseled to turn my life completely over to God. In addition to attending Sunday services, I began teaching high school Sunday school and volunteering in a variety of ways. I knew God was drawing me near, but still, it was hard sometimes. For two years I struggled with backsliding. With one foot in both worlds, I met a man by the name of Marcus Grodi, who was the assistant minister and singles group coordinator. My heart led the way while my brain pulled in the other direction. *Marry a minister? No way, not me*, my brain scolded. But my heart would not listen.

In spite of my misgivings, love won out, and we became engaged. I felt unworthy as a "baby" Christian to be marrying such a man so firm in his own faith. Marcus would remind me, "You are a new creation in the Lord." He did not worry about my past, but looked to the future. We were married in August of 1985.

Without so much as a workshop on how to be a minister's wife, I dove right in. I also became the director of a crisis pregnancy center. Our first child, John Marc, was born the day after our first anniversary. Life as a mother and minister's wife was an exciting roller coaster. Marcus, always full of ideas, often kept me on the edge of my seat. Since I tend to prefer the status quo, his creativity frequently challenged me.

When we moved from our small country church in central Ohio to a large evangelical congregation in northeast Ohio, I thought, *This is it*! I had arrived and was ready to put down roots. I threw myself into my job as a minister's wife. I was free to do whatever I wanted: teach Sunday school, redecorate the nursery, develop relationships with other like-minded people ... whatever I was led to do.

After only a year and a half, Marcus got another one of his ideas. This one would challenge me to the hilt. He was restless about his ministry as well as issues in our Presbyterian denomination. Falling back on his science background, Marcus decided to incorporate ministry with the study of bioethics. He left his pastoral position to study full-time while we also began investigating other denominations that might be a better fit. Both of us were unsatisfied at the way issues were dealt with at higher levels of our church. It seemed that personal opinions and politics, not truth, drove church teachings.

Marcus was now driving to Cleveland each day to Case Western Reserve University, while I cared for our preschooler and newborn son, Peter. I began to feel isolated. We continued to live in our old neighborhood near the church where we had left friends who did not understand what we were doing. To be honest, I did not understand what we were doing. While Marcus was studying genetics, he was also reading everything he could get his hands on about the Catholic Church. I was intrigued with all that Marcus shared with me, and we learned a lot together. Since both of us had written the Catholic Church off as being wrong, our minds were spinning with the beauty and revelations we were discovering in this ancient institution. But Catholic? No way, we both thought. Our prejudice against all things Catholic ran too deep. Yet, where were we to go?

We began attending Mass, just to see first hand what it was all about. I hated it. Where was the Sunday school program or nurseries for the little ones? The worst part was during the consecration of bread and wine into the Body and Blood of Christ because I struggled to accept what was actually taking place. The reality was immense, but I was not there yet in my learning. It was the cornerstone difference between Catholics and Protestants. Marcus was already blazing a trail to the Church, while I was not prepared to buy into all of it.

"I don't want you to feel like you have to come," Marcus assured me. "You and the kids can continue attending the Presbyterian services. This is not something I want to push you into."

The last thing I wanted was to split our family up on Sundays. I thought becoming a Christian would solve all my problems. I never envisioned that it would end up tearing me apart inside. "No, I will keep going to Mass with you," I determined. "I don't want us going our separate ways."

Each Sunday, I tearfully rode past our old church as we headed for Mass. We actually discovered a parish across town that had some of the Protestant customs that made us more comfortable. Coffee and donuts, an outgoing and friendly congregation and having CCD on Sunday mornings for children which felt like Sunday school, helped me relax a little. Once my guard came down, Marcus and I decided to begin taking the Rite of Catholic Initiation classes but discovered a road block that could impede our becoming Catholic. Since I had been married before, unless it was deemed that it had not been a Christian, sacramental marriage, the Catholic Church could not recognize my current marriage with Marcus. When I learned this fact, anger rose up within me. We could have been murders or thieves, but just because I had been married before, the Catholic Church was rejecting us. *Fine!* I thought. *It's just as well because I don't want to become Catholic.*

But we had come too far to just stop there. Marcus and I pondered our situation and put it to prayer. Slowly, we came to understand the wisdom of the Church's teaching. The requirement of obtaining an annulment was actually a reason to seek this traditional Church. Her teachings held that marriage was a sacred and permanent union blessed by God. If the first marriage met the criteria for being sacramental, then the Church stood by Christ's teaching that "what God has joined together, let no man put asunder." Our initial attraction to the Catholic Church was because it seemed to be the only one which held fast to those things that strengthen and preserve families. The other denominations had swayed from the historical teachings on abortion, contraception, and marriage, among many others. So, I swallowed my pride and took my first big submissive step. I bowed to the awesome power and majesty of the authority of the Church. The annulment process turned out not to be so daunting but rather a blessing to our marriage. Nine months later, we moved to Steubenville, Ohio, and continued learning about the Catholic faith. A month later, on December 20, 1992, with our five- and one-and-a-half-year old looking on, we were received into the Church at St. Peter's. At that same time, we also had our marriage blessed with a re-exchanging of vows and rings.

Marcus is no longer known as Reverend and I don't decorate church nurseries or teach Sunday school anymore. It was fun for a time, but I am eterernally thankful that my family and I ended up where we never dreamed we would tread—in the Catholic Church.

—Marilyn Grodi

Marilyn Grodi is married to Marcus, host of EWTN's program The Journey Home. *She earned bachelor's and master's degrees from Ohio State University and has read enough to have earned a Ph.D. in homeschooling the special-needs child. Two of their three boys are still at home in southeastern Ohio, where she and Marcus play at farming.*

Waiting for the Bus

To understand how I became acquainted with Minnie, you first have to understand about the Bus.

The Bus, as they call it, is the main source of public transportation around Oahu, the island where Honolulu is located.

Actually, the Bus is a lot of buses. Fox sixty cents, the yellow and black forty-seaters will carry you to just about any spot on Oahu you may want to visit. Or, if you prefer, you can stay on board the air-conditioned vehicles and tour the entire island, ending up back where you started your trip.

There are two types of buses on the line. The first is the early bus. It usually arrives a minute or two ahead of schedule and, no matter how fast you run, you can never catch up with it.

The second type is the late bus. If your bus doesn't come on time, you had better have a good book handy to read while you wait.

The ten-thirty morning bus that travels through Hawaii Kai, where I live, is a late bus. Fortunately, there is a stone bench, so your rest and relax while waiting for the Bus to come along.

That's how I met Minnie. Twice a week, I caught the Bus into downtown Honolulu. It beat the headache of trying to find a parking space in the downtown business district in the middle of the day.

I came across Minnie one morning a couple of years ago. She was a tiny, wrinkled Asian woman in her late sixties, possibly her seventies. Her hair was knotted at the back, and she always wore a muumuu, usually a dark color and faded from years of wear. She carried an umbrella, not to protect her from rain, but to keep the sun away. Most days, her umbrella was open when I arrived at the bench.

Minnie stored her valuables in one of those plastic bags you get at the super markets. She must have done a lot of shopping, because she had a different plastic bag every day, or so it seemed. What she stored in the bags remains a mystery, but it must have been important. She hugged her plastic bags close to her as we waited for the bus.

That first day I encountered Minnie, she pretended I did not exist. It was a long wait for the bus. It wasn't until the third or fourth time we shared the stone bench that she nodded when I arrived. By the seventh or eighth we had reached the "hello" stage. Once the ice was broken, small talk took over,. Once we boarded the Bus, Minnie and I always went our separate ways.

While waiting for the Bus, we both learned a lot about each other. She cleaned four or five condos in the nearby high-rise, which explained her presence in Hawaii Kai on a regular basis. I also discovered she lived alone in a small flat in Kaimuki. She was a widow.

"You're a Catholic," she said one morning. "I saw you outside Holy Trinity Church as I went by the other day."

I nodded.

Then she surprised me. "I was born a Catholic," Minnie said, matter-of-factly. "I was baptized, and I even had my First Holy Communion. I'm not a Catholic any more. Wish I was, but I lost track of being one."

Much to my regret, the Bus showed up about then.

"How come you quit the Catholic Church?" I asked her a couple of days later, while we were marking time on the stone bench.

"I didn't really quit," Minnie disclosed. "Things went against me, and I lost track of what it meant to be a Catholic. My oldest sister over in Hilo keeps shouting at me. She said I should return to the Church. She gives me a lot of trouble every time I go to visit her on the Big Island." (Hilo is located on Hawaii, the largest island in the Hawaiian chain.)

Bit by bit, and piece by piece, Minnie told me her story, as we waited for the Bus. In between, we discussed the weather, sports, politics, and a variety of other subjects. Eventually, the conversation came back to Minnie and the Catholic Church.

I had assumed Minnie was Chinese. She was not. She was born in a small town somewhere near Seoul, Korea.

"My family," she said proudly," was a good Catholic family. All of my sisters and my brother were raised as Catholics. They grew up and they married in the Catholic Church. I was the youngest, and I was preparing for my Confirmation, when the Japanese came. I hate the Japanese. They took over my country. Most Americans do not remember that.

"There were soldiers in our town, and we lived in fear. We dared not go out at night, and when we did, we had to sneak down side streets, and keep clear of the lights.

"Everything was locked up at night. You could not go anywhere. You could not get into the church. The doors were locked. The Japanese were watching the priest, and he had to say his Masses in secret. He had to be so careful.

"I went to the church about my Confirmation. The priest warned me to be careful, and he said he would let me know when there would be Confirmation. The years went by, and the Great War ended, and I was never confirmed.

"By then, I wasn't a young girl any more. I had grown to be a woman. I married, but not in the Catholic Church, and I lost track of my religion.

"My first husband died, and I came here to Hawaii. I married again, but we lost our only child in a fire. In time, my second husband died, too. Now I am alone." Though she did not come right out and say it, I sensed that Minnie wanted to return to the Catholic Church. She mentioned dropping by St. Patrick Church in Kaimuki for visits, and even stopped off at Holy Trinity, my parish church.

"I'm an old woman," she said one time. "I'm too old for Confirmation. Confirmation is for the very young."

I explained to Minnie that age was not the deciding factor when it came to Confirmation. I think I was getting the message across to her that day—but the Bus came along.

I don't recall if we ever talked religion after that. There were a lot of other topics for us to discuss.

One day, Minnie was hugging two plastic bags when I arrived at the stone bench. "Things I use to clean up," she explained. "I won't be coming back to the condos any more."

"Did you lose your job?" I asked.

"Not me," said Minnie with a trace of pride. "I quit. I'm moving to the Big Island. My older sister's husband has died. I'm moving over with her. My sister's a big boss. She'll make me jump. Goes to Mass every day. Probably make me do the same thing."

There was a warm glow in Minnie's eyes, and a look of contentment on her face. For the first time, since I had met her, Minnie looked beautiful. The old, tired lines were gone. We chatted for a while, but not for long.

The bus came about then, and we got aboard. I never expected to see Minnie again.

Several months later, I spotted a sweet little lady, all spruced up, sitting on the stone bench waiting for the Bus. It was Minnie—without her plastic bags.

"I figured you'd be along," she greeted me. "It's Tuesday. You always take the Bus on Tuesday."

Minnie had been visiting one of her former employees in the high-rise. "I came to Honolulu to see my eye doctor," she disclosed. "Need new glasses. Came to see old friends too. You're one of them."

I was pleased. For the first time, Minnie and I let the Bus go by that morning.

"I got big news," she said to me. "Big, big news!"

"What"? I asked quickly, figuring she had found a third husband.

"I'm a Catholic again," she said. "My sister had them confirm me with the young people at her little parish church. God has welcomed me home again."

"That's wonderful, Minnie," I told her. I should have given her a hug. I didn't. I wish I had.

"There's something else," she said.

"What?" I wanted to know.

"On the Big Island," she said, "I had to go to classes. I don't read or write well. A little woman about my age helped me so I would be able to get confirmed. After the young people had gone for the night, she would stay late and help me."

"Yes," I said, a bit puzzled.

"She was a little Japanese woman who came to Hawaii about the same time I did," Minnie went on. "She was so kind, so good. I don't believe I would have been confirmed if she had not been my friend."

Minnie waited for what she had said to sink in, and then asked: "Know what?"

"What, Minnie?"

My friend did not hesitate. "Maybe I don't hate the Japanese any more," she said, and she was smiling. "Maybe I'm beginning to like them. Maybe that was why God made me wait so long before he welcomed me home again."

Minnie and I took the Bus downtown together that day. She had an appointment with her eye doctor.

—Richard W. O'Donnell

Richard O'Donnell is a native of Boston. He has been a freelance writer since the early 1980s and wrote for the Boston Globe *for several years.*

Coincidence?

When my daughter Karen announced she was expecting her seventh baby, our family was elated. Each new life in our big family is cause for joy.

Karen was the seventh of our eleven children. As the seventh child of a seventh child, Karen felt this child was a great blessing. An ultrasound revealed that the baby was a girl, due on April 29. Karen looked up the date on the Church calendar. It was the feast day of St. Catherine of Siena, a doctor of the church. The feast day is always the day on which a saint dies. It is a celebration of the day he or she enters into eternal happiness with God. St. Catherine had come from a large family, too. She was the youngest of twenty-four.

Karen decided to name her baby after this great saint. Even her middle name would be Siena. Being born on the feast day of her patron saint would make for an especially close bond.

Unfortunately, Karen later discovered she had a condition called placenta previa. The placenta covered her cervix so it would block passage of the baby. Since this can cause hemorrhaging late in the pregnancy, she was watched closely. When Karen did experience serious complications, a C-section was planned on Good Friday, March 25. Although the baby would not enter the world on her patron saint's feast day, Karen and her husband still felt St. Catherine had a special connection with their daughter.

During the surgery, the doctor was surprised to discover that Karen's appendix was inflamed and could have reached the point bursting if it had gone undetected much longer. Once little Catherine Siena was lifted up into the world, the appendix was immediately removed. We jokingly call this her first miracle. This blue-eyed beauty among her brown-eyed siblings, had already made her mark.

A month after Catherine was born, Karen called me, one evening. "Mom," she said excitedly. "You'll never guess what I just found out. St. Catherine of Siena was born on March 25!" So, much to everyone's surprise, little Catherine Siena was born on the very birthday of her patron in heaven. Coincidence? Not in our book.

—Margaret Williams

Margaret Williams' biography appears after her story "The Tree" in chapter two.

A Mother's Sacrificial Love

We often pass through dark times when we question if there will ever be a light at the end of the tunnel. I know with certainty that this is how my mother, Paula Matchen, felt in the winter of 1972 when she discovered she was pregnant. However, when that peace finally did come, it was better than she could have ever imagined.

In January of 1972, my mother, a nineteen-year-old, unmarried freshman in college, discovered she was pregnant. The tiny baby she carried was not conceived with her consent.. She knew the young man who took her out to celebrate the end of the first semester, but wasn't aware of his malevolent intentions. When all was said and done, my mother's life was forever altered, while the perpetrator walked off as if nothing had happened.

The pain and confusion that followed my mother over the ensuing days, weeks, months, and years are still difficult for her to talk about thirty-three years later. Friends offered to help her obtain an abortion so she could "carry on with her life," but she knew that was never an option. Her child was a living human being, and despite the difficult situation, she was going to protect his life. Even still, my mother felt lost, and so that January she packed up her belongings, left the university, and moved in with her sister, far from her home.

While my aunt was there to care for my mother, the pregnancy was still extremely difficult, both emotionally and physically. Before the pregnancy, she weighed less than 100 pounds, standing only five feet tall. By the end, she was up to 150 pounds and delivered a nearly ten-pound baby. She suffered from severe toxemia and preeclampsia. Her blood pressure shot up to such dangerous levels that she had a stroke, leaving parts of the right side of her body paralyzed. She was forced to undergo an emergency C-section and had to receive seven pints of blood through transfusions just to keep her alive.

In the months leading up to the birth, decisions and arrangements were made. It was decided that placing the baby up for adoption would be the best option. My grandparents took care of the details, and my mother knew nothing about the individuals that her child would soon know as his family.

My mom says she remembers very little about the birth or what happened next, but will always have a clear memory of the nurses discussing her baby as she awoke from her weakened state. "I remember one of the nurses saying that he was the cutest, chubbiest baby boy she had ever seen," she said. "That was how I found out I had given birth to a son. I was still in a haze because of all the medication, but that was the first and last thing I would hear about my baby for a very long time. While the pain was deep, I knew I had made the right decision."

Following the tumultuous birth, my mother slowly began to recover. She regained almost total feeling in her body, with the exception of the right side of her mouth, which is still paralyzed today. She lost the extra weight and began to resemble the person she was prior to the pregnancy. While she was recovering physically, she was still an emotional mess. She knew that placing the baby up for adoption was the best thing for him, but she was never allowed the time to grieve her loss.

"I think that had I been given the chance to see him and touch him and tell him good-bye, I would have had some sense of closure," said Paula. "Unfortunately, I never did. I just prayed that he was healthy and in a loving, caring environment."

Not long after the birth, my mother became engaged and married. She and my dad have raised four healthy, happy children—myself included—and have now been married thirty-two years. While she always had the greatest love and devotion to her family, my mother would never forget her eldest, whom she did not know. She always dreamed of meeting him someday but was too afraid to begin that process.

While my mother's life went one direction, her son's went another. He was adopted by a loving family who named him Shawn. He grew up in a happy home where he loved to play outdoors and get dirty. He had one older sister, but his adoptive mother was unable to have more children after her. So Shawn was a true gift to them.

One day in the spring of 2000 my mom received a phone call. A very nice young lady called to ask my mother if the date September 14, 1972 meant anything to her. My mom was speechless. "I knew right away that this call was about my son whom I had never met," she said. "September 14, 1972 was the day of his birth. For the first time in twenty-eight years, a calm came over me concerning my son, and I knew that God had answered my prayers."

Shawn had married a few years before, and his wife was helping him to locate his birth mother. She was the one who made the call. Just like my mother, Shawn, too, had always wondered about her and entertained thoughts of one day meeting. That day came on Easter Sunday in 2000 at a church in Abilene, Texas.

"It was a dream come true," said Paula. "I always thought that if I just knew he was alive, that would be enough. I never imagined I would be given the opportunity to actually meet him and be a part of his life."

After a long, tearful embrace that Easter Sunday, Shawn, his pregnant wife, Toni, and their daughter Christine, all came back to our home to meet the rest of the family. We got along wonderfully and were overwhelmingly grateful to be in each other's lives after so much time had passed.

Five months later, for the first time in twenty-nine years, my mother visited the very same hospital where she had given birth to her firstborn son, whom she was never allowed to hold. This time, however, things were completely different. My mom was handed a newborn baby boy when my brother Shawn presented her with her first grandson.

Not long after the Easter meeting, my mother also met Shawn's parents, who were extremely appreciative of her decision to give Shawn life. Finally, my mother gained the true peace and closure for which she long had yearned.

Today, five years after that wonderful Easter Sunday, Shawn and his family are part of our family. We spend family celebrations and holidays together, never dwelling upon the roads that led us there.

—Amber Dolle

Amber Dolle is married to her best friend, Nick, and full-time mom to their young son, John Paul. Amber has been involved in the pro-life movement in different venues for the past seven years and currently serves as the Media Director for American Life League. In her spare time, she does freelance editing for Allan Wright, a Catholic author, teacher, and speaker with a focus on bringing the New Evangelization to the youth of the Catholic Church (www. allanwright.org). Amber also helps with the management of Mystical Rose Catholic Books and Gifts in Abilene, Texas.

Joy to the World

On a spring-like, San Diego morning, as my husband, John, went about his Saturday ritual of flipping pancakes, I was able to relax nearby reading the paper, as our little ones anxiously awaited their "panna-cakes." John was so good with the children and, consciously or not, was always creating memories.

An article caught my eye regarding the difficulty of placing Mexican American children over a year-and-a-half into adoptive homes. I casually asked John if he would ever consider adopting such a child and, equally nonchalantly, he said that he would. Little did he know that I would take his words and run with them.

The following Monday, while speaking with a neighbor about the article, she assured me that it would be impossible for us to adopt a child for several reasons. We already had several children, we could have more, and our children were so young. She had tried herself to adopt, but could not even get an appointment, having two small boys already.

I contacted the agency anyway. The phone counselor asked me about the ages of our three children. I replied, "Well, there's John Scott, who is almost four; Jennifer Anne, who is almost three; and six-month-old Heather Marie." There was a lengthy pause.

"When can you come in for an appointment?" she asked.

I thought I'd have to employ my most sophisticated tactics to get John to go along with this, but he was surprisingly docile to the whole idea of adopting. We were assigned a social worker, Libby Wilson. We filled out lots of paperwork, endured background checks, and entertained numerous home visits with Libby. We were soon approved as an adoptive family. It really did not take very long for the approval—perhaps a few months—but actually getting a child was another story.

Libby explained that once we were approved, then they would have to carefully consider what child would best fit into our family. We had no gender preference. At the time, the rule was that any child placed with us had to be of such an age that he *could* have been a biological child. So there had to be about a year difference in age, and the child could not be the oldest or under eighteen months of age. Wow, that sure narrowed the age window!

Once a child was identified as a possible good fit, there would be a few months of transition. First we'd get to see him at play, without his knowing we were there. If we were still interested, then we would meet him in his foster-home environment a few times. Next we'd meet in a neutral setting, spending more time with him. Then he would be brought to our home several times with a foster parent, until he was comfortable with us. Finally, we would keep him for good. Each step of the way, we were able to stop if we did not think the fit was right. The child would not feel rejection if that happened, since he would not know until the end that we were his new parents. John and I felt very good about the process and confident that it would insure a comfortable transition for our new child, as well as the rest of the family. But would they ever find a fit? We were not very hopeful, but we placed it in God's hands.

Months went by without any contact from the agency, and I stopped thinking about it daily or even weekly. We almost forgot about it entirely, as we went on with our busy lives.

John was a career Army officer, assigned to San Diego for two years while he worked on a master's degree. The time was rapidly approaching when we would have to move on and, as expected, he received orders to Ft. Bragg, North Carolina. As our moving day approached, I was busy getting our belongings organized for a cross country move, as well as preparing the children for what lay ahead. John was very busy trying to finish up his thesis. The kids were now five, four, and almost two.

I can remember the spot in the kitchen where I stood the day the phone rang and Libby's voice said, in a sing-song kind of way, "We have your little boy!" Not having spoken to her for so long, I didn't even remember who she was at first, so it took me a few seconds to recognize her voice and process what she had just said.

"Libby! Oh no, Libby! We are moving in two weeks," I said.

"That's OK," she replied. I was confused. She explained that this child was not in a good foster-home environment, and his natural mother had serious problems. The agency wanted to get him out of his current home soon, without the usual meeting procedures described to us earlier in the process. But since the child had been in this same foster home since he was six weeks old and was now almost three, this would not be easy. The foster parents might not cooperate and might try to prevent the county from removing him from their home. This happened with a previous child they had recently tried to place elsewhere.

Suddenly I realized that there was a very real possibility that we might soon have a new child in our family—very soon!

"What is his name?" I asked

"Jeffery Scott, but they always call him Scott," she replied.

Silence ... long silence.

When I was expecting our oldest son, we had decided that if it was a boy, we'd name him John Scott Wakelin. My maiden name is Scott, so this would honor my family and my husband. But to avoid the confusion of two Johns in the family, we'd agreed to call him by his middle name, Scott. For a week or so after his birth, we tried to call him Scott, but it wasn't working. We found ourselves calling him just, the baby, or he or him, and avoiding the name Scott. Finally one night I said to my husband, John, "Let's face it. He does not look like a Scott. He's a John." My husband agreed. And so our oldest son was also called John.

My brother's name is Jeffery, Jeffery Scott. I knew this child was meant to be our son.

Not understanding my silence, she then added, "You can change his name if you don't like it."

"Oh no," I said. "It's perfect."

We set up a time to meet, and she would have a picture for us, but that is all we would get until the day we took him home. No, he was not Mexican American. We were told he was 100 percent Italian. In later years, the kids would call him the Italian Stallion.

Libby explained what would happen next. The plan was that on the day that he would be placed in our care, the county adoption services would ask the foster mom to bring the child into court, as it often did for a periodic review. Once there, however, a social worker would take the child, and we would be waiting at another location for him to be given to us.

This was hardly the comfortable process we had expected. But we now believed he was destined to be our son, and if this was the way it had to be, God's grace would get us all through it. We would come to find out how much we needed that grace.

In the meantime, we had to move the family across the country to North Carolina, John's new duty station. Our furniture would be shipped, and we would drive with the children. The social worker did not want Scott to endure the long travel as his first experience with us. It would be hard enough on him already, so they asked that we move the family back East and then come back to the West coast to get Scott and fly him back. It would make his adjustment easier.

After turning the children over to my parents' care in New York, John and I turned around and flew back to get Scott. Friends put us up for our brief stay back in San Diego.

The morning arrived, and we went to the designated place to await our child. I clutched his picture. He was very tan, with beautiful skin and huge brown eyes. His hair was shiny and very dark brown. He was the cutest thing I had ever seen, and I was sure he was an angel. My husband was not as positive.

Stationed where directed, we waited and waited, checking our watches frequently. Then, from a distance, we heard wailing. It was getting louder and louder until the crying was so loud it hurt down deep in my heart. Here he was, and he was not happy to see us. "Mama, Mama," he kept calling, and that wasn't me. He would not be consoled. I tried to hold him, but his body became all right angles. He was perspiring profusely as he struggled and screamed.

What had we agree to? My husband and I looked nervously at each other. The social worker looked a bit more confident, but you could tell the scene had not been pretty in the courtroom. She assured us that he would be fine and helped us to our friend's car that we borrowed. We drove away, enduring screams without abatement. That night he cried, "Mama, Mama." I was mommy to him, but he was not calling me.

Once we arrived at my parents' home, John, Jenny, and Heather were waiting with gifts for him. My mother and father played with him and my dad made Scott and the others laugh with his corny antics. The next day it became evident that our two-and-a-half-year-old, Heather, was crazy about him. She followed him everywhere. Scott loved being the center of attention. He was having fun. A day or two later, we began our long trip from New York to North Carolina, and then the short-lived fun ceased.

We had a station wagon at the time, and the children were all in the back as we drove and drove. We began to see the wisdom of not driving him cross-country. He began to exhibit behavior that we would come to realize was his mode of operation. He teased, hit, screamed, and yelled without ceasing, and anything we tried to do to get him to stop would fail. Finally, at wit's end, my husband pulled over, stopped the car, and placed him to the farthest back part of the car, away from the others. Scott screamed and cried, and then sobbed. What was going through his little mind, I wondered? His whole world had changed in the past seventy-two hours.

It was dark now, and as we continued driving, a soothing silence began to fill the car. Then I thought, "Is he OK?" Out of the silence we began hearing a little voice making its way to our ears. "Joy to da woild, all you boys and goils, joy to da fisses in da deep bwoo sea, joy to you and me."

About three months after his placement into our home, we had a harrowing day that ended a harrowing week. Scott was pretty much spending the day in his room due to misbehavior and screaming with the cry I had learned to expect. "Mama, Mama." Our nerves were frazzled. My husband and I went into our bedroom, hugged each other, and cried. Any thoughts we might have had that we were super-parents or even mediocre ones were long gone, and we were at our wit's end. We did not know where to turn. Part of us wanted to give him back, but we knew we could never do that to him. He was testing us to the limits, and we felt like we were failing the test. But he survived, and so did we.

Adopting an older child is not easy, especially when you already have biological children. We, not the children, were the ones that had trouble adjusting to Scott, who did not respond the way the others did and who had all sorts of baggage that we were always tripping over. The other children were terrific and accepted him right away. Heather asked me one day where she and the other children came from. I told her that John and Jenny and she came from a special place (and I touched my abdomen), but because Scott's mommy couldn't care for him, Daddy and I said that we would love him and take care of him. She said, "So John and Jenny and I came from your tummy, but Scott came from your heart."

Five years after Scott's adoption, Jaclyn, our fifth child, was born. Scott was no longer the newcomer, and his mellowing came to completion soon after her arrival. Over time, love for him grew and grew and grew. A surprise phone call years later led to a wonderful reunion of Scott and two half-sisters and two half-brothers. We also discovered that Scott's biological dad was Puerto Rican and his mother Italian.

Patti, one of the half-sisters, made the call. She was in the foster home with Scott when he was taken from the foster parents. She was four and a half at the time of Scott's adoption. Scott often spoke of "Kimmy," but we thought Kimmy was just one of the other foster children. We did not know that she was a sibling. Years later we found out that Kimmy's name was changed to Patti after her adoption by, to our surprise, the foster parents that Scott was removed from.

Last year as Scott's foster mom was dying from cancer, Scott and Patti went to be with her, sitting with her, nursing her and just holding her hand during her last days on earth.

Scott is a wonderful son who has provided us with so many opportunities to trust God, and so many occasions to be proud. We are a better, happier family because he is a part of it. He is the one who worries about his sisters' safety. He remembers everyone's birthdays, calls his grandmother regularly, and gives gifts that are always thoughtful and personal. He is generous, loving, and kind. He has a successful career and scores of friends that love him. He is a strong Catholic, and he just made a beautiful choice in a wife. All his siblings and half-siblings were at their wedding. He just keeps adding joy to our world.

I asked Scott if he minded my sharing his story with others. He feels comfortable, hoping that it will help other families considering adoption. Surprisingly, Scott says that he has only happy memories of his family life at the time of adoption and beyond, and our other children, now all adults, are open to adoption within their own families. They all remember it as a positive experience. God is good in allowing only certain things to remain in our memory. I am in awe that a situation that seemed to be one of pain and separation worked together into a story of healing and love.

—Jan Wakelin

Jan Wakelin and her husband, John, reside in Poway, California, and have five adult children. She has degrees in psychology and business management, and a masters in theology. She is the director of radio and television at Catholic Answers, an apologetics and evangelization apostolate based in El Cajon, California.

In God's Hands

"Your baby has some form of leukemia." The doctor's words knocked the wind out of me. I was overcome with terror.

Markie had seemed perfectly healthy earlier that day. My mother-in-law and I had taken him to the pediatrician's for his eight-week well-baby visit. She and I planned to spend the day shopping for a combination baptism and graduation party we were going to throw the following Sunday. Our oldest son, David, was Markie's godfather and he was graduating from high school. We were looking forward to a memorable celebration, but it never happened.

As he examined Markie, the pediatrician wore a look of concern. He spent a lot of time probing Markie's belly area, which prompted me to question him, "What's wrong with his stomach?"

The doctor responded, "Has he been sick?"

"No. He's fine," I insisted.

The doctor told me that the baby's belly seemed enlarged and he wanted me to go right to the hospital for some tests. He was vague about his reasons for the immediate testing, so I figured Markie had some sort of infection. Still, I began to get panicky and I called Mark, my husband. He met us at home and went with me to the local hospital's radiology department, while my mother-in-law stayed at our house to wait for the other children to arrive home from school.

Sometime during our short trip from the local hospital back to the house, the doctor had called. He told my mother-in-law to send us back to his office with a change of clothes for the baby. I assumed the doctor wanted to do more tests that might soil my baby's clothes, but my husband suspected that we were going somewhere for the night.

The pediatrician instructed us to go straight to DuPont Hospital for Children in Delaware, which wasn't too far from the Pennsylvania border. He told us we had an appointment with a specialist but would not be specific until it was obvious to him that I had no intention of leaving until I had some answers. That's when he informed me that it looked like my baby had leukemia.

By six o'clock that evening, Markie was admitted to the Intensive Care Unit. He had been prepped to go to surgery the following morning to have a central line (a port) inserted for the chemotherapy. He was hooked up to more wires than imaginable, and every time he moved, something beeped or buzzed. Mark and I bunked together in a child-size cot in the baby's room. I kept looking at our son and wondering if we would leave together. I wept all night. Yet, it occurred to me that, had he not had his well visit the day before, the leukemia would not have been detected until it was too late. We were blessed.

We were also blessed with an abundance of support at home. Mark and I spent the entire summer of 1998 at DuPont, while family, friends, and neighbors cared for our four other children. Offers to help, food, and prayers came in constantly. Because he was so young, Markie's prognosis was not good, but no one could offer an exact probability. One oncologist said, "We are going to push Markie as close to the edge as we can [with treatment], and, hopefully, we don't push him off." During the three months of treatment that followed, Markie was sent back into ICU six times.

When the baby was well enough to move out of ICU, Mark and I began to pray together in the chapel. Mark began: "God, this is in Your hands. Whatever is Your will."

I angrily interrupted him, "No. You can't pray that way," I said. "You have to plead with God." I was accustomed to making deals: "I will do whatever You need me to do. Just make my baby well." However, as our trial unfolded, I came to understand that it is I who must bend to God's will and not the other way around. I began to pray like my husband.

Following another trip to intensive care, Markie developed neuropathy. He lost his voice as well as the ability to suck and swallow. It broke my heart to watch our infant son fuss and cry without making a sound. As difficult as it was to imagine losing him, watching him suffer hurt worse. "Lord," I would pray, "Whatever is Your will."

A short time later, a woman whose four-year-old son, Josh, was being treated at the hospital's clinic, visited the oncology floor to offer hope and encouragement. Josh had been critically ill with cancer when he was just two. His mother shared with us a story of startling revelation that had taken place a year after his diagnosis. She had been preparing his medicine at the kitchen sink with her back to Josh when the boy called out, "What are you doing here?"

Alarmed, she turned around quickly and found him staring at the back door. "Who are you talking to?" She asked. Josh pointed to the plaque of the Last Supper that was hanging over the doorway.

"Him," he replied singling out Jesus. "He was in my hospital room." From that point on, any time Markie went back into ICU, I thought of that story and found comfort.

Although Josh's incredible account gave me strength, the real test of my endurance came when I least expected. On a Monday morning following another episode in ICU, the doctor came to our room to discuss plans for resuming chemotherapy. Mark was holding the baby in the rocking chair, as he always did. He didn't seem to notice the doctor, so I tried to call his attention toward her. "The doctor's here," I said. He did not respond. Appearing fixated on the TV, Mark ignored a second call as well. Embarrassed by my husband's unresponsiveness, I quickly took the baby and listened to the doctor's plans.

After she left, I turned to Mark and said, "What was that all about?" With a tear rolling down his cheek, Mark looked up at me and said, "You don't understand. I can't listen anymore to what they're going to do to him. You're good at that. I'm good at praying." Mark's quiet strength had been holding me up all along, and now he needed my support. His reaction was my turning point. I stopped feeling sorry for myself and sought to be strong.

Toward the end of July, friends of ours brought their parish pastor to anoint Markie. A peaceful feeling came over me as the priest administered the anointing of the sick. Right then and there I sensed that Markie was healed. I wanted to tell the doctors, "We're good now, thanks. We can go home." I did not fully know what this feeling really meant, however, so I remained silent while Markie continued with the first phase of treatments.

The entire summer was a roller coaster ride – emotionally, spiritually, and, for Markie, physically. By August, Markie was at his lowest point, and our optimism was fading quickly when God sent yet another sign of hope. This time it was in the form of my neighbor Barb. She stopped my husband outside the house one day when he had gone home to check on the other children. Tearfully, she told him about a vision she'd had earlier that day.

I was a bundle of nerves when Barb came by the next day. The doctors were not feeling confident about Markie's current trip to the ICU. In the most serene manner Barb looked at me, gently rested her hand on my forearm, and said, "Jayne, it's all right. Everything is going to be all right." She blessed Markie with holy water from the river Jordan that had been given to her from her brother, and then she explained her vision.

"You know, Jayne, I've been praying so hard for Markie. I was saying my morning prayers on the way to work yesterday, when the most incredible thing happened. While I was stopped at a red light, I saw a picture in the sky. It was a bed with white sheets dangling over it. Your baby was lying on the center of it, and I was standing beside him with my hands over his abdomen. Jesus was way above us in a white robe surrounded by light. His hands were outstretched, and intense rays of light beamed from His palms through my hands and right through Markie and out the other side of the bed. It was so beautiful, and it brought me peace. I knew at that moment that Markie was going to be okay. I had never experienced anything like it."

I made Barb describe the vision over and over. Each time we cried together, and each time she reassured me that she was not a bit worried about our baby.

Markie was released from DuPont in early September 1998. Later that month, he began phase two of his treatments. He has been completely off treatment since August of 2000. We recently learned that infants with Markie's type of leukemia are only given a fifteen percent chance of survival. Truly by the grace of God, Markie is still with us. We can see now, that all the pain we went through was not without purpose because our family has grown closer with each other and with God. He held us in His hands during the darkest moments and reshaped our hearts with strength and the understanding that God will never abandon us.

—Jayne Rodgers

Jayne and Mark Rodgers have five children, David, Jason, Sean, Danielle, and Mark. They live in Springfield, Pennsylvania, where Mark works as an insurance agent and Jayne operates an interior decorating business, Painting Jayne. In addition to being active members of their community and church, the Rodgers help raise awareness and financial support for The Leukemia & Lymphoma Society. They are also actively involved with First Connection, the society's peer-to-peer support group.

The Miracle Tailor

In 1935, when my brother and two sisters and I were young children, we went to a parish run by Dominican priests in Somerset, Ohio. Our pastor, Father Robert Kircher, loved to gather the children together for solemn church processions to celebrate special feast days. One of the most special was the procession for the May crowning of our Blessed Mother. My brother Danny, who was seven at the time, was really looking forward to being in the procession. It was customary for all the boys to wear white shirts. Times were hard for our family, so Danny had only one white shirt. It was the one he wore when he made his First Holy Communion.

After Mass one Sunday, Danny and my youngest sister, Agnes, who was three, were outside the house. Somehow Danny tore a big hole in his white shirt. He was devastated, fearing that he would not be able to march in the procession. He decided to ask God to mend it. He held the pieces together while Agnes prayed with him. According to both children, the shirt became whole again. They ran screaming and laughing into the house and related their miracle to me and Middy, who were nine and eleven, respectively. Their enthusiasm was sincere. With my sister there as an eye witness and the two of them wild with excitement, we never doubted their story.

Several weeks later, I was climbing over a barbed wire fence and tore my good dress. Looking down at the rip, I gasped. I knew better than to be climbing a fence in my nice dress. Recalling Danny's miracle, Middy suggested that we pray as Danny and Agnes had. I held my dress together and prayed, "Dear God, please mend my dress for me." I prayed and prayed, but nothing happened. Finally, I realized there was nothing to do but admit my misdeed to my mother. With tears streaming down my cheeks, I went into the house expecting the worst. I showed my mother the dress and told her I prayed and prayed to God for it to be mended, but nothing happened.

Instead of being angry, my mother seemed to understand. She gave me a mild scolding and then proceeded to patch the hole. As a child, I thought God had not answered my prayer. Years later as an adult, I knew that he had. I am to understand that my brother Danny had a pure motive for his prayer. He wanted to please God in the procession. God in His goodness and mercy answered a little boy's cry for help. God answered my prayer in a far different way. Instead of being punished, I was actually consoled by my mother but convicted of my wrong doing.

—Mary Pitstick

Mary Pitstick grew up in a devoutly Catholic family, the sixth of ten children. She and her husband, Paul, reside on a farm near Fairborn, Ohio. They have seven children, nineteen grandchildren, and six great-grandchildren.

Holy, Innocent, and Cured

Ever since I was a child, I saw the Feast of Holy Innocents as one of particular sadness, in such startling contrast to the joyous celebration of Christmas. On December 28, 2001, this feast day took on a new meaning for my family and me: my four-year old son, Leo, was diagnosed with acute lymphoblastic leukemia (ALL).

In 2001, Leo was as innocent as any child his age. I took him to our pediatrician to investigate some strange symptoms. After a blood test Dr. Peterson told me to take Leo to St. Paul Children's Hospital, to the oncology clinic. I asked if we could go home for lunch first. She said, no, we should go now. My wife, Joan, was at home with our other three kids, including our two-month-old daughter, Emily. It wasn't until that evening that we could arrange for childcare, so Joan could join Leo and me at the hospital.

Thus began a series of blood draws, x-rays, and doctor consultations. I will never forget the oncology doctor who conducted Leo's intake into the oncology clinic. He was patient, kind, and sat with Leo and me for some time. Doctors, in my experience, never do this. They don't sit down to talk, and listen, and just be with their patients. Dr. David Slomiany did.

My most poignant memory of that day was when Leo and I arrived back at the oncology clinic's waiting room, a room we would come to know so well. We had just come up from the blood lab. It was late afternoon and Leo, remarkably, was happy and lively. He saw the toys in the waiting room and immediately began to play. He played in earnest with puzzles, cars, and colorful plastic toys. I looked at him and noted his handsome face, his quizzical expressions, his trusting smile. He knew nothing of what lay ahead, how his little life had just radically changed forever. Here was a test of a father's love—to lead your child, with his innocence and complete trust, into a nightmare of chemotherapy, sickness, pills, needles, tests, waiting rooms, labs, and hospitals. I wept for love of Leo; I wept for pity of myself.

Leo's story has a happy ending. December 28, 2006 marked the five-year anniversary of his diagnosis. The doctors told us from the beginning that he had an eighty-five percent chance of cure, and that if he stayed in remission for five years, they would consider him cured. Today we celebrate that milestone. We thank God for allowing us to keep our son! We are also painfully aware that other families' stories do not end so well. We often pray for other children and families dealing with childhood cancer and other illnesses. I know that every week new families are brought into that same waiting room, and are introduced suddenly, painfully, to a new and frightening life.

Another holy, innocent boy figures into Leo's story. Four-year-old William, the son of my wife's friend, knew about Leo's cancer, and he and his family prayed for Leo every day. In early 2002 William's family learned that he was suffering from cardiomyopathy. When William was hospitalized and underwent tests and medication, he did something that touched our family deeply: he offered his sacrifices for Leo as well as himself. Among his prayers he would say, "Mom, I don't like this, but I'll offer it for Leo."

William died in June 2002 at age four. Leo and William didn't know each other well, but William became the best friend a four-year-old with leukemia could have. Leo now has an advocate in heaven!

Children and suffering; children and death. These things simply should not ever go together. Yet even our Lord's birth was followed by a great tragedy in Bethlehem. It is part of the fallen human condition that with joy in life, inevitably, comes sorrow. It was in the midst of such sorrow that Jesus came into our world, just as it was through his horrific death that he gave salvation to the world.

The suffering and sacrifices of children, of holy innocents, must bear fruit. God, in His infinite goodness, mercy, and mystery, would not let it be otherwise.

Holy Innocents of Bethlehem, pray for us!

—Mark Dittman

Mark Dittman is a husband, father, freelance writer, and parish administrator. He lives with his wife, Joan, and four children in Maplewood, Minnesota.

Chapter 6

A Family's Character

Courage Under Fire

Looking down over the Omaha beaches of Normandy, France, my son Thomas Jr. pointed to the stretch of land which is now a cemetery holding more than 9,000 American soldiers. "That's where some of the fiercest fighting took place," he explained.

My son had planned this trip of a lifetime with me. As a history buff, he was enamored with the heroism of the men who stormed the beaches at Normandy over sixty years ago on what become known as D-day. The operation remains the largest invasion from sea to land in history, involving close to three million troops crossing the English Channel to take back France from German occupation. It was a bold and bloody mission in which rapid enemy fire failed to halt these heroic men from marching forward into almost certain death—all in the name of freedom.

Although I knew well of the history, I listened intently as my son explained the battle. "Here they were, coming in under all that fire," he said with an otherworldly expression on his face. Then he looked thoughtful for a moment. "I wonder if I would have had the courage to come onto that beach under such a hail of fire." I said nothing. Tom was deep in thought. But I knew my son would never lack for courage. He was thoughtful and loving and never backed down in the face of adversity.

Just a few months later, on September 11, 2001, my wife
Beverly and I would be desperately praying for our courageous
son. After seeing the World Trade Center and the Pentagon
get struck by terrorist-commanded planes, Tom's wife, Deena,
called to tell us that Tom was on United flight 93 from Newark.
He was returning to California from a business trip. When
Islamic terrorists had taken over the plane, he called his wife.
"Are you OK?" she had asked.

"No, I'm not," he reported. "I'm on a plane that has been
hijacked." The crew had been killed and a passenger knifed.
The rest of the passengers were herded to the back of the plane.
Tom became determined to take back the plane before the
hijackers could reach their target, later discovered to be the U.S.
Capitol building in Washington, DC. He directed Deena to
call the FBI and police.

We sat by the phone and television, shocked by the surreal
plot our own dear son was entangled in. We prayed unceasingly,
waiting frantically for word from Deena. Both the FBI and the
police were at her house within minutes to monitor Tom's calls.
He would call her a total of four times, keeping her posted and
asking for prayers.

When Tom called again to report that the knifed passenger
was dead, Deena told him about the other hijacked planes
hitting buildings in New York and Washington. "Oh my God,
it's a suicide mission," she heard him tell others. Tom noticed
the plane turn and head south. "We're over a rural area," he told
Deena. "It's fields. I've gotta go."

Minutes later, he called again. "They're talking about
crashing this plane into the ground. We have to do something.
I'm putting a plan together." The last time he phoned, Tom
announced: "We're going to take back the plane," he said. "We
can't wait for the authorities. I don't know what they could do,
anyway. It's up to us. I think we can do it."

"What do you want me to do?" Deena had asked.

"Pray, Deena," said Tom. "Just pray." Then his last words were, "We're going to do something."

Moments later, the plane crashed in a field in Pennsylvania. When we listened to the black box recordings, Tom's voice could be heard barking commands as they attempted to take back the plane. Tom was a tall, strong, former football player. His leadership skills led him to become chief operating officer of his company. I believe that if he had not been on the plane that day, the terrorists would have killed a lot of other people.

Tom's success in life went deeper than anything you could put on a score card. He was a devoted husband, father, and son who put God at the center of everything he did. In recent years before he died, Tom had given up his lunch hour to attend daily Mass. His desire was to discern God's will and always follow it. Surely, God led him during his last moments in this world.

My wife, Beverly, and I are still grieving our son's loss. We always will. But we have drawn on Tom's courage and our faith in God to help us through. We will never put our son behind us. Sometimes I look up to the sky and find strength in the knowledge that our son is in heaven and we will see him again some day. He did his best, and it seems certain that Tom prevented a worse loss of life. He was truly a man of courage.

—Thomas Edward Burnett, Sr.

Thomas Edward Burnett resides in Minnesota with his wife of fifty-three years, Beverly. He graduated from the University of Minnesota and retired from Richfield Public Schools after thirty years of teaching.

The Bully

Most of us have had to deal with a bully at some point in our childhood. In my case, his name was Butch. Butch was a couple of years older than I. He had a reputation for being fast with his fists. If he did not like someone, watch out.

Butch had pretty much ignored me up until I was nine years old. Suddenly, at the beginning of the new school year, even though I was a girl, I became his favorite target. It was the year I returned to school after recovering from polio.

Within the first few weeks of school, it became apparent that Butch had decided to make my life miserable. He did an excellent job of it.

Each day at recess, Butch would lay in wait to trip me and knock me down in the dirt. That really was not a challenge, as I still had to use crutches sometimes to walk long distances. Butch would take my crutches and hold them over me, taunting me so I would cry. Being pretty tough, I refused to cry. This would infuriate him all the more. Day after day, the bully game continued. Day after day, I plotted my revenge. In my mind's eye, I could picture the day I would make Butch sorry he had ever messed with me.

For the entire school year Butch's game of bullying continued. And during that time, I gained more and more strength in my legs. I was so happy on the day I was able to go to school without my crutches. But that did not stop Butch. His next tactic was to taunt me about my limp. He nicknamed me the "gimp."

And so day after day, as the game continued, I worked even harder to overcome my limp. Every night after school, I practiced walking without favoring my bad leg. I finally managed to overcome the limp through hours of practice, which, no one but a bully could have inspired me to undertake. Then I began practicing running. It hurt to run, but I was determined to run as fast as any kid in school. It was imperative if my revenge was going to be successful. Butch was very proud of the fact he held the school track record. Every spring at the close of school, we had a track meet in which all the grades ran against one another. No one had ever beaten Butch at track, but I was determined to show "Butch the Bully" that this little gimp wasn't afraid of him.

Winning the race when the entire school, parents and teachers would be present to see me beat the school Bully, was my plan for my revenge. My dad had observed my diligent training for the track meet. He finally asked me what was that driving me so hard? I told him of the taunts and humiliations Butch had subjected me to through the school year. Dad, with his usual wisdom, said: "Christy, you know, revenge isn't all it's cracked up to be. Don't let anger and bitterness become your motivation for running a good race."

I loved my dad and respected his opinion, but I could not back down from my desire for revenge against Butch, who had made my life so miserable. I wanted to let it go, but my anger held on. I was determined to beat Butch so he would feel as bad as he had made me feel.

Finally, the day of the race came. As luck would have it, I was placed right next to Butch in the starting line-up. True to form, Butch made his usual derogatory comments. They just fueled my resolve to outrun him and beat him at his own game. With my heart pounding, I bent down in the runner's starting stance. Saying a quick prayer for victory, I set my eyes on the finish line.

BANG! The sound of the starting shot echoed over the field, and we were off. I ran and ran and ran, never taking my eyes off my goal. I passed Butch as though he were standing still and kept on going. I relished the thought of crossing that finish line. It held the key to my victory and the defeat of my archenemy, Butch.

Just as I crossed the line, a cheer went up. I had won! Then, just as quickly, the sound of gasps came forth from the crowd. I turned around, prepared to make Butch wallow in his defeat but I was not yet aware of why everyone had gasped. As I turned to deliver my final note of revenge, there, in the dirt, lay Butch. He had tripped just before crossing the finish line and was crying. He seemed to be in a great deal of pain.

Seeing him on the ground crying, somehow stole the satisfaction I had anticipated my victory would bring. Sprinting over to Butch as fast as I could, I instinctively tried to help him up. A crowd quickly gathered, and Doc Albee checked him over for injuries.

It was then that I suddenly realized that Dad was right. Running a good race and winning were admirable goals, but winning to get revenge, was not so sweet. Looking at Butch in tears, gave me no satisfaction.

Instead, I soon found something I had never expected—a new friend. In the following weeks and days of that summer, Butch and I became good friends. He had broken his ankle, so I taught him how to use crutches. I spent time playing checkers with him and just generally passing the time since his buddies were all too busy playing baseball and swimming. In the end, I learned how to make a friend out of an enemy. Butch was often around the house, and my big brother Bill ended up becoming good friends with him.

Isn't it funny how God sometimes uses challenging people to make us stretch and grow? I shall always be grateful for my father's advice and for a bully named Butch, who motivated me to overcome both my limp and my notion of how to defeat and enemy.

—Christine Trollinger

Christine Trollinger's biography appears after her story "Lucy's Star" in chapter two.

More Words of Wisdom for Families

No matter what you've done for yourself or for humanity, if you can't look back on having given love and attention to your own family, what have you really accomplished?

—Lee Iacocca

The history of mankind, the history of salvation, passes by way of the family ... The family is placed at the center of the great struggle between good and evil, between life and death, between love and all that is opposed to love.

—Pope John Paul II

Only a life lived for others is worth living.

—Albert Einstein

Children seldom misquote you. In fact, they usually repeat word for word what you shouldn't have said.

—Anonymous

Families are like fudge... mostly sweet with a few nuts.

—Author Unknown

In raising my children, I have lost my mind but found my soul.

—Lisa T. Shepherd

Children have never been very good at listening to adults but they have never failed to imitate them.

—James Baldwyn

The best inheritance a person can give to his children is a few minutes of his time each day.

—O. A. Battista

Other things may change us, but we start and end with the family.

—Anthony Brandt

A baby is God's opinion that the world should go on.

—Carl Sandburg

Husband: a man who buys his football tickets four months in advance and waits until December 24 to do his Christmas shopping.

Our most basic instinct is not for survival but for family. Most of us would give our own life for the survival of a family member, yet we lead our daily life too often as if we take our family for granted.

—Paul Pearshall

The first thing that a person finds in life and the last to which he holds out his hand, and the most precious that he possess, even if he does not realize it, is family life.

—Blessed Adolph Kolping

A Lunch, a Marriage, and a Bald Head

He looked terrified. He was thirteen years old, diagnosed with lymphoma, and a guest at a Leukemia/Lymphoma Society fundraiser with which my husband was helping and I was attending. He wore a baseball cap to cover his bald head and kept pulling it down as if no one would know as long as he kept it on.

When I saw him from across the room, I immediately recognized the look on his face. It was a look of panic and fear, one that I had had myself when I had first been diagnosed with Hodgkin's lymphoma. *Why did this happen? What does this mean? Am I going to die?*

During the fundraising auction I never saw him smile, although I did see him mouth "thank you" when the master of ceremonies presented him with a gift certificate for a trip with his family to Indianapolis. Thousands of dollars were raised for research that day as Notre Dame banners and footballs were auctioned off, as well as guitars signed by rock-and-rollers whose names every teenager would recognize. In the air was frivolity and generosity. But the success of a fundraiser and its light-hearted manner means little to you when you're fighting for your life. That queasy feeling of uncertainty doesn't go away just because you break for a fancy lunch with your grandma and a bunch of other nice people. Even when you're thirteen; especially when you're thirteen.

So after the lunch, I wanted to connect. Having just finished treatment myself for lymphoma and being declared in remission, I wanted this boy to know he'd be okay, that the pain of the chemo would end and his life could go on. I filtered through the crowd to the other end of the restaurant and found him standing against the wall. After introducing myself and telling him I had just finished treatment myself, I tried to encourage him. Things would get better, I said. That crummy taste in his mouth would go away and his muscles would stop hurting from treatment.

No more nausea. No more sleepless nights from shooting pains in his arms and legs. Then, for good measure, I did what any other mother would do in such circumstances. I lifted my wig to show him our common denominator—a bald head. He broke a small smile.

Some things are easier dealt with when someone else has been there first. Something that would mortify my own children should I do it in public in front of them seemed like the right thing to do in those circumstances. Two bald heads made a perfect bonding moment. My hairlessness gave credibility in a way nothing else could. When I told that boy he'd be okay, I hoped he'd believe me because I had actually been where he was. I hadn't thought life could go on when I became ill, but it did.

Similarly, when my sister-in-law Theresa lost her husband in a tragic plane crash, she didn't think life could go on. For months afterward, she exchanged emails with a young woman who had experienced the sudden loss of her own husband. This woman completely understood what Theresa was experiencing. The wondering, "Why?" The excruciating hurt. What to tell her two young toddlers? In time, Theresa's heart began to heal. She began to find joy in her life again. One day Ken came into her life. They fell in love. On a brisk fall evening, as the leaves began to change color, Theresa and Ken married. That night, Ken gave Theresa his ring, and he also produced, out of his pocket, two small rings for Theresa's two little daughters. He placed the rings on their fingers, as he had placed a ring on their mother's, and promised to love, honor and protect them all. There wasn't a dry eye in the whole chapel. Today, two kids later, Theresa fields phone calls from young widows. She knows what to say and her answers ring true because she has been in their shoes. They believe they can live again and love again because she has.

Our tragedies are chances to be angels to others. And opportunities are everywhere. At a PTA meeting, down the pew to the left, right next door. And, of course, across the room at a fundraising lunch. To have a companion down an uncertain path, if even for a moment, is a gift indeed. And while one follows today, he may lead tomorrow. And the cycle of community goes on. "Church" with a little "c." That's us. There for each other when things get tough. Our gift to one another can be as simple as sharing our experiences and trials, and sometimes, when the time is right, even a bald head.

—Theresa Thomas

Theresa Thomas' biography appears after her story "The Sibling Bond" in chapter one.

Inflation Manipulation

"I hate to bring this up, Dad, but a lower allowance than
other kids have could emotionally scar me for life."

A Saint for Siblings

Every big brother or sister has those moments when he or she sees the younger siblings as pests. But those same little pests usually idolize the older ones. This was surely the case for Macrina who was the oldest sister of ten children.

Macrina was considered "hot" in her day. She was as beautiful as she was bright, so it was no surprise that she had men lined up with marriage proposals. But when she did finally select a suitor and become engaged, her fiancé died before the wedding.

There were plenty of others who promised love and happiness, but Macrina was not interested. Instead, she decided to stay at home and care for her parents and oversee the education of her siblings. Macrina gave her brothers and sisters a strong foundation in the basic subjects, particularly in the faith of her family.

Her sisterly influence must have been exceptional, because she herself was canonized a saint after her death at the age of fifty in the year 379. Her legacy shone forth in her young siblings. Among them were some very important figures in the fourth-century Church: St Gregory of Nyssa, St. Basil the Great and St. Peter of Sebaste. Gregory and Basil, both bishops, became known as two of the greatest teachers in Church history.

Gregory's own written testimony credits Macrina for their strong education and spiritual growth. Gregory once said in a speech that his sister was quick to point out when any of her brothers strayed from the right path. In one instance, Basil has just returned from a university in Athens. Apparently quite prideful, Macrina warned him not to be so full of himself— something only a big sister would have the guts and the right to say.

Sainthood is earned and not something one can be born into, but good family ties sure seem to help. Macrina came from a God-centered family. Her parents faithfully practiced their Christian beliefs, and she had grandparents who were martyred for their faith.

So for every big brother or sister tempted to tell the younger ones to scram, he or she should consider Macrina and how her love and influence helped lead the family straight to heaven.

—Patti Maguire Armstrong

Patti Maguire Armstrong is an editor of the Amazing Grace for Families. *Her biography appears at the end of the book.*

Vacationing on a Dime

When I lowered the sun visor of my windshield as I headed home from work, it occurred to me that the days had gotten longer. It was springtime, Easter was just around the corner, and I always felt good this time of year because it was the season of renewal.

My wife, Bev, sensed my good mood when I walked in the house so, after I had a chance to say hello to our boys, she carefully broke the news to me. "We got a call about your brother John from Florida a little while ago," she began. "He will be fine but he was in a car accident."

I called right away. He told me that he was in traction with a compound fracture in his left leg, and that he would be hospitalized for two months.

When I got off the phone with John, Bev and I discussed visiting him. We weren't sure who would watch the children if we flew from Pennsylvania to Florida, but we could barely afford airfare for two. Then it occurred to us that school would be closed for spring break, and we could make a vacation on a budget out of it by packing up the station wagon and driving down the coast with the children.

After spending a few days with John in Boca Raton, we drove to Orlando. Our boys were young at the time and very excited, even though we prepared them for a low-key day at the Magic Kingdom. In the early 1970s, admission to the amusement park did not include the rides and attractions. At lunchtime, we took the boys back to our station wagon to eat the peanut butter and jelly sandwiches. When we went back into the park, I noticed Bev was lagging behind. I turned around to find her chatting with another woman. I thought, "Oh, great. She's going to hold us up." I walked over to them and learned that the woman's two children had taken sick, and she was giving us her unused ride tickets because it was the last day of their vacation. A family we didn't even know enabled us to enjoy a complete day in the park.

If not for my brother John, we probably would not have taken a vacation that year, but it made us realize that we did not need a lot of money to begin a tradition of family vacations. We were creative and frugal and found a multitude of ways to make lasting memories while finding rest, relaxation, and fun.

Camping as a family created some of our most cherished memories. We spent hours talking and sharing stories around the campfire at night. Sometimes we'd simply sit staring quietly together into the magnificently star-studded night sky. Each boy felt a sense of duty and importance as he pitched in to keep the campsite tidy or help prepare meals.

Our vacations were always an adventure. Many times, we didn't have firm plans or enough money, but we put our faith in God, and things always worked out. Apparently ours wasn't the only family vacationing on a dime because the campsites were always crowded. Sometimes we needed reservations months ahead of time. Several times, we took our chances and drove down with reservations for only a few nights.

Such was the case when we planned to camp at Fort Wilderness one year with our friends Bob and Mary Helen Inforzato and their family. We were only able to reserve one night in advance, but we drove down anyway, praying the entire time that something would become available. Before entering the site, both families got together and prayed hard. I pulled up to the entrance first. As the woman at the campground checked our reservation, I explained that the family in the car behind us was part of our group and that we'd like to extend our stay for a week. She looked at me like I had two heads and said, "Are you kidding? You have to book a year in advance." I asked her to kindly check her computer, and sure enough, within minutes from her last check, a cancellation had come in— and by a party of two families, no less! She was so astonished that she nudged the woman working next to her and explained what had just transpired. The other woman looked at me and dropped her jaw. I just shrugged my shoulders and proceeded to drive into the campground, knowing that sometimes it's just a matter of having the right connections.

—Joseph M. Oliver

Joseph M. Oliver is a husband, father, grandfather, and deacon. Joe was born and raised with his six siblings in Connecticut but has resided in suburban Philadelphia with his wife since the mid-1960s. Together they started Oliver Heating & Cooling, a successful HVAC company that operates in the Philadelphia tri-state region.

I Proposed in a Chain Letter!

Last August my wife, Ramona, and I celebrated twenty years of married life—most of them good ones. It's a curious thing, reaching this milestone. When I was a boy, the only ones celebrating twentieth anniversaries were old people with ample wrinkles, high foreheads, and starchy clothing—people who were so old they'd reached their forties and had little time left. Most of them seemed happy. Others looked like love was a dream and marriage was the alarm clock.

In my case, twenty years together is nothing short of miraculous, considering that I proposed to Ramona by chain letter. This is what it said:

> *Dear Ramona Bjorndal,*
> *Do not throw away this letter! It was started by my ancestors just after The Great Flood and it's NEVER BEEN BROKEN! To keep the chain going, all you have to do is marry me. This will include providing decent meals, clean laundry, and lots of love for the next 60 years. In return, you will receive my undying devotion, occasional flowers, chocolate, and access to my car keys until death do us part. If you break the chain, you'll be destined to live a life of misery and boredom, much like the math class I'm sitting in now.*

It was pretty clever stuff for a tenth grader, I thought, and four years later, when I summoned the courage to show it to her, she laughed. She also agreed to marry me.

A few years ago, we returned to the same hotel where we first shared a pillow more than two decades ago. I gasped at the price, reminding myself that it cost $39 in 1982 ("Did they even have hotels back then?" my thirteen-year-old later asked). The staff was so impressed that a couple could stay together this long that they couldn't spoil us enough. They wheeled in complimentary chocolates and a large bottle of champagne on ice. I've always had enough fun sober, so we bypassed the tiny bubbles and went straight for the chocolate, and then sat in a hot tub talking of our sweet years together.

I suppose there are a hundred reasons we still share the same phone number and address. Here are my top five:

We left no alternatives. The first three years of our marriage were miserable—until I got a divorce—a divorce from loving myself and seeking my own way. What a difference it has made. Finding the right person, I've since discovered, is less important than being the right person.

We even golf together. My wife enjoys golf about as much as I enjoy shopping for curtain fabric. Still, she comes along sometimes and cheers as I putt. Our fifth anniversary was celebrated on a golf course at her suggestion. Perhaps that's why I find it easier to move furniture when she asks. Or vacuum carpets. Or bathe the dog. One of these days I'll get up the nerve to enter a curtain fabric store.

We sweat the small stuff. Early on, I left mud on the carpet, whiskers in the sink, or my underwear where it landed. Worse, I often hurt her with a biting comment. Small things can create quite a pile (trust me). So I'm learning to take care of the minor details, before they become major ones. If I'm last out of bed, I make it. If I'm late for supper, I call home. We go to bed at the same time even when I'm not tired, and I kiss her lips before I shave each morning. Twice in the last year I lit candles in our bedroom, four times I've said "I was wrong," and just the other day (drum roll please), I even located the laundry hamper.

We travel together. Whenever possible, Ramona goes along with me as I travel across the country speaking. Sure, it costs money, and I haven't had a window seat in years, but who cares? Our retirement savings plan may be smaller, but I'd like to grow old with someone with whom I share more than money; I share memories.

We pray together. One of Ramona's first wishes for our marriage was that we'd pray together, and I've honored this. Bringing our desires, our dreams, and our concerns before God together has united us as a couple.

Lately we've been thanking God at night for his amazing grace. For taking two selfish kids who hardly knew how to spell love and drawing them close to himself and closer to each other. In the end, I suppose you could chart our marital happiness on a graph that would parallel the depth of our relationship with Jesus. His power dwarfs that of any self-help book or chain letter. For these twenty years, he gets the credit.

On our way to our overpriced hotel, we heard Huey Lewis and the News sing, "I'm happy to be stuck with you," and we both smiled and tapped our toes. But glue or chains don't hold a marriage together. A hundred tiny threads do. Threads like trust, commitment, kindness, humility, gentleness, respect, and flowers on an anniversary.

As we checked in, I told our hostess the significance of this day. Her eyes grew wide. "Wow," she said, "that's a long time with one person!"

"Yes," I replied with a grin, "but it would have been a whole lot longer without her."

—Phil Callaway

Phil Callaway is a writer from Alberta, Canada. He is a popular speaker and author of thirteen books, including With God on the Golf Course *(Harvest House). You can visit him at www.philcallaway.com.*

The Crossbearer

I felt chilled as I sat in the sacristy listening to the story Charlie Carroll was telling. It was almost like I was standing out in the cold damp of a West Virginia morning, listening to the machinery grinding and clanking; watching my family and friends standing silently and waiting for the word—good or bad —which would end our vigil.

Danny, Charlie, Victor, and I had just come from swimming at the YMCA as guests of Jim Hoch. Danny suggested stopping at the sacristy to see if Sister St. Patrick had posted the list of assignments for Holy Week.

The list had been posted—except for Easter itself—and we carefully noted what we were supposed to do. Sister St. Patrick puttered around joking that since we had all graduated from Saint Columbkille and were in high school, she had to put us down on the list to make sure we didn't forget our loyalties.

I remembered how, a couple of years earlier, Charlie Carroll had reacted when he learned about one of our "traditions," which said that any kid who showed up for the First Mass of Easter could "suit up" and be in the procession and on the altar, whether he was on the list or not. For some reason it seemed very important to the skinny, red-headed kid from West Virginia to do something special on that day.

Sister didn't have the assignments for Easter Sunday down yet, but Victor joked that Charlie would be there for sure, so it didn't matter if she bothered to assign anyone else.

"What's so important about servin' on Easter, Charlie?" Danny asked.

Sister was folding a surplice but put it down when Charlie Carroll began to tell us an almost unbelievable story, which we had never heard before.

When Charlie was eight or nine—a couple years before the mine closed and the family moved up to our city—Charlie remembered being called out of school because someone had come to say that there had been a cave-in at the mine.

It was on Good Friday morning.

Charlie hurried home, where his mother and sisters were waiting for him. Then, together, they hurried breathlessly over to the mine area where their father was trapped to joint the hundreds of others who were assembled.

"I remember it was cold and rainy," Charlie told us quietly as we sat there in the warmth of the sacristy. "Not really raining but sort of wet out. The ground was muddy because my old shoes kept slidin'."

Rescue people were bustling around. Large machines which were used to pump air into the mine whirred and hissed while daylight faded to dusk and dusk to darkness.

There were lights set up all around the mine entrance where the work was going on, Charlie said. But the big shelter—a wooden lumber-storage area where the families were gathered— was dark, and they had to huddle together to keep warm.

I had never remembered Charlie talking so much. As he told his story, his voice seemed to become quietly intense, recalling what must have been a terrible ordeal for the small family.

"I guess we slept some, on the piles of lumber. In the morning there were Red Cross people there with blankets and with food for us. No one left the mine or went home or anything."

He said that they waited all the next day—Holy Saturday— watching and praying. The Protestant minister from the church was there as well as the "mission" priest who travelled the hills on Sundays to minister to the handfuls of Catholics in them. Charlie said that the two clergymen knelt on the muddy ground and prayed together. Then, they went from family to family regardless of which church they belonged to - or if they belonged to any, at all.

"How was your mother, Mr. Carroll?" Sister St. Patrick asked. She was as caught up in Charlie's story as the rest of us.

"She kept tellin' us that it was goin' to be OK, S'ter," Charlie said, "that our daddy was goin' to come walkin' out of that mine straight and strong..."

Sister shook her head and let Charlie continue.

"Well," he said, "we waited the whole second day. I remember I was really scared when the second night started comin' because I was always kind of scared of the dark. To me, it seemed like we'd been there in the dark forever..."

Charlie said he had stayed awake most of that second night. His sisters were sleeping under the gray blankets. His mother was awake, like him, watching the mine entrance with a fierce concentration.

Some of the people were gathered over by the mine office praying with the minister and the priest. No one seemed to notice that it was Easter morning as the sun began to rise over the towering hills.

"The sun started comin' up over the hill," Charlie said, "and it was a warm sun. Not all misty like it had been. The steam was risin' up off the damp ground, and there was a lot of hustle goin' on over by the mine entrance."

The sun rose higher, and the shadows began to disappear. Charlie said he heard some yelling and saw a lot of movement going on over by the mine, so he pushed through the crowd of people to see what was going on.

"They was yellin' and hollerin'," Charlie said in his faint West Virginia drawl, "that the rescuers had broken through and that a lot of miners were comin' out. I looked over at the big ol' entrance and saw the rescuers comin' out with big smiles and turnin' back to look while they made room for the other men to pass through."

He said that the rescuers formed two lines and that the saved miners came on through them like they were in a parade. The very first miner he saw was his father. Charlie was deathly quiet when he told us about his first sight.

"I don't know if he was the first one out or not. But, to me, he was the only one I could see. He was walkin' out with his big smile and wavin', lookin' around to see if he could see us.

"I ran right out and grabbed onto him, and I started cryin' and laughin' all at the same time."

Miraculously, no miner had been killed. Several were injured, but not a single life was lost.

"Bet you really had an Easter Mass that day, Charlie!" Victor grinned.

"Didn't have no Mass. Nothin' except the prayin' and the cryin' right there at the mine. The priest and the preacher were goin' from family to family, huggin' them and prayin' with them..."

"You never told us that story before," Victor said.

"No.," Charlie replied and then lapsed into silence.

Sister wiped at her eye.

"A fine, fine Easter, indeed," she said.

Sister went over to her table and took out her papers to work on the rest of the serving assignments. We still sat there peppering Charlie with questions about what it was like at the mine accident, unable to fully comprehend what he must have gone through.

When she had finished writing, Sister came back and tacked the serving list for the First Mass of Easter on the corkboard with the rest of Holy Week.

Anyone could be there, like I said, but only a handful were assigned to specific jobs. Right after Kevin's name Sister had written: "Crossbearer – Charlie Carroll."

Charlie beamed his thanks at the powerful nun.

"Your tellin' about your father walkin' out into the sun of Easter made me think of how beautiful our processional cross is on Easter," Sister told him. "And how we have taken a symbol of shame and made it triumphant. It seems right you should carry it, Mr. Carroll."

I recalled how Charlie and his family always went up to the Blessed Virgin's altar after the Mass on Easter and knelt there for a few minutes. I mentioned this, and Charlie said that was when they always said their own prayers of thanks.

Sister started laughing and went over to her "work drawer" and pulled it open.

"I guess that explains these..." she grinned and took three small pieces of coal from the drawer.

"Every year I find a lump of coal on the Blessed Mother's altar," she said, "and now I think I know who puts them there..."

Charlie blushed and smiled. He said that it was dumb, perhaps, but that was what they did.

Sister said it wasn't "dumb" at all.

When we gathered for the Easter procession that year I felt somehow different. I had always loved Easter. But this year I saw it shining in the eyes of a skinny fifteen-year-old from Mingo County, West Virginia, who stood holding the flower decked processional cross, waiting to begin.

After Mass I watched Charlie go on out to meet his family for their traditional visit to the Blessed Virgin's altar. Sister St. Patrick and Danny were watching, too and were smiling as they realized what it was all about.

"It must have been somethin', S'ter," Danny said, "to see his daddy comin' out of the mine on Easter morning. I wish I could have seen somethin' like that."

Sister had her arms folded on her ample bosom and looked at my brother and then out at the Carroll family again. I guess she knew there would be another lump of coal to put away after they had gone.

"I think we just did, Mr. Patrick," she said simply, "I think we just did."

—Sean Patrick

Sean Patrick recently celebrated his twentieth anniversary as a regular monthly columnist in Catholic Digest. *Having retired from a lifetime of service in law* *enforcement Sean and his wife 'Trish now relax in rural Ohio surrounded by one of the largest communities of Old Order Amish in the world. Sean has published two collections of his stories (*Patrick's Corner *and* The Best of Sean Patrick*) and continues writing for* Catholic Digest *and other magazines. He and 'Trish are active in the music ministry of St. Edward's parish in Parkman, Ohio.*

Don't Hope, Friend ... Decide!

While waiting to pick up a friend at the airport in Portland, Oregon, I had one of those life-changing experiences that you hear other people talk about. You know, the kind that sneaks up on you unexpectedly? Well, this one occurred a mere two feet away from me!

Straining to locate my friend among the passengers deplaning through the jetway, I noticed a man coming toward me carrying two light bags. He stopped right next to me to greet his family.

First, he motioned to his youngest son, around age six, and laid down his bags. They gave each other a long, and movingly loving hug. As they separated enough to look in each other's face, I heard the father say, "It's so good to see you, son. I missed you so much!" His son smiled somewhat shyly, diverted his eyes, and replied softly, "Me too, Dad!"

Then the man stood up, gazed in the eyes of his oldest son, about ten, and, while cupping his son's face in his hands, he said, "You're already quite the young man. I love you very much, Zach!" They, too, hugged a most loving, tender hug. His son said nothing. No reply was necessary.

While this was happening, a baby girl was squirming excitedly in her mother's arms, never once taking her little eyes off the wonderful sight of her returning father. The man said, "Hi babygirl!" as he gently took the child from her mother. He quickly kissed her face all over and then held her close to his chest while rocking her from side to side. The little girl instantly relaxed and simply laid her head on his shoulder and remained motionless in total, pure contentment.

After several moments, he handed his daughter to his oldest son and declared, "I've saved the best for last!" and proceeded to give his wife the longest, most passionate kiss I ever remember seeing. He gazed into her eyes for several seconds and then silently mouthed, "I love you so much!" They stared into each other's eyes, beaming big smiles at one another, while holding both hands. For an instant, they reminded me of newlyweds, but I knew by the age of their kids that they couldn't be. I puzzled about it for a moment, and then realized how totally engrossed I was in the wonderful display of unconditional love not more than an arm's length away from me. I suddenly felt uncomfortable, as if I were invading something sacred, but was amazed to hear my own voice nervously ask, "Wow! How long have you two been married?"

"Been together fourteen years total, married twelve of those," he replied without breaking his gaze from his lovely wife's face. "Well then, how long have you been away?" I asked. The man finally looked at me, still beaming his joyous smile and told me, "Two whole days!"

Two days?! I was stunned! I was certain by the intensity of the greeting I had just witnessed that he'd been gone for at least several weeks, if not months, and I know my expression betrayed me. So I said almost offhandedly, hoping to end my intrusion with some semblance of grace (and to get back to searching for my friend), "I hope my marriage is still that passionate after twelve years!"

The man suddenly stopped smiling. He looked me straight in the eye, and with an intensity that burned right into my soul, he told me something that left me a different person. He told me, "Don't hope friend ... decide." Then he flashed me his wonderful smile again, shook my hand, and said, "God bless!" With that, he and his family turned and energetically strode away together.

I was still watching that exceptional man and his special family walk just out of sight when my friend came up to me and asked, "What'cha looking at?" Without hesitating, and with a curious sense of certainty, I replied, "My future!"

—Michael Hargrove

Michael Hargrove is a published author, professional speaker, and is currently serving as CEO of My Success Company. His work regularly appears in many magazines, websites, and books throughout the world. He is also a contributing author to the Chicken Soup for the Soul *book and television series.*

An Unexpected Gift

Five years ago, my wife and I seemed to have finally embarked on the good times within our marriage, in both finances and in our careers. We were enjoying life and working very hard to move our careers forward. The last thing we expected was the doctor's news: "You're pregnant."

My wife, Roxanne, was distraught, to say the least. Both our boys were teens, and one was just about to graduate from high school. For days all she could do was cry. On the other hand, I was ecstatic. As time went by, though, Roxanne grew used to the idea of having another child to the point that she soon shared my enthusiasm.

Then things grew complicated. Roxanne's doctor had her do blood work. When the results came back, she had high numbers for Down Syndrome. The doctor said that since the numbers were so high, the diagnosis was almost a guarantee. We were told to seriously think about "terminating the pregnancy." We were speechless. It seemed there were no words to describe our pain.

Many good people tried to help us through this difficult time. For instance, a very special person offered to set up a meeting with a doctor in town and his wife who had a Down Syndrome baby. But when you are in this situation, it feels as though you are alone and no one can really help. Although we were both numb at first, Roxanne finally told God, "This is my son, however he is born, and I will love him with all I have. However he is born, that is between Caleb (that is what we chose to call him) and you, Lord."

I struggled with the news. I am sorry to say that I even turned against God for a time. But in the end, I knew I could not go on without Him. Finally the thought came to me. "I have always lived my life to love children. I always prided myself on being what God wants me to be: a man of love. Just because life is getting hard, am I going to change?" I knew I had to continue on my path even though my world was changing. The Holy Spirit was moving through me and filling me with the strength I needed.

By the time Roxanne and I went to the hospital to welcome our son into the world, we felt God's divine presence giving us the love we needed as parents. By then, we already loved Caleb so much it was as if he was already with us.

Roxanne and I had come to realize that there is nothing "wrong" with a child born with Down Syndrome. Every baby is a precious and gift from God. Each child is perfect, according to God's plan. We anticipated Roxanne's labor with joy, knowing our "perfect" son would soon be born. But to show that even a test which seems indisputable can be wrong, Caleb is now three years old without a single sign of Down Syndrome. In fact, he is incredibly precocious for his age. What a gift we have in him! Before Caleb, we thought a pregnancy would put a strain on the good times with our careers and finances in full swing. We were so wrong. There is nothing greater than being a mommy and daddy. No job or amount of money can compare with such a blessing.

When some one asked Roxanne about the situation later, she said: "Don't ever worry about a test or numbers; you just have to have enough faith in God." You never know when something that you fear will end up being the greatest miracle in your life."

—Troy Brown

Troy Brown, a devoted husband and father of three, resides in Chataignier, Louisiana, and belongs to the Sacred Heart of Jesus Parish in Ville Platte, Louisiana. He has been a CCD teacher for nearly ten years and involved with the RCIA program for about two years. To see his writings and blog, visit www. troybrownonline.net.

Power of the Powerless: A Brother's Lesson

I grew up in a house where my brother was on his back in his bed for almost thirty-three years, in the same corner of his room, under the same window, beside the same yellow walls. Oliver was blind and mute. His legs were twisted. He didn't have the strength to lift his head nor the intelligence to learn anything.

Today I am an English teacher, and each time I introduce my class to the play about Helen Keller, *The Miracle Worker*, I tell my students about Oliver. One day, during my first year teaching, a boy in the last row raised his hand and said, "Oh, Mr. de Vinck. You mean he was a vegetable."

I stammered for a few seconds. My family and I fed Oliver. We changed his diapers, hung his clothes and bed linens on the basement line in winter, and spread them out white and clean on the lawn in the summer. I always liked to watch the grasshoppers jump on the pillowcases.

We bathed Oliver. Tickled his chest to make him laugh. Sometimes we left the radio on in his room. We pulled the shade down over his bed in the morning to keep the sun from burning his tender skin. We listened to him laugh as we watched television downstairs. We listened to him rock his arms up and down to make the bed squeak. We listened to him cough in the middle of the night.

"Well, I guess you could call him a vegetable. I called him Oliver, my brother. You would have liked him."

One October day in 1946, when my mother was pregnant with Oliver, her second son, she was overcome by fumes from a leaking coal-burning stove. My oldest brother was sleeping in his crib, which was high off the ground, so the gas didn't affect him. My father pulled them outside, where my mother revived quickly.

On April 20, 1947, Oliver was born. A healthy-looking, plump, beautiful boy.

One afternoon, a few months later, my mother brought Oliver to a window. She held him there in the bright sun, and there Oliver looked and looked directly into the sunlight, which was the first moment my mother realized that Oliver was blind. We wondered if the gas leak my mother suffered from during pregnancy was to blame. My parents, the true heroes of this story, learned with the passing months, that blindness was only part of the problem. So they brought Oliver to Mt. Sinai Hospital in New York for tests to determine the extent of his condition.

The doctor said that he wanted to make it very clear to both my mother and father that there was absolutely nothing that could be done for Oliver. He didn't want my parents to grasp at false hope. "You could place him in an institution," he said. "But," my parents replied, "he is our son. We will take Oliver home, of course." The doctor answered, "Then take him home and love him."

Oliver grew to the size of a ten-year-old. He had a big chest and a large head. His hands and feet were those of a five-year-old, small and soft. We'd wrap a box of baby cereal for him at Christmas and place it under the tree; pat his head with a damp cloth in the middle of a July heat wave. His baptismal certificate hung on the wall above his head. A bishop came to the house and confirmed him.

Even now, years after his death from pneumonia on March 12, 1980, Oliver still remains the weakest, most helpless human being I've ever met, and yet he was one of the most powerful I've human beings I ever met. He could do absolutely nothing except breathe, sleep, eat, and yet he was directly responsible for action, love, courage, and insight. When I was small my mother would say, "Isn't it wonderful that you can see?" And once she said, "When you go to heaven, Oliver will run to you, embrace you, and the first thing he will say is 'Thank you.'" I remember, too, my mother explaining to me that we were blessed with Oliver in ways that were not clear to her at first. Loving Oliver was our gift to him, but it was also God's gift to us to allow us to do so.

So often parents are faced with a child who is severely retarded, but who is also hyperactive, demanding, or wild, and who needs constant care. So many people have little choice but to place their child in an institution. We were fortunate that Oliver didn't need us to be in his room all day. He never knew what his condition was. We were blessed with his presence, a true presence of peace.

When I was in my early twenties, I met a girl and fell in love. After a few months, I brought her home to meet my family. When my mother went to the kitchen to prepare dinner, I asked the girl, "Would you like to see Oliver?" for I had told her about my brother. "No," she answered.

Soon after, I met Roe, a lovely girl. She asked me the names of my brothers and sisters. She loved children. I thought she was wonderful. I brought her home after a few months to meet my family. Soon it was time for me to feed Oliver. I remember sheepishly asking Roe if she'd like to see him. "Sure," she said.

I sat at Oliver's bedside as Roe watched over my shoulder. I gave him his first spoonful, his second. "Can I do that?" Roe asked with ease, freedom, and compassion. I gave her the bowl, and she fed Oliver one spoonful at a time.

The power of the powerless. Oliver showed me which girl I should marry. Today Roe and I have three children.

—Christopher de Vinck

Christopher de Vinck is the author of The Power of the Powerless: A Brother's Legacy of Love *(Doubleday), in which he shares further insights gained from Oliver. He has written eleven books and lives with his wife, Roe, in Pompton Plains, New Jersey.*

Editors' Note: *The above article appeared in the April 10, 1985 issue of the* Wall Street Journal.

It Takes a Heavenly Village

When I first heard the phrase "It takes a village to raise a family" uttered by then-First Lady Hillary Clinton, I bristled. A village? *No, thank you, I do not want the village of Washington, DC, raising my children.* But honestly, I knew I could use some help, so, I began looking for it.

First, I hired some really good security guard-nannies—ten, in fact. I actively, openly, and prayerfully hired my ten children's guardian angels. They are a theological fact. Guardian angels are given by God to watch over us. When my family said the familiar Guardian Angel prayer every morning and evening, I admit that I did so lightly. Not anymore. I now say that prayer with deep conviction and peace, knowing that there are angels watching over each and every one of my children. "For he will give his angels charge of you to guard you in all your ways" (Psalm 91:11). Security detail done. I'm still on the ground crew for this detail, but it is very reassuring to know that I've got air coverage, so to speak.

Still, I felt I needed some more help. Remember that conversation Jesus had with John at the foot of the cross? "Woman, behold your son … Behold your mother." But of course, my kids have another mother and she is a much better one than I could ever be! Therefore, every morning I give over the care of my children to their heavenly mother, Mary and her earthly spouse, Joseph, in a simple, honest prayer: "Mary, Joseph, I'm not sure what I'm doing, so your inspiration, grace and guidance would help. Thank you," or similar words admitting my ineptitude and acknowledging their proven abilities. The way I figure it, they were reliable with their son, Jesus, so I think I can trust them with my crew.

Now, I know about the whole temple episode and "losing" Jesus for three days, but I think that by age twelve children need to take some responsibility for themselves and their whereabouts.

And I also think that Jesus wanted to get left behind. I am especially impressed with Jesus' behavior after getting "lost." Whatever Joseph and Mary said to Him on the long walk home worked because we are told, "He went down with them and came to Nazareth, and was obedient to them" (Luke 2:51). And later we are told, "Jesus increased in wisdom, and in stature, and in favor with God and man" (Luke 2:52). Joseph can lecture my children anytime he wants. For a man of few words in Scripture, he is impressive. There are times I have sent my children to sit quietly and talk to Joseph about what happened. Their time in silent lecture (on the couch) often works much better than my fifteen-minute lecture of words would have.

My heavenly village was still pretty empty, so I went about and hired on all of my children's name saints. Much as I do with Mary and Joseph, I say each of my children's names out loud in the morning and ask their saints to fill in all the holes I'll miss and things I'll forget. While most of them have two saints' names, one does not, but that didn't stop me. My one daughter is named for her father's godmother, a beautiful Catholic woman who is still living and prays for her namesake every day. Her middle name is that of a long-ago babysitter who died suddenly of meningitis at the age of twenty, while a senior in college. Christa is not a beatified saint, but that wonderful girl's life remains an inspiration to us, so I've hired her, from heaven or from purgatory, perhaps, to look out for her twelve-year-old namesake as well.

Not done, I looked in *Butler's Lives of the Saints* for some obscure saints who didn't seem to be already busy. St. Anthony is already working at my house full-time keeping track of my keys and purse, and John Paul II is kept quite busy, I'm sure, keeping watch over the thousands of boys who received his name both during his papacy and since his saintly death. Although the saints have no limitations on interventions, I looked for saints that no one was naming their children after. I imagine they wish they had more to do in the battle of winning souls. I wanted to ask them to share their time viewing the beatific vision with looking in on our home and our chaos. I found St. Zama—interesting name, easy to remember, and fun to shout out in time of need. "St. Zama, your intercession is needed now!" When I discovered that he was the first recorded bishop for Bologna, Italy, I laughed out loud. No longer do I need to seek the help of Oscar Meyer. I also found St. Wisdom, who, along with her daughters Faith, Hope, and Charity, died under Hadrian. My prayers for the necessary doses of those virtues every day now include asking their namesakes for extra help.

And finally, Bobo. Yes, we have a St. Bobo. Another easy name to remember, and since he was both a knight and later a hermit, I will ask him to watch over my sons in particular. May their busy days growing up end in days of prayer with God. It was fun teaching my children about their newest friends.

So, the house is pretty full. I'm feeling less lonely as my husband and I raise our kids, and I've come to admit that Hillary might have had something there. You do need a village to raise a family—a heavenly one. I depend on a village inhabited not by politicians but by saints. Isn't it wonderful to know that a veritable metropolis of heavenly citizens will take the raising of your children just as seriously as you do?

—Rachel Watkins

Rachel Watkins, wife of Matt and mother of ten, is a contributor to Heart, Mind, Strength Radio *program and the blogsite, www.execeptionalmarriages. com. She is also the creator of The Little Flowers Girls' Club. Visit www. eccehomopress.com for more information.*

I Gave My Husband Away

Like most teenage girls, I often dreamed of my ideal man. He would be loving, patient, kind, and considerate. We would marry, and his undying love would care for me and whatever children we had. But this guy I imagined was not just the man of my dreams; he was the man of my prayers. Every day, I stopped in the chapel and prayed that the Lord would send me just such a man.

On September 8, 1973, I walked down the aisle and said "I do" to Rex, the man of my hopes and prayers. As the years passed, Rex proved to be exactly everything I had requested. We were blessed with five children. With each baby, it seemed that our love deepened for each other and for God.

Together, we volunteered for various ministries in our parish and diocese. Slowly, the feeling grew within us both, that Rex was called to be a permanent deacon, to serve in an official capacity as an assistant shepherd of our church's flock. While attending the ordination Mass of a neighbor, Rex and I suddenly looked over at each other. No words were necessary. At that moment, we both knew for certain that Rex was being called. Silently, we simply nodded at one another.

Although only the man is ordained to the office of deacon, spouses participate in the formation classes. It was during this time of preparation that I came to realize that this was not just one more way in which Rex would volunteer for our parish. It was a commitment beyond any he had ever previously made. Rex had to agree not to remarry in the event of my death. He would have a flock to help shepherd. Rex's pact with God would not just be between the two of them, either. I had to give away my husband. For the first time in our married life, I'd be alone in the pew with our children.

Rex and I had always attended Mass as a family, sitting together and praying together. My husband and I sat side by side as we believed this was a symbol of our union in Christ. Our children knew that we were inseparable, and even they did not sit between us. It is what I had envisioned as a young girl so many years before when I prayed for a good husband.

Now, there would be many Sundays, holidays, and major feasts days when I would have full responsibility of the five children in the pew with me. With three boys and two girls, getting through any Mass on my own would be a challenge. Looking ahead to a long future as the lone adult in our pew was intimidating. Our youngest would be one years old when Daddy was ordained! The other children were all in their formative years in between the ages of three and twelve. The whole group together was like a bouquet of helium-filled balloons that wanted to flitter away. I wish I could brag that the children sat as quiet little angels during Masses, but my crowd's personalities just did not fit that description. Keeping order in the pew and not providing huge distractions to those around us was something Rex had always been there to help with. Taking on this daunting task alone was one of the toughest things I would have to adjust to as the wife of a deacon.

As part of our preparation for ordination, we had occasional interviews in front of the deaconate board. These interviews were meant for further discernment about whether we'd be ready for ordination. One of these important interviews happened to come on our wedding-anniversary date. At first, I did not think anything of the coincidence, but after the interview, I was hit by the immense significance. I was asked how I felt about Rex's ordination. The Holy Spirit illuminated my thoughts as I responded.

"In high school I had prayed for the Lord to send me a wonderful man," I explained. "He heard my prayer and answered it. Now, I am being asked to give Rex back to the Lord in service of His people. How can I say no?"

It has been nineteen years since I willingly gave Rex back to our Lord when he was ordained a permanent deacon. I still remember the joy flowing through me like a fountain. Over the years, I have missed Rex sitting next to me, especially at our children's special events such as First Communion and Confirmation. Even on ordinary Sundays, I sometimes wished for Rex's help with the children during Mass. One memorable Sunday, I took the baby to the back of the church since he was being rather fussy. Before long, I heard the patter of little patent-leather shoes coming down the aisle. There was his teary-eyed three-year-old sister, who missed us. Next around the corner appeared the smiling face of my seven-year-old child, coming to see if I needed anything. After a few minutes, my ten-year-old son came to see what was going on. Finally, our twelve-year-old daughter showed up, thinking maybe I needed her help. It felt as though my bouquet of helium balloons was let loose in the church. With everyone accounted for, I rounded the children up and trekked back to the empty pew. We made quite a procession.

The years have since passed, and the children are grown. Our youngest son is away at college and a leader in the campus Catholic youth group, so most Sundays I am alone in the pew. However, I know that my husband, Rex, is a very gifted man and that the love he shows me and our children is not just for our family. The small sacrifice of sitting in a pew alone I have accepted so that others may be blessed by the Lord through my precious spouse. I rejoice in having such a wonderful gift I can lovingly share with others.

—Rita Pilger

Rita Pilger lives in Arvada, Colorado, with her husband. She's now a grandmother of two. She works part-time in a fitness center and volunteers as a victim advocate with a local police department.

Daddy's Irish Wake

Late in January of 1984, I had driven 750 miles to be with my father as he underwent his latest cancer surgery. With each mile of the trip, my mind clicked off the years spent at my father's knee—years of always knowing my dad was there for me. Years that now sadly threatened to come to an end.

Just as I had feared, the surgery did not go well. The doctors quickly opened my father up and closed him again. As the surgery was much shorter than predicted, I knew the news was not good.

Parting with a loved one is truly one of the hardest things we must do in this life. But, in my family, we always had a clear perspective of the beginning, middle, and end of life on this good green earth, as my dad liked to call it.

It was a perspective, which my father had learned from his father, and generations before them had handed this Irish wisdom down to each succeeding generation.

My dad was always such an inspiration. He possessed a special Irish sense of humor, full of wisdom, love, and a great trust in God.

When the doctor told my dad he could do nothing more to stop the spread of cancer, my dad pondered this for a moment. He then looked his doctor in the eye and with a weak but familiar grin, said: "Well now, it's January and Saint Paddy's Day would be a perfect time for an Irish wake, don't you think?" Then he added: "I have always thought it was such a sad thing that the poor bloke who died, never got to enjoy his last party."

The doctor agreed since a wake is the part of the funeral where everyone celebrates the life of their deceased loved one. Later, the doctor told us Dad was very weak and probably would not last but another week or two at most. Obviously, he did not know my father well. Dad made out a list of final things he needed to get done. On the top of his list was to throw his own Irish wake on Saint Patrick's Day, more than two months away. Even more startling, to those who did not know him, was a list of things Dad wrote on his personal calendar covering the whole year of 1984 until Valentine's Day of 1985. The doctors humored my dad, but all the while were planning his hospice care and the end of his life, which they were certain would be just a few short days away.

Within a week of recovering from the last surgery, my dad had had enough of doctors and hospitals. He wanted to go home to die. The doctors agreed, so we took Dad home, for what we thought would be a short time.

Even we could not envision that Dad would live much longer. He was so frail and weak that the end seemed imminent.

My father was to surprise us all. A few days after he returned home, he disappeared when mom was shopping. Now, that was no easy feat since he was bedridden and on oxygen. He had had gotten up, dressed, and walked over to the funeral home to plan his Irish wake. He expected his good friend Randy, the undertaker, to help him pull it off. And while he was at it, he made all of his funeral arrangements and had Randy take him to pick out the gravestone.

As the weeks passed, Dad seemed to grow stronger just through anticipating his goal of spending one last Saint Patrick's Day with his friends. Never mind it was to be his own wake ... that thought didn't faze him at all. If anything it seemed to give him strength and joy to be checking each item off his calendar, which he felt the Good Lord wanted him to get done before heading Home, as Dad called it—home to heaven after finishing his mission.

To everyone's amazement, Dad made it to Saint Patrick's Day. His wake was one which none of us shall ever forget.

Dad would have no tears. There was joy, and story telling and remembering all the good times of our lives together. His best friends from childhood luckily were of a mind like my dad. They played up the Irish wake to the hilt, with Irish toasts and general foolishness born out of the spirit of love. One of Dad's buddies reached over and stuck his hand in Dad's pocket to turn it inside out. It was an old joke among friends that, whether they were rich or poor, they would always stick together. And in the end, they would all go out with empty pockets, except for their rosary and an abundance of trust in God's love and mercy.

All in all, it was an Irish send off, which was better than any Saint Patrick's Day we had ever celebrated in past years. From that day to the day he died, my father remained optimistic and happy. Of course, his doctors were a bit incredulous to say the least. Dad lived right up until the day he marked off the second to last "to do," item on his calendar. The only item not crossed off was Valentine's Day 1985, the day he died.

Dad passed away shortly after midnight. As if to punctuate his love for us, his grave marker was heart shaped and engraved with roses and butterflies. I guess the Good Lord must have agreed with my dad, that he had a few loose ends to tie up before heading home. And through His grace nothing was left undone.

—Christine Trollinger

Christine Trollinger's biography appears after her story "Lucy's Star" in chapter two.

Chapter 7
A Family's Strength

God Made Us a Family

"It looks like you are not ovulating," my doctor said. Well, that explained why I was not getting pregnant. My husband, Calvin, and I had been married for one year and were in our early twenties. We wanted to start a family right away, but now, it appeared unlikely to happen. I knew of other couples who had paid thousands of dollars to fertility specialists. Calvin and I both agreed it would be better to spend our money on adoption. It was Wednesday. By Monday we were the parents to four-month-old Samuel.

My mother-in-law had been caring for Samuel as a foster mother. The original family backed out. He was a mixed-race baby, and the parents were concerned his skin was too light compared with their other adopted children.

As licensed foster parents in Indiana, we had been taking care of infants while the paperwork was completed before they went to their permanent adoptive homes. I received a phone call from Adoptions of Kentucky on Monday morning informing us that we could have Samuel right away since we had a foster-care license.

"Calvin," I cried, calling him at work. "We're parents!" He came home right away. We hugged and cried in a deliriously happy state of shock. God had answered our prayer for a child of our own, with mind-boggling speed. But God was not done building our family yet. And again, things would happen quickly.

Calvin and I had applied to work as house parents with Noah's Ark Children's Village. This is a specialized Christian foster care agency. While Calvin and I waited for an opening, they had contacted me to help out one of their foster families by taking over for the weekend.

I walked into the door and into the gaze of five children of varying ages. Dylan grabbed my attention immediately. The diminutive little guy in diapers appeared much younger than his three years. And instead of the eager and curious young face he should have worn, Dylan looked deeply sad. In his short little life, he had already experienced so much pain. This was his fourth foster home. I cared for the kids for about two hours that day. In Dylan's case, my attempts at interaction were rebuffed. He did not talk much, instead using grunts and his fists to communicate. Dylan's verbal ability was poor, but he excelled at hitting the other children.

Although Dylan wanted nothing to do with me, I was captivated with him. I thought about him all the way home. A few days later, the agency asked Calvin and me to baby-sit the entire weekend for the same family. It was the perfect way for us to determine if we wanted to work at this eighty-eight acre village where homes, support, and other amenities were provided to the on-site foster families.

It was an exciting, albeit exhausting weekend. Dylan was no more interested in me than he had been the first time. He had diarrhea all weekend—which was a challenge—and he remained withdrawn. But I was drawn to him even more. I cried all the way home for Dylan. "I know he's suppose to be our son," I revealed to Calvin.

Calvin thought I was nuts, but he just smiled. "Don't get your hopes up," he tried to reason with me. "Parental rights have not been terminated, so he's not even available for adoption." It did not seem to make sense, but I've learned to trust my instincts as long as I stay close to God in prayer. I asked God to lead us regarding Dylan. I could not get that poor little guy out of my mind. I trusted that if it were meant to be, Calvin would eventually agree with me, and God would lead the way.

A couple months later, we moved into a Noah's Ark home and began doing foster care for them. Dylan was placed in another home on the premises after the other foster family moved on. We started getting Dylan during the day from this new foster family to help them, since they were struggling with his behavior. They had other small children, and he was very violent. He had pushed a two-year-old down some stairs, knocked kids down and was still not talking. He could only say "truck" and "blue" and kept repeating those words.

During babysitting, Dylan started warming up to me. I was not worried about Samuel's safety because I was in the room at all times. Two months later Dylan proved too much for the other family and was placed in our home. He had been diagnosed as autistic. Dylan would often rock back and forth, and his behaviors were very repetitive. Even though all indications were that this little guy would be a handful, I could not squelch my yearning to be his mom.

A few months after he was in our home, parental rights were terminated. We immediately filled out the paperwork to begin the adoption process. Dylan's violent behavior continued unabated, however. Often, he would not respond to me. When I tried to soothe Dylan and told him: "Mommy is here," a typical response for him was to scream at me. But I would not give up. I kept showering him with love and patience, and little by little, he started responding. The first time Dylan crawled up on my lap on his own, my spirit soared. I looked over at Calvin and caught his eye with the unspoken message: "Are you seeing this?"

"Thank you, thank you, God," I joyfully prayed.

But it would be many more months before Dylan allowed Calvin to have anything to do with him. He did not even want to get into the car if Calvin was there. Calvin did not force himself on Dylan, but he tried playing toys and games with him. Dylan would have none of it.

One day, I took Dylan to the playground. Then, while Dylan warmed up and began having fun, Calvin joined us and took Dylan horseback riding. "Look at you," I gushed with tears in my eyes. Dylan grinned. He really looked happy and Calvin was trotting along beside him.

But Dylan's pain would not let go. For the first four months, not a day went by that he did not hit others or act out in some way. One day, I put him in the corner for time out. He began screaming and banging his head against the wall.

I wrapped my arms around this broken little boy. "I love you, Dylan," I cried. "You're safe now. Daddy and I are never going to leave you." Dylan kept swinging his arms, so I held him tight and tried not to get hit. Then, I prayed: "God, should we be doing this? Help this to stop. Help Dylan not to hurt and be afraid anymore. Lord, whatever his frustration and anger is, please take it away."

We sat there for a good thirty to forty minutes. At that point, I wondered if I had been wrong. Maybe I was not supposed to be his mommy. "God, are we in over our heads?" I asked. "Can we help this poor, dear boy?" Finally, Dylan calmed down. He was crying, and I was crying. I was scared that I might not be able to help Dylan. But then I remembered all the promises I had made to love him forever. If we did not keep Dylan, who would? I realized he needed us, so we could not give up on him.

Calvin and I prayed hard for Dylan's healing. We did not want him to hurt anymore, but we were powerless to stop it. It was in God's hands. Calvin and I, our families, and some of the members of our church began adding fasting to our prayers. We were going to do everything possible to fight for our little boy.

The first year was rough, but after six months, we began seeing improvements. Dylan's speech was getting better through speech therapy, and it became clear that he was not autistic. The pain from his past often came out, but we kept reassuring Dylan with our love. He also had the love and security of our extended families.

We taught Dylan about God, and we prayed together as a family at bedtime. By the time his adoption became final, he was four years old and still lagging behind in some areas, but his progress was incredible. Instead of being trapped by his pain, a happy little boy was emerging. Dylan was bonding with us and had begun to play with other children without the violence. Once the progress began, it never stopped. There were still bad days and struggles, but Dylan had let us into his heart, and he was firmly in ours.

Today, at nine years old, Dylan is no different from any other boy his age. There is absolutely no sign of autism. He is outgoing and loves skateboarding, and tae kwon do. He is also very affectionate. Often, Dylan will come up to Calvin and me out of the blue and hug us. "I love you, Mama; I love you, Dad," he will say. And he and Samuel are typical brothers. They love to wrestle and sometimes fight but are fiercely loyal to one another. They will even make excuses for each other if one gets into trouble.

Calvin and I thank God for our family every day. He gave us our boys, and then He gave us the grace and love we needed to become a happy family.

—Donna Bader

Donna and Calvin Bader continue to do foster care. Donna says she loves it so much that she cannot imagine ever not being a foster parent They live in Jeffersonville, Indiana, where they homeschool and enjoy riding motor cycles. Donna can be reached at BaderDonna@yahoo.com.

Risking All for Life

Kathi Clapham opened her eyes after two weeks in a medically-induced coma, and the first person she saw was her mother.

"Don't worry, Kathi," her mother said. "You're going to be just fine. Now go be a mommy to those babies."

What makes this moment so extraordinary is that Kathi's mother, Dorothy Novelli, had died three months earlier.

"I just remember her face because she looked healthy and young, like she did when I was a little girl," Kathi said about the mother who was her lifelong "best friend." "I believe the Lord allowed her to visit me that day."

It was certainly a momentous occasion in the life of this thirty-four-year-old mother of two from West Chester, Pennsylvania. Only weeks before, and against all odds, Kathi gave birth to twins, Sarah Dorothy and Paul Anthony. At twenty-six weeks gestation, the babies weighed less than two pounds each. While they lay fighting for their lives in the neonatal intensive care unit at the Hospital of the University of Pennsylvania, Kathi had her own battle to fight.

Kathi has cystic fibrosis (CF), a condition that causes progressive lung failure. As dire as it might sound, the disease never stopped her from living.

"There wasn't much I didn't do while growing up," she said. Although she always had to take medication and avoid infections, she was only hospitalized twice during childhood.

After marrying her husband, Drew, a computer-information specialist, on September 1, 2001, they decided to start a family, even though there were plenty of risks involved.

"If both parents are carriers of the disease, there's a one-in-four chance the child will have the disease," Kathi said. "We knew my husband wasn't a carrier, which means that there was less than a one percent chance that one of our children would have it."

As a result of today's pre-natal screening, some studies have found that ninety-five percent of couples whose unborn babies test positive for CF choose to terminate the pregnancy.

Kathi can only shake her head at those sad statistics, knowing that life with CF isn't bad enough to warrant a death sentence. In fact, the disease comes in degrees from mild to severe, and even if a fetus is correctly diagnosed as having a severe case, the severity of the disease can change during life.

However, the main worry for the Claphams was how much the pregnancy would aggravate her condition. This was why her CF doctor openly advised women with the disease not to get pregnant. But when she told him the good news, "he responded like a father," Kathi said.

Although he didn't agree with her decision, "he treated me with love and respect and gave me the best medical care he could give me," Kathi said.

His gentleness was even more appreciated because only two weeks before, Kathi's mother had been hospitalized and suffered serious complications after a hernia operation.

"I got pregnant a couple weeks after she went into the hospital," Kathi said. "Of course your mom is the first person you want to tell after your husband, but she couldn't even talk to me because she had a tracheotomy."

This was doubly hard on Kathi because she learned very early in the pregnancy that she was carrying twins. Sadly, she would never hear her mother's voice again. Dorothy Novelli remained on life support until she died on October 30, 2003, of chronic sepsis infections.

Two weeks later, Kathi was hospitalized. "I kept getting lung infections. I wasn't gaining the weight I needed. The babies were pressing on my lungs, and I couldn't breathe."

As the babies continued to grow and thrive, Kathi's condition steadily declined. At twenty-two weeks, she consulted with a high risk maternal fetal medicine specialist, who said her only choice was to terminate the pregnancy.

"My husband wasn't there at the time," Kathi said. "I had one of my sisters with me, and you never heard two women scream and cry so loud. And while I was sitting there listening to him tell me all the reasons I needed to do this, these two babies were kicking like crazy, as if they were saying, 'I want to live! I want to live!'"

She was given a week to decide whether to have an abortion before the babies reached the legal age of viability, which is twenty-four weeks. Naturally, she chose life.

"I was just stunned," she said. "That day still doesn't seem like it really happened. It was so surreal. Personally, I think the trauma of aborting two babies that I wanted so badly would have killed me, or at least killed my spirit to live. That's the part they didn't factor in."

From then on, she began to experience first-hand the hot-button topic of abortion. While many nurses and aides prayed with and supported her, others couldn't hide their agendas. "It was scary. You could read people's faces when they came into my room whether they judged me or not. I was definitely the talk of that floor."

One social worker was so unprofessional she actually cornered Kathi's sister and husband to say, "What's going on with Kathi? You know she needs to have this abortion!"

"This is how people's agendas became clear," Kathi said. "It wasn't about me. It was about their agenda."

By the end of the twenty-fifth week, everyone knew Kathi wouldn't survive another week. Doctors performed an emergency C-section on January 7, 2004 at three p.m., and delivered two tiny babies. Paul Anthony weighed one pound twelve ounces; Sara Dorothy, named after Kathi's mother, weighed even less, at one pound nine ounces. The children were rushed to the neonatal intensive care unit, and Kathi returned to Intensive Care where she seemed to be doing well for two weeks.

"They were getting ready to move me to a regular floor when I went into respiratory failure. I had double pneumonia, and it just took over my lungs."

To save her life, the doctors put Kathi into a medically-induced coma and hooked her up to a ventilator. It would be two weeks before she opened her eyes again, and that was when Kathi saw her mother telling her everything was going to be fine. Although her mother had died three months earlier, so it had to be a vision, it was as if she were right before her daughter in flesh and blood. Kathi knew she could always trust whatever her mother told her. By the end of February, she was able to go home, but her babies remained hospitalized until June.

"The babies have a clean bill of health and are on their way to a normal life," she said, while cradling twenty-seven month old Sarah on her lap. "I'm always going to tell them that they were meant to be on this earth. They have great things to do."

As for Kathi: "My prognosis is to take care of myself. I'm already blazing trails. The average life expectancy for people with CF is thirty-five, and I'm going to be thirty-five in June."

She's not worried. The Claphams are people whose faith was strengthened, not weakened, by the trials they've endured. "The Lord comforts us and gives us the strength to do what we need to do to face it," she said. "The older you get, the more you realize that no one gets out of this life unscathed. We all have our hardships. We all have our crosses. Mine just came at a younger age than others—and that's OK."

Right now, she couldn't be happier. "I always wanted to be a mommy, and some days I just want to pinch myself because I can't believe I have these two little angels."

But she does believe, and every time she looks at them she's reminded of the most important lesson to be learned from experiences like hers. "Life is precious," she says. "It's just so precious."

—Susan Brinkmann

Susan Brinkmann's biography appears after her story "A Mother's Ultimate Sacrifice" in chapter one.

Never Say Never

Paul Walsh was seventeen years old when the car he was driving hit a tree on Chester Pike on an icy December night in 1983. One doctor described his head injuries as the equivalent of dropping an egg on a cement sidewalk. Not only was his skull shattered, every bone in his face was broken, and there was a tear in his brain. Doctors at Crozier-Chester Medical Center in Pennsylvania said he was irreversibly brain damaged and would never regain consciousness.

As the old saying goes, "Never say never." On Saturday, May 14, 2005, Paul Walsh received a bachelor's degree in liberal arts from Neumann College in Aston, Pennsylvania.

"I'd like to teach special education," said the thirty-eight-year-old graduate, who is employed as a full-time health care associate with Elwyn, Inc., a residential day program for the mentally disadvantaged. "I'd like to continue working with mentally disadvantaged persons."

Paul's recovery from massive head injuries in 1984 was "unexplained, on a purely medical and scientific basis," said one of the physicians who treated him, Michael Ryan, MD. In a written statement, Dr. Ryan said: "It is my feeling that without the help of the supernatural influence, Paul would today be dead or continue to be in a comatose state."

Although he recalls little of his four-month ordeal following the accident, his mother, Betty Walsh, remembers every detail, from the moment she got the phone call on the night of the accident.

"The nurse told me to come to the hospital right away," said the mother of ten. "It was hard to even recognize Paul. His face was so swollen, like a pumpkin, and totally wrapped in bandages. It didn't look very good, but he did recognize my voice because he moved when he heard me."

After ten hours of surgery the following day, during which Paul lost four-and-a-half times the amount of blood in his body, he was transferred to Crozier-Chester Medical Center, where his condition remained critical.

At first, he seemed to be improving and was even talking a little, but there was a suspicious fluid dripping out of his nose. Everyone thought he had a cold, and a month went by before doctors discovered the fluid wasn't from nasal congestion—it was spinal fluid. A cat scan revealed a tear in Paul's brain.

"That's when they realized he was worse off than they thought," Betty said.

Doctors tried to repair the tear, but the inside of Paul's head was too shattered. They resorted to draining the fluid with spinal taps and then a catheter, but Paul's condition continued to deteriorate. He began slipping in and out of consciousness.

Another cat scan revealed that he had hydrocephalus and the ventricles of his brain were filling with fluid. Doctors prepared him for emergency surgery to put a shunt in his head to drain the fluid when they discovered yet another serious complication —he had also developed spinal meningitis.

"At this point, there was no hope," Betty said. "The ventricles just kept filling with fluid, and it flattened the frontal lobe of his brain which one doctor told me was his whole personality."

Even though Paul was alive, in essence, he was gone.

"They kept saying 'you have to stop hoping. . . the way he is now is the way he's going to be. He is permanently and irreversibly brain damaged.'"

But Betty was not about to give up on her son. Even though she had nine other children at home, she felt like the woman in the Bible who had ten coins but lost one and couldn't stop searching until she found it.

"We just decided Paul needed a miracle," Betty said. "In the end, if Paul didn't get better, I would accept it, but in the meantime, I was really going to believe I could have a miracle, and I would at least pray with faith."

A woman from St. Madeline's gave her five prayer cards for people who were in the process of beatification and needed a miracle. Every day after Mass, she and her mother would go to the hospital and pray the Rosary over Paul, then say the five prayers. "Whenever I came to the Padre Pio prayer, Paul blessed himself, even though he was totally unconscious," Betty said.

Several people witnessed the phenomenon, including a few nurses. Betty decided to call a local group of Padre Pio devotees and report what was happening. They decided to send someone to the hospital with one of the gloves worn by Padre Pio over the bloody stigmata wounds in his hands. On Monday, March 12, Paul was blessed with the relic, and within days, one of his many serious ailments had miraculously vanished.

Betty called the group again and on April 6, 1984, the glove was once again brought to Paul and laid on his head.

"I knew immediately something had happened because it was like an electric shock went through him," Betty said. "He opened his eyes and looked around the room, very clear-eyed. Then he fell back into the coma again but I just knew something had happened."

She was right. The next day, when she returned to the hospital, she was shocked to find her son sitting in a chair and watching television. "He turned and said 'Hi, Mom.' The nurse rushed in and said 'He's been talking all day!' She said that when she called the neurosurgeon to tell him Paul Walsh was talking, the doctor said, 'It's not possible' and hung up on her."

But it was true. "They gave Paul another CT scan, and all the doctor kept saying was, 'I don't believe this. I don't believe this.' The frontal lobe of his brain wasn't smashed anymore."

Even more inexplicable was what happened days later, on Easter Sunday morning, when Paul and his roommate woke up to find a man standing at the foot of Paul's bed. Described as "an old priest in a brown robe," Paul thought it was Betty's brother, Charley, who bears a remarkable resemblance to Padre Pio.

"I remember being very certain that my Uncle Charley had been in to visit me," Paul said. "I did see him. He was very happy and smiled at me. And then he left the room."

Betty knew it couldn't have been Charley because he lives in Boston. She folded up a picture of Padre Pio, hiding the name, and showed it to Paul. "That's who visited me," he said. "Isn't that Uncle Charley?"

Weeks later, Paul Walsh walked out of Crozier-Chester Medical Center, completely healed.

If there was any doubt in their minds that Padre Pio interceded in Paul's healing, those doubts were put to rest a year after the accident when the family received an unexpected phone call from Bill Rose, who lived on the property where Paul hit the tree. Rose claimed he heard the crash the night of the accident and ran outside to find Paul laying on the ground with his face in a gutter. He knew the person was dying, and while someone called for an ambulance, he held Paul's head up out of the gutter and prayed for his soul.

"Within three to five minutes of your son's accident," he told Betty, "I dedicated him to Padre Pio."

To this day, Paul admits he still wonders "why me?" But that doesn't stop him from telling his story whenever he can. "I'm not doing this for myself," Paul said. "I want to give other people hope."

—Susan Brinkmann

Susan Brinkmann's biography appears after her story "A Mother's Ultimate Sacrifice" in chapter one.

Not What I Expected

"Daddy, I'm pregnant."

My unmarried daughter's announcement forever changed our family. No longer could "unplanned pregnancies" be spoken of in abstract terms as things that only happen in other families.

This was a flesh-and-blood reality that challenged us to renew our commitment to Christ and to our beloved firstborn daughter.

The early weeks of 2006 had some remarkable twists. On New Year's Day, hours before heading to Boston for my annual Ignatian retreat, my wife, Maureen, gave me the surprising yet wonderful news that she was pregnant. In February, we learned that she was carrying twins, but the joy turned to sadness as they died *in utero*. While Maureen was still recovering from her seventh and eighth miscarriages, we learned that we were to become grandparents for the first time. Over the course of the next several months, we had our ups and downs, but we've come to see God's providential love for our family in a more profound way.

Like all Catholic parents, we strive to provide all our children with a solid formation in the Christian faith. While parents might disagree on the exact amount of "sheltering" that needs to take place, clearly during our children's formative years it's crucial to maintain some control over their environment and activities. Yet when our children become adults in their own right, we can't exercise the same type of control. We desire good things for our adult children, but we can't make decisions for them.

Maureen jokingly says, "I hate free will," when our children make bad decisions. If it were only up to us, our children would always choose Christ and His Church, and they would always choose that which is morally good. Yet they are all on their own journey home to God, and we have to trust that the Lord in His time will lead them to repentance and conversion.

In this particular situation, we obviously could not undo the sins and bad choices our daughter had already made as an emancipated adult. We could not "control" the outcome, despite my conviction that "Father knows best" how to handle the situation. Maureen and I had to learn that what was needed was not control and coercion, but love, support, and wise guidance. Our daughter had to make her own difficult decisions, and that was scary.

In the weeks following this "announcement," my daughter was inclined to choose to place her child in an adoptive home. There is substantial irony in this, as Maureen and I have had several experiences of adoption as the adoptive parents.

As a matter of principle, I knew that adoption would be a good, loving decision. At the same time, what grandparent does not want to be part of their grandchild's life? I have frequently called upon grandparents in that situation to be generous in supporting adoption and not to lay undue pressure on the mother to keep their grandchild. The shoe was now on the other foot, and so I learned to have more compassion and understanding for grandparents who don't want to "lose" their grandchildren.

As it turned out, however, our daughter really wanted to keep the child and be a full-time mother. I continued to encourage adoption and lovingly set forth the harsh realities of single motherhood. Even more, we encouraged her in her spiritual and personal life to grow in faith and responsibility.

Over time, it became increasingly clear that her heart was set on keeping the child. We did our best to change gears and support this decision once it was firmly made. We invited her to move home rent-free so that she could be a full-time, nursing mom. She accepted.

Our daughter's moving home required an adjustment for everybody. After being on her own for several years, our twenty-six-year-old had to deal not only with meddling parents, but also five younger siblings ranging in age from fourteen to less than two, as well as her elderly grandmother. For our part, we had to get used to having an adult child in our midst, learning to balance parental concern with the desire to give her appropriate freedom and space.

Slowly but surely, our daughter blended back into our household. She grew accustomed to the rhythm of our daily life, from prayer time, family meals, and our busy homeschool day. I have commented in recent months that she has become, in some sense, more a part of our family than ever before. I'm very proud of her.

I realize that our society in general is too accepting of many evils that touch upon human sexuality and marriage and family life. All the same, as the pregnancy became more obvious to all the world, I was so grateful for the love and compassion showed us by the families in our parish and community. I don't recall hearing any judgmental or condemning remarks.

For myself, I remember a priest once saying that God's love, when focused on us sinners, shows itself as mercy. I want my daughter and all my family to come to a profound experience of God the Father's love for us. As a human father, I thought it was absolutely necessary to communicate to my daughter God's fatherly love and mercy. It surely wasn't the only thing, but it was the most important and God-like thing.

Similarly, I always want my family to see the Church as the family of God, our true and lasting home. Even though we might stray, the Good Shepherd goes looking for us, and there's great rejoicing in heaven when He finds us and brings us back into the fold. If my family is truly to be a "domestic church," or as Pope John Paul II called it, a "sanctuary of life," I felt it was imperative to extend an arm of assistance, welcome, and unconditional love to my daughter in her time of need.

On June 13, the feast of St. Anthony, little Alexandra ("Alex") Marina Terese Suprenant was born. It didn't take much for this beautiful little child of God to steal her grandpa's heart.

Our daughter and Alex are a gift to the entire family. They share a room with my daughter Mary Kate, who loves being their "roommate." Alex has two doting uncles (Samuel, five, and Raymond, two) who consider themselves her bodyguards.

Meanwhile, our daughter continues to grow and mature as a full-time mom. She has been a big help to her ailing grandmother, and she has become an indispensable part of our homeschooling operation. But beyond all that, her face looks happier than it has for many years.

We have traveled down roads we never dreamed we would tread, but God's grace has illuminated our path and brought us joy as we chart a new course in the life of our family.

—Leon Suprenant

Leon Suprenant is the director of outreach for Catholics United for the Faith (www.cuf.org). His book credits include the bestselling Catholic for a Reason *series, and he is author of dozens of published articles on living the Catholic faith. He is a board member of Catholic Athletes for Christ an also serves on the advisory board of the Institute on Religious Life, the Mater Ecclesiae Fund for Vocations, and Catholic Scripture Study.*

Changing the World, One Child at a Time

"Look at this," Jean Gaunt said, showing the Sunday newspaper to her husband, Tom. Their hometown paper, the *Indianapolis Star*, featured a story about nine siblings who were available for adoption. It was Mother's Day 1999, and the irony of the date did not escape Jean.

"I had not thought about adopting for quite a while, until I saw the article," says Jean. "One of the little girls, Samantha, was seven at the time, and she looked quite a bit like I did at that age. It really tugged on my heartstrings, especially since it was Mother's Day." Jean says that she rarely reads the newspaper and she just happened to read it on that day. If she hadn't seen the article, she never would have known about the kids.

When Tom read the article, he immediately began thinking about the kind of parents it would take to raise these kids. It needed to be an older, mature couple with a good married relationship. There couldn't be any other children in the home because the needs of these nine would overrun the needs of any other kids. "Who do I know like that?" Tom had wondered out loud. It seemed like no one, but the question just kept coming back to them.

Tom and Jean Gaunt already had six children—four of them were their biological children, and two of them were adopted on previous occasions. Their older children were grown and out of the house. They had been empty nesters for the past three years. Jean had always dreamed of owning a bed and breakfast and nine months before, they had finally purchased their dream home. Jean dreamed of their bed and breakfast, but God had other plans for their new home.

A few weeks later, while Tom and Jean were still considering the adoption, they attended a Billy Graham seminar. "Billy Graham pointed out to us in the audience and talked about how people have to get out of their comfort zones and make a difference in their communities. We left that night convinced that this was something God wanted us to do," says Tom.

These nine siblings ranged in age from eighteen months to fifteen years. They had been the victims of almost unimaginable abuse at the hands of their stepfather, and they desperately needed a fresh start with a loving family.

The Gaunts decided to become that family.

Tom and Jean knew they were taking on a challenge. Nine kids would be tough for anyone, but *these* nine children were going to be especially challenging.

Several of the children had special needs, including autism and other developmental delays. Many of the kids suffered from Reactive Attachment Disorder, an emotional result of the abuse they endured. This disorder makes it difficult for children to trust others and make emotional attachments.

At the time Tom and Jean adopted them, the children were still mourning the loss of their tenth sibling, a brother named Kyle. Kyle, who was twelve at the time of his death, had always promised his brothers and sisters that he would find a way to help them escape their life of abuse, and through his death, he fulfilled that promise. When Kyle's body was found on the banks of the White River, the children were immediately removed from their home and placed in foster care. The media picked up the story, and Tom and Jean learned of the children's plight. Tom and Jean feel that they actually adopted ten children, rather than nine, and in their hearts, Kyle is their son as well. The family added the last name "Gaunt" to Kyle's headstone, and they take the children to his gravesite often.

It took the children several years to trust Tom and Jean. Jean says that for years the children would ask her if they were going to eat dinner that night. Not *what* they would eat, but *if* they would eat.

"We've had lots of therapy," says Tom. "At first, all Jean did was transport the kids to and from therapy. In the beginning, we spent thirty hours a week, but after about three years, it dropped off." They are down to only weekly sessions now so the family takes karate as a way to spend time together.

Tom and Jean's message is one of permanency. Children must have a safe, permanent place to grow up. "Our world, our society is no better than the children we raise into it," says Tom. "Every time a child is moved, it creates another shell, another layer of padding that has to be broken through. There is more emotional damage, more distrust.

"When a child is removed from their birth home, they are unplugged. They lose everything, their home, their school, their family, their toys and clothes, and their pets. They are completely unplugged," says Tom. "Then they are brought into another family. Really the job of the adoptive family is to rebuild those connections."

Jean goes on to say, "These kids must have adults that they can count on to be there. Merely surviving is not enough. Kids need a place to thrive."

And thrive these children have. The oldest daughter, Stephanie, recently graduated from high school. She was the first one in her family to accomplish that. She is now taking college courses at a nearby university. The younger children are doing well in school.

The Gaunts admit that there are days when they wonder if they did the right thing.

"Your commitment overrides your feelings on those days," says Jean. "For every day that I question what I did, there are a million days when I know exactly why I did it," Tom adds.

Right now, there are nearly half a million children in our nation who are waiting to be adopted. Jean likens what she and Tom have done to the story about the man who is throwing a beached starfish back into the ocean. When someone tells him that he'll never reach all of them, he throws back another starfish and answers, "But it makes a huge difference to that one." Tom and Jean know that they have made a difference in the lives of these nine children.

Tom and Jean speak to church groups through their adoption ministry. They travel to various churches, show their son's film, and tell their story. They counsel other families who have adopted or are considering it.

"As a country, and as people, we've got to commit to our children," insists Jean. "God gives children to people in different ways. We're just ordinary people who decided to act."

"We've got some homemade children and some hand picked children," say the Gaunts, and they wouldn't have it any other way.

—Diane Sonntag

Diane Sonntag is an elementary school teacher and freelance writer in Indiana. She has written for a variety of print and online publications. She can be reached at DianeSonntag@comcast.net. The Gaunts' oldest biological son made an award-winning documentary based on the adoption called A Place Called Home: An Adoption Story. *The film was on PBS in January 2006. For more information about the film, visit www.aplacecalledhome.info.*

If I Could Just Phone Home

While saying my prayers one night just before 11:00, I was praying for comfort for the families of two relatively young men who had recently died. Both were dedicated physicians. Both were men of faith. As I pondered their passing, I was fervently wishing that I could somehow comfort their families, either by figuring out a good reason that God would have called them home, or by giving them a glimpse of God's promise:

"No eye has seen, nor ear heard, nor the heart of man conceived, what God has prepared for those who love him" (1 Corinthians 2:8).

Suddenly, I remembered the time when my oldest son, Jerome, was given the opportunity to go to Mexico for two weeks with one of our priests and several boys from our local Catholic high school. He was fifteen at the time, and I had never "let him out of my pocket" so to speak. I am a stay-at-home mom, very cautious where my children are concerned. I've never been to another country, so needless to say, my view of Mexico was skewed by television. I was picturing banditos and constant drug busts and my son being unjustly arrested by the Mexican police. I know it sounds silly; it was, but it was hard to let go. I prayed for peace and for his safety and finally along with my husband, said yes.

It was a tearful day when he left. I repeatedly told God that I was sorry for crying over a two-week trip to Mexico, but I suppose there was more to my tears than just worry. I think it was the whole "he's growing up" thing. Anyway, I knew I was going to miss him.

The very next night after he left, the priest had all the boys phone home. I'll never forget that call. Jerome was so excited, he couldn't talk fast enough:

"Mom, you should see the *ocean*! It is so *beautiful* here! Mom, you should *taste* the food! We are living with this little

Mexican woman who makes us *fresh* tortillas and real refried beans! Mom, you should see the all the flowers! You would love them! The weather is so perfect here! I am having so much fun!"

He went on and on and on. The joy in his voice alone was enough to put a stopper in my tear ducts! When I replaced the receiver I thought to myself, how could I possibly be sad that he is gone when he is so happy? It was at that very moment that a thought came to me. It's too bad that our loved ones can't "phone home" from Heaven. If they could just tell us how happy they are, then our pain would be greatly reduced.

As I lay in bed remembering that specific memory, I realized that maybe I could write a song about "phoning home." Though it was late, I sprung out of bed and went to the computer. I knew from experience that when God calls me to write something, it would come out very quickly. It did. I knew it was from God and I cried. I always feel so humbled and in awe at His ability to work through me.

There were two problems that suddenly arose regarding this new song, "If I Could Just Phone Home." One was that I had just completed the long and costly process of recording my second CD, *Walk On*, not to mention that I needed to get it submitted for printing soon so that I could have it in time for Christmas deadlines. The second problem was cost. I just didn't think I could swing payment for another song. I decided to leave it in God's hands by praying, "Okay, God. If this is really Your will that I add this song to my CD at this late date, then please help me write the music tomorrow, and let it flow quickly."

He did. The music came very easily, and so with joy, I added the song to the CD.

Needless to say, however, I had never really gotten very much feedback from that particular song. It was strange. I couldn't imagine that something that was "so from God" hadn't had a bigger impact than it did. I have learned, however, that we don't always see the outcome of the seeds we have planted.

Recently, a woman whose relatives live in the apartment building with my mother, lost her seventeen-year-old autistic son, Alex. I had the opportunity to meet him several times and he was just a big sweetheart. Always smiling. Always a kind word.

For some unknown reason, he just fell over and was gone instantly. A heart attack or aneurism was suspected. My own heart just ached for his family, and though I didn't know the mother well, I kept thinking that I would like to give her a copy of the song, "If I Could Just Phone Home." I kept putting it off, thinking it was too soon. Another time I would think about it and realize I didn't have her address. There were several times the idea would pop up and I would say to myself, *I've got to get that song to Alex's mother!*

One morning after Mass, I stopped by to see my mother, and on the way, thought of taking the song over. I dismissed the thought when I realized that there was probably very little chance of seeing Alex's mother that day, since I had only met her there a couple of times.

Sure enough, she walked into the apartment building. I excused myself from the group of residents who were sitting in the lobby having coffee and ran home to get it. I quickly printed off a copy of the words and headed back over to catch her before she left.

I wasn't even sure of her name, so I felt a little awkward. As I handed her the CD and the folded up words, I told her how sorry I was to hear of her son's passing and what a good young man she had raised. Tears filled her eyes as she thanked me and began talking about her pain.

Then she said something I will never forget. She patted her shirt pocket that held her cell phone and sadly said, "My phone used to ring all the time. I used to get calls many times a day from Alex. He would call me to tell me little things, like what he was eating ... and now, my phone never rings."

I could not believe my ears. I had not told her the name of the song. Tears welled up in my eyes as I marveled at God's goodness and mercy. I had just handed her a song entitled, "If I Could Just Phone Home". Through God's grace, this hurting mother, and good Christian woman, was going to get her phone call after all.

—Elizabeth Schmeidler

Elizabeth Schmeidler's biography appears after her story "Just Do It!" in chapter one.

Escape from Tower Two

The clock had just passed 9:00 on the morning of September 11 when the phone rang in Stanley Praimnath's office in the South Tower of the World Trade Center. About fiftteen minutes earlier, Praimnath, an assistant vice president for Fuji Bank, had taken the express elevator down to the lobby after hearing of "an incident" at the North Tower. But when he got there, security guards assured him that everything was okay and advised him to return to his office.

Back on the eighty-first floor, the offices were still mostly empty. He picked up his ringing phone. "Are you watching the news?" asked a woman in Fuji Bank's Chicago office. "Are you all right?" "I'm fine," Praimnath said, wondering why she had called.

Just then, he turned to gaze out the window toward the Statue of Liberty, like he had done so many times before. But this time, the breathtaking view was disrupted by the surreal sight of a low-flying commercial jet. And it was headed straight for the tower!

Screaming, Praimnath dropped the phone in mid-sentence and dove to the floor. Curling under his desk in a fetal position, he began talking to God.

"Lord, help me!" He continued to pray desperately, as a hard whine filled the air; it sounded like a steel cage being ripped to shreds.

Praimnath had no idea that the earlier "incident" had been another jetliner smashing into the North Tower. When United Airlines Flight 175 crashed into his building, all he knew was that this might be his final day.

At first Praimnath didn't even know the plane had exploded or that the building was on fire. Looking outside, he saw a blue flame dancing on one wing and thought it might ignite the building. "Had I known the truth, I probably would have panicked more," he says now.

Although those initial moments remain a blur, when he finally stood up, the office looked like a war zone. Equipment lay scattered about like matchsticks. Rubble covered the floor. Dust filled the air, as if someone had ripped open bags of cement and tossed them skyward.

Clawing across mounds of debris, everything he climbed on collapsed. Soon cuts and bruises covered his body. His white shirt had disappeared.

"Lord, I have to go home to my family," he wheezed. "I have to see my daughters."

Just then he saw a light poking through the darkness. Amazed that someone had appeared on his floor with a flashlight, he thought, *This is my guardian angel! The Lord sent somebody to help me!*

"I see the light! I see the light!" he screamed.

"Come toward the light," said an unseen voice. "I'm here to help you."

But as Praimnath pushed on, another wall tumbled down. Shielding his face with his right hand, he winced when a nail embedded itself in his palm. When he told his rescuer what had happened, the man urged, "Bite it out. Suck the blood. Spit it out."

"I can't," he said. Fatigue overwhelmed him. The smell of jet fuel filled the air. Somehow, he summoned the strength to grab the nail. When blood spurted, he wiped it off on his tattered undershirt. When he got closer to the light, though, another fallen wall blocked his path. Electrical circuits and wires dangled from the exposed ceiling above. The voice told him to climb over the debris, but he felt too tired. Finally, Praimnath asked the man if he believed in Christ. When the voice answered affirmatively, he suggested they pray. Afterwards, the 5-foot-9 karate student felt strength surging through him. Punching away at the wall, he kept driving dents deeper until the other man exclaimed, "I can see your hand!"

Praimnath's "guardian angel" was Brian Clark, an executive at a brokerage firm three floors above him. After Clark pulled him through the wall, they hugged quickly and darted into the stairwell. Fortunately, the tower's walls were coated with a luminous paint that had been applied after an earlier terrorist bombing in 1993.

Fear and anxiety filled Praimnath as they raced down the stairs. Sagging with exhaustion, he locked arms with Clark. He remembers telling him, "You're my guardian angel, who the Lord sent to help me."

"I was rambling on," Praimnath recalls. "I never would have made it out were it not for this man." When they finally reached the concourse at the mezzanine level, some firemen asked if there were others. When we replied, "Yes," they pushed past in a frantic ascent.

The two businessmen looked around at a gruesome scene. Shards of glass fell from above. Miscellaneous body parts lay scattered about. Flaming debris darted through the air.

Looking at one of his rubber-soled shoes, Praimnath declared, "These things are going to melt." Seeing water cascading down the steps, Praimnath, Clark, and others stood under the sprinkler system and drenched themselves before fleeing the building. Two blocks later, they stopped outside historic Trinity Church and grasped its gates. Soon, they watched in horror as the South Tower wobbled and shook ominously. Flares of smoky debris shot from the building like Roman candles. Then, finally, the South Tower—the building in which Praimnath had just stood minutes earlier— began to fall upon itself. Only forty-seven minutes had passed between the plane's impact and the tower's collapse.

Today, Praimnath, forty-five, is filled with a profound mixture of awe and gratitude when he considers the fact that he is a September 11 survivor. "I believe the Lord's hand saved me that day," he says. "There is no other way to explain it."

A year after the hijackings that claimed thousands of lives and changed the course of history, the British Guyana native still wrestles with the question of why he made it out alive when so many others didn't. He can only surmise that, for reasons only God knows, it wasn't his day to leave this earth. What he's certain about, however, is that God still has work for him to do. "My Lord has some unfinished tasks for me," he says softly. And he's sure that this work is not just as a loan operations officer for Fuji Bank, but as a husband, a father of two young girls, and the Sunday school superintendent of his church.

Most of all, Praimnath wants to offer himself as a living witness to God's power to save. The story of his miraculous escape from the World Trade Center has inspired many people.

Praimnath, who came to America in 1981, is still saddened by the thousands of lives that were wiped out on 9/11, and he knows that thousands continue to grieve the loss of loved ones. His heart breaks for the families of the twenty-three people from his office who were killed. He realizes he'll never be able to completely shake the horrific images, smells, and sensations that overwhelmed his senses that morning. Still, he knows that his faith was strengthened because of that day. In a sense, he was raised from the dead, called out from the darkness. And he rejoices that he's alive today to tell the story at churches, on television, and to anyone who wants to hear it.

Says Praimnath, "The people who used to not want to hear anything about the Lord are now coming to me and saying, 'Stan, tell me about your God.'" Praimnath admits that he's been on a spiritual high since 9/11, and he hopes that passion doesn't wane.

"I took the tattered clothes I was wearing on that day, put them in a box, and wrote DELIVERANCE all over it," he says. "I told my wife, 'If ever I get [spiritually] cold, I want you to bring this box to me, open it up, and show me what the Lord brought me up from.'"

—Ken Walker

A freelance writer from Huntington, West Virginia, Ken Walker has written more than 2,500 magazine and newspaper articles during his career. He has also co-authored or contributed to more than a dozen books and devotionals. Among his awards are the "Pacesetter" award given at the nation's largest Christian writer's conference and one for in-depth reporting from the Florida Magazine Association.

Momma Never Gave Up

My son Randy was born with a special brain defect from lack of oxygen in the birth process. In the early days it was called "minimal brain dysfunction," which some psychologist's refer to as a "Racing Brain syndrome." (The brain fires commands so fast that a person cannot always sort them out.)

I always knew my son was special but worried constantly about how to teach him to put on the brakes. By the age of six, he had already gained a reputation as being incorrigible and a holy terror. Instead of sitting quietly and learning like other children, he rushed headlong into everything. When he did not understand something, he started acting out. His kindergarten teacher told me she was letting him advance to first grade so she would not have to see him back in her classroom.

After another dismal school year in first grade, my husband and I took him out of public school and enrolled him in the Catholic school. In the beginning, his new school didn't quite know what to do, either, but they took a real interest. By the time Randy was in second grade, he had been held back twice. Not because he was unable to learn, but because he did not learn things in the usual classroom setting. He needed one-on-one teaching to be able to slow down and concentrate. In second grade (the second time around), he was blessed with a wonderful teacher. She was very interested in the field of special education, which had discovered this particular problem in some children. It was a whole new frontier in education, back then.

For the next few years he attended a special clinic for children who were gifted, and he excelled. Children diagnosed with attention deficit, as Randy was, are usually above the learning curve. They just learn differently. Randy was also diagnosed with dyslexia. Back in the early days of special ed, it was hunt and peck for a method that worked to overcome the reading barriers. Once he got the special help he needed, things got much better. Until, that is, the teen years hit.

Most teenagers rebel somewhat, but his "racing brain" kicked into high gear. My husband had a re-occurrence of his cancer, and it turned our world up side down. Randy quickly distanced himself from the nightmare of cancer and illness. For Randy, that meant he was angry and frustrated. The doctors had diagnosed my husband's cancer as hereditary and found through testing, that all of our children had inherited the propensity. From that day onward, Randy traveled on a path of destruction. Drugs were readily available in his high school, and Randy latched onto them.

I started taking him to school myself when he was on report for major truancy. But before I even turned the corner, Randy was out the backdoor heading off to get his latest fix. By age eighteen, he had been suspended so many times he had missed most of the school year. He finally dropped out of school and began selling drugs. By the age of twenty, Randy was completely out of control. One day the police came to the house with a search warrant as they suspected Randy was a drug dealer. They found nothing and left. Randy thought he had fooled everyone, but the smug look on his face told me he was guilty. After the police left, I turned the house upside down and found his stash and contact book in the rafters of the basement. I don't think I ever felt such utter hopelessness as I did on that day. When I confronted him with the evidence, he broke down for the first time in many years and cried: "Momma, I don't know why I do such stupid things. I promise to try harder to be in control. I promise I will not do it again."

My mother's heart wanted to believe him, but deep down, I knew better. I had to draw courage and strength in prayer. After hours of tears and praying, I knew God would not just reach down and fix the problem. He expected me to administer

some "tough love." I trusted God to give me the grace needed at
the proper time.

Randy was shocked when I told him to get in the car—we
were going to the police station so he could turn himself in. I
assured him the only way to change was to take responsibility. I
said, "It will take time to change, and it won't be easy. First you
have to take responsibility for your actions."

Randy got off with a slap on the wrist but was soon caught
in a drug sting operation when a "narc" turned him in. I was
again there to the rescue—at least at first. My husband and I
paid the bail and Randy came home promising to change. By
the next day, he had broken his agreement and was arrested
once more.

This time, I hired a lawyer who worked with troubled
youth. Mr. McGee was known for taking cases and working
with them. He would take no guff, but his young clients always
knew he was there for them. Mr. McGee agreed with my
husband and I when we insisted that the judge give him some
jail time. Randy served six months in the county jail. Time
in a big-city jail was not a walk in the park. Randy was scared
straight by that experience and never took or sold drugs again.
But that was not the end of his self-destructive ways. By the time
he got out of jail, Randy was twenty-one, and alcohol became
his drug of choice. He quickly became an alcoholic bum.

Randy continued to wander aimlessly through life for the
next few years. I continued to pray and cry and trust that God
would help my son. I knew Randy was very ill. When he ran
out of money, he slept in the back of a garbage truck parked in
the City dump or crashed under a tree in the park. Randy kept
jobs just long enough to get money to buy more booze and party.
When he was too sick to go it alone, he crawled back home to
dry out once again.

By the time Randy was twenty-five, he still kept promising us
that he would change, but he continued his destructive lifestyle.

He returned home one last time after a week of binge drinking. When Randy arrived, I had his bags packed and waiting. I gave him a hug, and said: "Get in the car. I am taking you to the life you seem to want so much." The destination was a fleabag motel charging twenty-five dollars a week. I paid his rent for the first month and wished him well. With tears in my eyes, I quietly whispered: "I love you forever, but I will not stand by and watch you destroy yourself. Call me when you're ready to get the help you need. In the meantime, just know, God has great plans for you. He loves you even more than I do." As I drove away from that horrible place, I could barely keep from turning around and bringing him home again. I felt as though I would surely die from a broken heart.

By Christmas of that year, Randy had burned himself out once again. He was sick, broke, and out of work. Randy called and asked if he could come home. It broke my heart further to have to say "No, son. I love you forever, but I will not allow you to come home just to get well and continue destroying yourself." Instead, I went to his motel, paid his rent for the month, and nursed him back to health. When he was strong enough, I drove him around to look for work once again.

I believe it was in that terrible dirty motel that he finally began to seek God. For years, he had ridiculed anyone who brought up God. But that day in the depths of despair, I think Randy realized that God was his only hope. He finally accepted my assurance that "God loved him." His anger at God disappeared. Finally, Randy was ready to change, although it did not happen overnight.

An older man named George, who had a carpet-cleaning business, hired Randy when no one else would. He treated Randy like a son and taught him the business. After a year, when he was ready to retire, he helped Randy start his own carpet cleaning business. George was an earthly kind of angel. Working with George, Randy still was drinking but had slowed it down to weekends only. George kept him clean and sober throughout the work week.

Randy continued to fight the battle of alcoholism for a few more years, but the important thing was that he *was* fighting. Even though he struggled with reading, he faithfully read the Bible each day. Slowly but surely, Randy began to overcome his frustrations. One day, I told him that Sr. Teresa of Calcutta and her nun's in India had a special prayer line to God. I put Randy on their prayer list.

During the Labor Day weekend of September 1997 though, at the age of thirty-two, Randy was busy partying once again. On September 5, he woke up so sick from drinking, I thought he would die. But within a short time, he felt completely well. From that moment on he could no longer bear the smell or taste of alcohol. As this was the day that Mother Teresa of Calcutta died, I think her intercession before the throne of God saved my son. Since that time, he has built up his own business, and life has finally settled down. He is a wonderful man, and I am very proud of him.

Randy asked me recently why I never gave up on him. I just smiled and answered: "God never gives up on any of His children. He loves you for the person He created you to be." I could never give up on my son. God carried us both through this experience for a purpose. Many rough stones become precious gems only after getting rolled and tumbled, cut and polished. After many rough years, Randy, my precious son, has become a gem.

—Christine Trollinger

Christine Trollinger biography appears after her story "Lucy's Star" in chapter two.

The Most Important Thing Is Love

If you had met my son Josh, you would have loved him. Everyone did. But then, he always loved everyone. At his funeral, the church overflowed with people from across the country. They came from California, Massachusettes, New York, Nebraska, and Texas. An entire family from the country of Libya tried frantically to fly here but could not get through the red tape of international travel fast enough.

For a man who lived a mere twenty-six years, Josh had touched the lives of so many. He was truly a superstar like none I've ever known. But that is not what drew so many people to Bismarck, North Dakota, to pay their final respects. "Josh was brilliant," one of his professors from the Massachusettes of Technology (MIT) stated at his funeral. "Even for MIT, Josh was brilliant. But there are a lot of brilliant students at MIT. We loved Josh because he was good and he loved everyone."

Losing my beloved son—my intellectual soul mate—took away a spark in my heart that can never be replaced. At the time, I thought it would kill my own spirit. I was furious at God for snatching away such a gift that had filled my life with so much joy. But thanks to the wisdom of my wife, I've been able to see our loss in a different way. And rather than destroy me, that spark put there by Josh has lit a flame in me that will burn forever.

As a teenager, I was too restless for the demands of college. It was the seventies, and my hair was long enough to be tucked into my belt. I found a job in a unisex clothing boutique in a mall in St. Charles, Missouri. When I met Cathy, who worked at another store in the mall, sparks flew. Our romance began in April of 1974, and we married six months later, out first child already on the way. I was nineteen and Cathy, eighteen. At the wedding, there were quite a few relatives speaking in hushed tones, questioning my suitability as a husband.

Our daughter Angela was born in 1975 and twenty-two months later Josh came along. Cathy and I were back-to-nature hippies with a decidedly conservative bent. God, church, a stay-at-home mom, and bread-winner dad meshed in with our counter-culture lifestyle. We had headed out to Montana and I partnered with a friend to build custom log homes in a remote area of northwest Montana, amid thick pine forests and Rocky Mountains vistas. Unfortunately, the roller coaster economy of the area often left us with barely enough money to eat. During the dry times, I commiserated with Cathy that I should have gotten a college degree.

"Either do something or shut up about it," my usually sweet-natured wife told me. "Crying about it isn't going to help anyone."

Cathy was right. I did not want to live a life of regrets at what could have been. My hair was short by now, thanks to losing a big contract due to my appearance, and I was ready to trade our tenuous lifestyle for something more conventional.

We moved to Oklahoma in the fall of 1982 where Cathy and I took part-time jobs and started college together. In between work and school, I delighted in my family. As I watched Angela and Josh grow, I often stepped back in awe that God had given me two such bright and precious souls. I've always loved numbers so I often used them to play with my children. Converting temperatures from the Celsius to Fahrenheit scale and other math games were fun competitions for Angela and Josh when they were just five and seven. It was around this time, that Josh began to really amaze us with his intellectual abilities. Sitting in the grocery cart one afternoon, Cathy handed him items as they went through the store. With the cart half full, Josh looked at the last can she handed him, paused just a moment and then informed her of how much the total was thus far.

"What?" Cathy asked, confused as to what Josh was getting at. He repeated the amount and told her he had been adding everything up for her. It turned out that Josh was exactly right. After that, he made it his job to keep track of the totals so his mom would know how much money was left to spend.

While I was attending college, it was the only time in our married life that Cathy and I decided it would be a bad time to have more children. Even so, when Angela was nine and Josh seven, Roseanne and Lea were conceived one right after the other. Cathy found house cleaning jobs that allowed her to bring the girls so they could stay together. I plowed ahead and earned my masters in geophysics and got a good job right way. By the time the children ranged in age from fifteen to four, I took a job in North Dakota as a hydrologist with the U.S. Geological Survey.

I chose a rural home so the kids would be each other's best friends. Josh often played with his little sisters and taught them algebra and geometry when they were still in grade school. I don't think Rose and Lea were particularly interested in math, but if it meant spending time with their big brother, they wanted in on it.

As Josh made his way through the teen years, he developed deep friendships easily with both kids and adults. In spite of getting straight A's and scoring 99% on every standardized test he ever took, Josh was humble. Never did he lord his superior intellect or accomplishments or even appear to acknowledge it.

While still in high school, Josh set his sights on attending MIT for college. He was easily accepted and got a masters in computer science and electrical engineering. While there, he designed a course in computer operating systems which is still taught there and at other universities across the country. Josh did not go straight through, however. He and a couple friends started a software company. On paper, the company was worth millions. Josh called once and chuckled with me that even through he was meeting with lawyers and business men, talking about millions of dollars, he was riding a fifteen dollar bike and wearing thrift store clothing worth no more than a dollar an item. Josh wanted to return to school, so the relinquished his share of the company. Money did not mean much to him. As a matter of fact, the less he owned the happier he was.

Josh was fluent in German, Arabic, and Spanish, and knew a good amount of Italian. During one of his breaks from school, he traveled throughout Europe and delighted in playing the American tourist only to surprise the locals when he started speaking their language fluently. Angela joined him once for a two-week trip to Morocco. It was there that she came to understand her brother's love of languages. It was not just to make travel easier. It was a way for Josh to truly get to know people, such as the family in Libya who welcomed him into their home and treated him like one of their own.

Josh and I talked by phone weekly. Our deep conversations could travel the universe in content ranging from physics and computers to my newspaper column. One of the best pieces of advice on my opinion column came from Josh. "Just because you can stomp on people doesn't mean you should," he told me. "If you want people to listen, you first need to understand what they fear, *then* persuade them."

Josh was back at MIT half-way through a Ph.D. when I called him one day to ask for suggestions to deal with Lea who was in the midst of teenage rebellion. "Let me think about it," Josh told me. A short time later he called back. "I'm taking her with me to Barcelona, Spain for the summer and we are going to learn Spanish," he informed me. "I set aside a savings from my software company's retirement fund when I left, which I can use for this." At the time, he was in the middle of his dissertation, co-authoring three other papers and tutoring underprivileged children in mathematics.

Later, when I spoke with one of his co-authors, I asked if he was surprised that Josh put everything on hold to help his sister.

"No," he had replied. "It did not surprise me that he did that for his sister because Josh would have done that for anyone."

When they returned, Lea was invigorated with goals and determination. Josh had taken a job with a software company in California to earn money to return to school. He invited Lea to drive out with him to explore possibilities for her college. Since he had taken trips with two of his sister's before leaving, he promised Roseanne that they would go to Europe together the following summer. It was New Year's Day when Josh and Lea left.

The following morning, the phone rang while I ate breakfast. "I'm calling from the Rock Springs, Wyoming hospital. We need permission to treat your daughter Lea for injuries from an automobile accident she was in this morning. We don't think she was hurt badly but we need permission to treat her."

"What?" I cried incredulous, "What happened?" When Lea came to the phone, she was crying and apologizing.

"I'm so sorry Dad, I'm so sorry," she cried.

"How is Josh," I asked.

No one knew. Josh had not regained consciousness yet.

It was snowing and Lea was driving on Interstate 80 in Wyoming. A semi-truck passed and caused a complete white-out. Lea slowed, waiting for visibility to return, when they were hit from behind by another truck. It took almost two hours for rescue workers to cut them out of their mangled car. "We are taking him in for an MRI now," I was told.

My brain kicked into autopilot, and within the hour, I arranged a flight from Bismarck to Wyoming for the rest of our family. Gripped by fear and helplessness we prayed desperately to God to take care of our beloved Josh. As I went through airport security, my cell phone rang. It was the doctor. "Josh stopped breathing on his own," he told me solemnly. "When people are unconscious that long and can't breathe on their own, they don't come back. I'm sorry," he said.

All hope drained from within me. Josh was gone. I looked at the pain in eyes of my family and said nothing. If I told them now, there would be an hysterical scene on the plane. We walked to our seats like zombies and everyone kept praying.

Lea had only minor injuries and met us, crying, at the hospital entrance. We were taken to Josh's room, where the doctor explained he was gone. We were asked about organ donation and told that, the longer they waited, the less likely his organs could help others.

We looked at our Josh who was hooked up to a ventilator to keep his organs from deteriorating before they could be donated. Other than a bandage at the top of his head, he looked fine, as if he were just sleeping and would open his eyes any minute. Yet, my son was no longer there, his soul had left this world. We all broke down crying. Even though I already knew the truth, hearing it out loud cut through my heart. This could not be happening to us. As a father, I had always been able to step in and help my children. I never dreamed such crushing pain existed in this world.

Roseanne, refused to accept that her brother was gone. "No," she sobbed. "We can pray him back. Let's all pray."

We touched Josh and held his hand and told him how much we loved him. Then, we all held each other tightly and wailed hysterically. After a time, a social worker took us into a room to talk about organ donation.

"He's going to be all right, " Rosanne cried.

"No, Rose," I choked out the words. "He's gone. We need to accept reality. Josh had on his driver's license that he wanted to be an organ donor. He would be the first one to want others to benefit."

We clung to each other and returned to Josh's room to cry and touch him. The hospital had arranged for us to stay in a room at a hospitality house across the street. His organs would be removed in the morning. Although we had gone back several times to say our good-byes, I went one last time by myself.

Tears poured down my face as I gripped his hand for the last time. "My baby boy, my beautiful baby boy," I sobbed. "I love you so much." I could not imagine a world without him.

In our room, we had put the mattresses on the floor so we could remain close to one another in our pain. As the four of us talked about Josh, it occurred to me that in twenty-six years of being his father, I had never once felt angry at him. "Has anyone ever been angry at Josh?" I asked. No one ever had. I added up all our time lived of knowing Josh—113 years. "We've known him for 113 years, and in all that time, no one was ever mad at him," I realized. I asked if anyone ever remembered him being unkind, or ever lying or bragging. There was never a time.

Although we all knew Josh was an incredible human being, not until that moment did we truly understand the immensity of the life he had lived. I felt the pain of losing him would overwhelm me. "Why would God do this?" I asked Cathy in anger. "How can this be?"

Cathy's eyes were swollen from crying. "Steve," she said, her voice shaking. "We can't be angry. Think of the gift God us for twenty-six years. We've talked about all the good things about Josh. Look at what we've had."

In an instant, Cathy's words cut through my anger. "God does not want us to be thankful *for* everything, he wants us to be thankful *in* all things. Then you will look up instead of down."

I knew that we had instilled our love of God in Josh, but I realized then that Cathy's gentle heart had been imparted so powerfully upon Josh.

"I need to be more like Josh," I stammered.

"No," Cathy said. "You need to be more like Christ, and then you will be more like Josh."

Cathy's words had touched my heart and soul. We were blessed with Josh as we were blessed with all our children. The

pain did not end, for I will always miss Josh. I would live under
a highway bridge and never have another penny for the rest of
my life if I could spend just five more minutes with Josh. But
there is no anger; only acceptance.

In my fifty-two years of life, my dreams have always
contained just bits and pieces of irrelevant junk, expect for one.
Three weeks after losing Josh, I dreamt he and I were walking
around in the woods. I moved some sticks out of the way so we
could sit. He looked at me and said: "Hey, Dad. I died in that
car accident, but I'm really happy helping other people now." I
awoke knowing that Josh had truly been with me.

Death holds no fear for me now. Through Josh, I have come
to a deeper understanding of both life and death. We must
accept how tenuous our mortal existence is, and in the end, it is
not what you have acquired or accomplished in life that really
counts, but how much you have loved and are loved.

—Steve Cates

*Steve Cates is a consulting geophysicist. He is the chairman of the board of the
North Dakota Family Alliance, served as North Dakota commissioner since
1992 to the Education Commission of the States, and is a past President of the
North Dakota Geological Society. Steve is also the publisher of the monthly*
Dakota Beacon *magazine.*

Running the Good Race

When we accepted Joash, an AIDS orphan from Kenya into our home, we had expected it would be as successful as it had been with his older brother, Calvin. Instead, my husband Mark and I now sat across from Joash, prepared to tell him it was more than we could handle. Already, I had begun looking for an alternative home. Much prayer and soul searching had gone into his placement with us, but in the end, it seemed we could not properly meet the needs of everyone in our family of ten children.

Not until we started having challenges, did our missionary friend in Kenya, Evan, the one who had originally asked us to take Joash in, admit that he was aware of some of the problems. "I believed that if I put him with a good family, he would come around," confessed Evan in an email. "Things worked out so well with Calvin." Our emails had kept Evan posted on Joash. "Just send him back," Evan directed. "You've tried your best."

Calvin was then a senior at St. Mary's High School. He was on the National Society and had received a four-year academic scholarship for college. He had been with our family for three years. His coming to us was an amazing answer to his seemingly impossible prayer. Years earlier, Calvin had read a book about a boy who left Kenya to go to school in the United States. "Maybe I could go there someday," Calvin dreamed.

"Dear God," he began praying, "Please let me go to the United States." Calvin prayed with the faith of a child, even though at thirteen, his childhood had been lost long ago. Both his parents had died of AIDS, leaving Rogers, fifteen, Calvin, eleven, and Joash, eight, among Kenya's 650,000 AIDS orphans.

When Calvin revealed his prayer to his older brother and an aunt, he was laughed at but he kept praying.

Then, Evan Beauchamp came to Calvin's school as a missionary for the diocese of Bismarck, North Dakota. He learned of the boys' hardships and invited Calvin to live with him during the week and then return to help his brothers on weekends. Calvin kept asking Evan to take him back to the United States. Since Evan was seventy, he knew the U.S. State Department would never agree to such a scenario.

When Evan was back in the United States for sabbatical, he asked Mark and me if we would take Calvin in. After prayers of discernment and an agreement of financial support from two other couples, we agreed to do so. We obtained legal guardianship for Calvin and although there had been adjustments on both sides, Calvin became a much-loved member of our family. He and my son Tyler, only a month apart in age, were especially close.

A year later, Chuck and Tip Reichert, one of the couples helping to support Calvin, took him back to Kenya for his brother Rogers' wedding. Tip, the mother of seven who had also fostered seven more, was drawn to Joash. "He looked so lost," she told me. "He needs a mother."

Joash had been continually moved around between Rogers and relatives with varying problems on both sides, Evan agreed with Tip that maybe he could follow Calvin to the United States. "I know this seems crazy," Evan emailed me, "but what would you think about taking Joash in, too?"

Could I handle one more? I wondered. *No, I could not*, I determined. I found another family who wanted to take him in. Mark insisted that Joash belonged with his brother and told me he was going to pray about it. "Fine," I said. "Go ahead, but I'm not going to change my mind."

A few days later, I changed my mind. One morning, I read an email Mark had stayed up late to write, full of reasons why we should take Joash in. "If we died, wouldn't we want *our* kids to stay together," Mark argued. I called him at work.

"Okay, Mark. He can come." I said to his happy surprise. Then, I hurried off to morning Mass, as was my custom. I was not really paying attention to the reading, when the words from Hosea 14:4 penetrated my reverie: "In you the orphan finds compassion." I was in awe at the timing.

A few months later, Joash arrived. We assumed the loss he had experienced was much the same as Calvin's. Only later did we gradually learn that his pain cut deeper and affected how he encountered the world. Joash was only eight when he sat desperately by his mother's side as she lay dying. Joash adored his mother, Yovencia, and she always loved and protected him—her youngest. Although caning—hitting with a large stick—was accepted discipline in Kenya, Yovencia never allowed Joash to be caned. The older boys had grown more independent, but Joash usually preferred to be at his mother's side.

When she was taken to a separate hut, Joash was told to keep away, but he would sneak through the window at night just to sit by her side. He hoped that his mother would not die, like his dad and so many others in his village had done. Charles had been away from home, working to earn money for the family. There was no AIDS education, and people lacked understanding as to how it spread. Teenage girls and young women, needing money for their own families, often gathered around male work crews offering their services as prostitutes. Although Christianity is spreading, the Kenyan culture traditionally has not been strict about sexual fidelity in marriage. Charles died of AIDS on December 14, 1996. Fourteen months later, Yovencia followed.

Joash had been at his mother's side only moments before she died. Someone told him to go take a shower, but then he heard loud weeping. He ran back towards the hut and forced his way in to see his mother. In horror, Joash realized she was gone.

Joash ran to the river to be alone. There, his body shook as he cried out in anguish. How could he go on? Now there was no one to love him and care for him. *God must be punishing me,* he thought, *He has taken my mother and left me all alone.* Joash sobbed for hours before a cousin came for him. His grandfather took him in for a time, but the gruff old man resented the responsibility. Joash bounced between relatives and his brother Rogers. Since Rogers had begun attending school for masonry, he could not adequately supervise his younger brother and was just a teenager himself. Often in frustration, he disciplined Joash by caning. *If my mother was still alive, they would not be treating me this way*, Joash often thought. He built a wall around his emotions. If people did not care about him, he wanted them to know he did not care about them either. His angry defenses became ingrained.

At the airport, five years after his mother died, Joash again broke down and cried when Calvin left for the United States. Calvin had always been kind to him and he loved his brother very much. Now, he would not even have him. One evening, after Rogers had been angry, Joash grumbled, "I wish Calvin were here."

"Then you better start praying if you want to go to the United States and see Calvin again," Roger had answered.

That night, before bed, Joash said the first prayer he had ever said on his own. He prayed the Our Father, a prayer he had learned in school. And every night after that, he said an "Our Father" before going to sleep.

About six months later, Rogers let Joash know that Evan wanted to make arrangements for him to join Calvin. Initially, Joash could not believe it was true, fearing it was some kind of a joke. For the first time since his mother's death seven years earlier, he had something to look forward to. But Joash's defensiveness and pursuing his own agenda for so long had become habitual. Very soon after his arrival in July of 2005, struggles began. I knew his negative behaviors were born of pain, but I could not seem to make things better.

Joash was the same age as my son Jacob—both fifteen. Joash often viewed Jacob as bossing him around. In turn, Jacob had a short fuse. Joash seemed to enjoy being contrary with everyone, but would sulk if corrected. When school started, things got worse between the two boys. After about seven months, Mark and I decided the situation was more than we could handle. I wanted to teach my kids not to jump ship in the face of trouble, but our limping along seemed to be hurting everyone. Joash knew he had crossed a line one day, and for a couple of days, we were all pretty quiet around each other. On the evening Mark and I planned to reveal our plans to find another placement for him, Joash approached us first.

"I know I've messed up," he said, with pleading eyes. "I stopped at the chapel at school today and prayed. I've asked God to help me. Please give me another chance. I promise I will try harder."

His pledge was salve to my heart. I did not want him to go away; I just wanted a manageable family life. Afterwards, for the first time, things started getting better.

Instead of grudgingly doing chores now, Joash worked at being helpful. He also worked hard at his studies. We could see Joash actually trying, although sometimes, situations were beyond him. His vulnerability often left him feeling attacked by others when such was not the case. But I also noticed something Joash had no idea I was aware of. When one of the younger children was upset about something or sullen over getting punished, Joash comforted them. He would try to stop the tears or just talk with them and suggest a fun activity. I knew this boy, who had built a wall around his heart, had a big one indeed.

Then, while taking each day at a time and putting his best foot forward, Joash made an amazing discovery that changed his life dramatically. After lackluster seasons in soccer and basketball, track season began. Joash had once tried to run a race in sixth grade but quit when people laughed after he tripped. In eighth grade, he entered a race once more and seemed to be off to a good start; running past everyone. Unfortunately, he was quickly pulled out and disqualified. He had no idea it was a walking—not a running—race.

As a freshman at St. Mary's, he decided he would try track one more time. That's when he discovered that he had wings on his feet and could fly. At his first track meet competing with nine schools for the western region of North Dakota, I accidentally brought Joash two hours early; not realizing the track events started an hour after the field events. Joash ran around the track for well over an hour to warm up. *He's going to wear himself out,* I feared. When the starters gun fired, Joash bolted ahead of the pack for the 1,600-meter race. *Oh dear,* I thought, *he does not realize he needs to pace himself; he'll never keep that lead.* Then, he kept turning and looking behind him—another big no-no that slows a runner down. Still, Joash managed to cross the finish line at 5:07, nine seconds behind first place. Not bad for his very first race.

At one meet, I watched nervously when Joash again took a big lead right from the start, fearing he would tire out. The crowd on the inside field ran from one side to the other yelling: "Go, Joash, go!" When he crossed the finish line in first place, tears came to my eyes—not because he had won, but because I knew that his victory was far more than just a foot race. I understood how much those cheers meant to him, lifting him off the ground in more ways than one.

At the end of his freshman season, Joash took seventh at state for the 1,600 meter at 4:40 and fourth in the 3,200 meter at 9:47. At the end of his first cross-country season as a sophomore, Joash was the second fastest runner on the 5K course, four seconds behind the winner. By the end of sophomore track season Joash came in third for both the 1,600 and 3,200 with times of 4:33 and 9:37. During his junior year of cross-country, Joash broke a few course records and won the state cross-country championship coming in a full eighteen seconds ahead of the second place runner for the 5K event.

Running has brought Joash great joy and self-confidence, which permeates our family. He is respectful, helpful, and full of zest for life. We are all very proud of his accomplishments. I thank God we never let him go in the quest for a happy family because now we are much happier with him than we would have ever been without him. Seeing him grow into a responsible, young man is immensely rewarding. Watching him run is just the bonus.

—Patti Maguire Armstrong

Patti Maguire Armstrong is one of the editors of Amazing Grace for Families. *Her biography appears at the end of the book.*

Acknowledgments

Many thanks to all the families who shared their stories of faith, inspiration, hope, and humor with us; to the staff and associates of Ascension Press for all their assistance in making yet another inspirational *Amazing Grace* book a reality; and to designers Kinsey Caruth and Devin Schadt for a wonderful cover.

— Jeff Cavins, Matthew Pinto, and
Patti Maguire Armstrong

Editor and Contributor Contact Information

To contact one of the contributors, please write them at the following address:

> *(Name of writer)*
> c/o Ascension Press
> P.O. Box 1990
> West Chester, PA 19380
> Or email: info@ascensionpress.com

To contact one of the co-editors, please write them at one of the following addresses:

> Jeff Cavins
> P.O. Box 1533
> Maple Grove, MN 55311
> Or email: jcavins@attbi.com

> Matthew Pinto
> P.O. Box 1990
> West Chester, PA 19380
> Or email: mpinto@ascensionpress.com

> Patti Maguire Armstrong
> P.O. Box 1532
> Bismarck, ND 58502
> Or email: patti@bis.midco.net

About the Editors

Jeff Cavins served as a Protestant minister for twelve years before returning to the Catholic faith. His story is chronicled in his autobiography, *My Life on the Rock* (Ascension Press). Jeff is best-known as the founding host of the popular EWTN television program *Life on the Rock*. With Matthew Pinto, he is the co-creator of the *Amazing Grace* series, and is the author of *I'm Not Being Fed: Discovering the Food that Satisfies the Soul* (Ascension, 2005). Jeff is also the creator and principal author of *The Great Adventure*, a popular Bible study program. He and his wife, Emily, reside in Minnesota with their three daughters.

Matthew Pinto is the author of the best-selling question-and-answer book *Did Adam & Eve Have Belly Buttons?* (Ascension, 1998), co-author of *Did Jesus Have a Last Name?* (Ascension, 2005), and creator of the *Friendly Defenders Catholic Flash Cards* series. Matt is co-founder of several Catholic organizations, including CatholicExchange.com and *Envoy* magazine, and the creator, with Jeff Cavins, of the *Amazing Grace* series. Matt and his wife, Maryanne, live in Pennsylvania with their five sons.

Patti Maguire Armstrong worked in the fields of social work and public administration before staying home full-time to raise her children. As a freelance writer, Patti has written more than 400 articles for both secular and religious publications. She has authored the book *Catholic Truths for Our Children* (www.raisingcatholickids.com) as a guide to help parents pass on the Catholic faith to their children and served as co-editor of four *Amazing Grace* books. Patti and her husband, Mark, live in North Dakota with their ten children.